Advance Praise

For

The CEO's Guide
to Training, eLearning & Work

Will Thalheimer has once again provided us with essential wisdom. In his inimitable style, he lays out the flaws in the L&D business, peppered with the too-often neglected realities of how humans learn. This is a book that needs to be understood throughout the organization, from the CEO down to L&D.

Clark Quinn
Research-to-Practice Consultant, Speaker, Author at Quinnovation.com

Will has written a book that is passionate and pithy. He's not taking it anymore. After a lifetime researching and reflecting on what not to do, he's come up with a two–barrel shotgun blast that says – listen up – let's stop mucking around and get this right. It's a plan... no a masterplan... by a master of his craft.

Donald Clark
Author of AI for Learning and other books

The book is a most remarkable collection and an indispensable resource for not just the CEOs, but any learning professional – whether at expert or entry level. It also proves a valuable text for master's programs offering an in-depth research-backed glimpse of all the intricacies that go into the work and decisions for training and performance support.

Elham Arabi, PhD
Researcher, Speaker, Global Learning Consultant in Higher Ed. & Corporate

There are so many things I like about Will Thalheimer's latest book, The CEO's Guide to Training, eLearning & Work. Will anchors learning to performance requirements, encourages collaboration between L&D and business stakeholders, and guides us to the learning sciences and away from poor practices influenced by myths and misunderstandings in learning practice.

Guy W. Wallace
President, EPPIC (retired)

(Fanboy. When people ask me about Will that's what I say.) I admired Will's work from afar for more than a decade then close up for a year. I learned something in every article, post, and conversation. This book gets to the heart of the matter: how to make learning work. Direct, research-informed, and clear... just what every leader needs. Highly recommend!

Jerry Hamburg
Performance Consultant

Will Thalheimer's book is an indispensable resource for CEOs and learning leaders who are serious about cultivating talent and driving performance in their organizations. With a laser-sharp focus on empirical evidence and practical strategies, Thalheimer demystifies the complex world of corporate learning. He goes beyond the conventional wisdom to offer a guide that is thought-provoking, evidence-informed and actionable. This book is a must-read for anyone committed to fostering a culture of continuous learning. It provides the tools to recognize and utilize the inherent potential of learning in organizations. Thalheimer's expertise shines throughout the pages, making it an authoritative text that will undoubtedly contribute to the future of the learning field.

Jos Arets

Will Thalheimer writes the book so many in our field need. It is aimed at CEOs and they need to read it but, really and truly, anyone in the L&D field would benefit from the ideas, concepts, and advice expertly presented by Dr. Thalheimer. Buy multiple copies of this book and share with the executive as well as the L&D leadership teams. The entire organization will be better for it.

Dr. Karl M. Kapp
Professor of Instructional Design and Technology at Commonwealth University
and an expert on the convergence of learning, technology, and business.

Will Thalheimer is one of a handful of people I turn to all the time to explain the practical and applied side of research related to our profession in L&D. What many don't know about Will, is he also has a tremendous background as a business and leadership consultant. So, this book is a marriage of the science of learning and the "careabouts" executives should have when it comes to that science. In other words, he streamlines what execs should ask for, expect, demand, measure, and more. He gives them a prescription for learning when learning is not their day job. And even more importantly, he provides a blueprint for CLOs and learning pros when they engage those same execs. If this book doesn't change your life... you haven't read it!

Matt Richter
The Thiagi Group and Learning Development Accelerator

No kidding, I'm buying copies of this for my entire team and our clients, too. Whether you're the CEO, a senior leader, someone with a great idea for a course, or you can simply spell the acronym, this is the wake-up call that you need about the training you're developing. Will pulls no punches.

Megan Torrance
Chief Energy Officer, Torrance Learning

Great book! Through indexed bite-sized snippets of shared wisdom and experience, CEOs will quickly learn why their organization's training isn't contributing to the performance results their organization needs. They'll also learn how they, in partnership with their learning team, can fix it.

Michael Allen
Chairman and CEO, Allen Interactions

An essential read for both L&D leaders and CEOs, Thalheimer's book is a crucial tool for enhancing the synergy between senior executives and L&D. It not only deepens the dialogue on elevating L&D's impact but also fosters a stronger, more aligned relationship for organizational growth.

Michelle Ockers
Organisational Learning Strategist, Learning Uncut

Will does an exceptional job of encouraging the C-suite to actively engage in the learning process while also holding learning professionals accountable to business impact. The CEO's Guide is for all executives and learning professionals who want to increase employee engagement, develop productive teams, and show meaningful improvement at the organizational level.

Nikki Vassallo, MBA, CPTD
Vice President Learning and Development, Workers Credit Union

After reading most of what has been written on the management, design and evaluation of training and performance improvement over the past couple of decades, I have no qualms about recommending this engaging, succinct, evidence-based, and accurate discussion as absolutely the best. Will Thalheimer not only describes what needs to happen in all organizations but clearly points out what is most often happening in training that works against the bottom line, how to get rid of the negatives and what should replace them. The book also clearly and accurately describes the myths and misconceptions that often support expensive but damaging initiatives. Problematic training initiatives exist in all large organizations and are not a popular topic, but the best outcomes most often begin by acknowledging, eliminating and/or changing programs and beliefs that are preventing success. It is rare for anyone to have Will's broad and deep knowledge and experience in organizational management, learning and performance research, as well as expertise in training design and development. He has not only done all that but can write in a way that engages, entertains, and enlightens readers. Many of us who have invested our careers in this area look to him to answer questions and pull it all together in a useful way. Now this book provides his excellent summary of what we know that would be useful to managers at all levels. I'm often frustrated by authors who discuss needs in a general way but fail to clearly describe how to accomplish a desired program or strategy. This book excels at describing how to do what is recommended.

Richard E. Clark
Professor Emeritus, USC, (and Legendary Learning Researcher)

Another excellent offering from Will Thalheimer who does the heavy research lifting and provides straightforward and practical guidance. Ignore at your peril.

Robert Brinkerhoff
Professor Emeritus Western Michigan University, Research Advisor Promote International

You won't like this book, which is exactly why you must read it. Will Thalheimer continues his no-nonsense, no-holds-barred style to speak truth to power: to tell business leaders what they need—but don't necessarily want—to hear about the current effectiveness of training & development and what to do about it.

Roy V.H. Pollock, DVM, PhD
Chief Learning Officer at The 6Ds Company
Co-author, The Six Disciplines of Breakthrough Learning

Make a short investment of your time for a big return. Read this book. Encourage anyone associated with workforce learning to read this book. Then apply the wisdom packed in the short conversational chapters to maximize your organizational ROI in performance improvement.

Ruth Clark
Legendary Author and Learning Research Translator

The complex world of L&D is distilled into an essential guide for any senior leaders to digest in 'The CEO's Guide to Training, E-learning, and Work'. The book's brilliance lies in its clarity and directness, making sophisticated L&D concepts accessible and actionable. What impresses me the most is how each chapter unfolds as a revelation, challenging conventional wisdom and offering practical insights. The author's expertise shines through in the honest, relatable, and often humorous narrative, effortlessly guiding leaders through the fundamentals of learning and performance support practices and the nuanced world of evaluation and research. This isn't just a book; it's a roadmap for CEOs and learning professionals alike, empowering them to unlock the full potential of their teams and make learning a pivotal aspect of their success. An indispensable guide in the ever-changing era of workforce development and organizational learning.

Stella Lee, Paradox Learning Inc.

THE CEO'S GUIDE TO TRAINING, ELEARNING & WORK

THE CEO'S GUIDE TO TRAINING, ELEARNING & WORK

Empowering Learning for
a Competitive Advantage

Will Thalheimer, PhD, MBA

Work-Learning Press
SOMERVILLE, MASSACHUSETTS

Work-Learning Press
www.worklearning.com

The CEO's Guide to Training, eLearning & Work/ Will Thalheimer

ISBN: 978-1-941577-06-6 (paperback)
ISBN: 978-1-941577-07-3 (hardcover)
ISBN: 978-1-941577-08-0 (eBook)

Library of Congress Control Number: 2024907253

Dedication

This book is dedicated to the best among us—
those who teach us with love and wisdom.
They help us rise.
They help us see.
They help us live deep.
We owe them almost everything.

Reflection

Professionals aim high with firm principles and commitments.
They are open to learning, improvement, and transcendence.
They do not bow or grovel to whims, popularity, or authority.
They know who they are and who they aspire to be.
They build their profession as they live it.

Contents

Section One   Foundations to Get You Started 1

Chapter 1   Introduction... 3

Chapter 2   First Do No Harm.. 7

Chapter 3   Training and Development Related to Organizational Success........... 9

Chapter 4   Weakness at the Heart of the Learning Field 11

Chapter 5   Remembering and Forgetting 13

Chapter 6   Author's Introduction... 15

Chapter 7   How to Use This Book 17

Section Two   Fundamentals of Training Practice 19

Chapter 8   Learning Data Is Often Crap Data 21

Chapter 9   Other Learning Evaluation Failures 23

Chapter 10   Training Is NOT Always the Answer 25

Chapter 11   Training Does NOT Work Alone 27

Chapter 12   Your Learners Don't Always Know Learning 29

Chapter 13   Why Your Experts Aren't Always Great at Teaching......... 31

Chapter 14   Avoiding Myths and Misconceptions 33

Chapter 15   Managers and Learning 43

Chapter 16   Managers' Performance Checklist 45

Chapter 17   Stop Your Managers from Demanding Stupid Stuff 47

Section Three   Learning and Technology 49

Chapter 18   Technology and Learning.. 51

Chapter 19   Classroom Training vs. eLearning 53

Chapter 20   Large Course Repositories: Be Very Careful................. 55

Chapter 21   Generative AI: How Learning Can Help 57

Chapter 22   When Training Pollutes 59

Section Four   The Powerful Practicality of the Learning Sciences 61

Chapter 23   The Amazing Power of Learning Research: Retrieval Practice 63

Chapter 24   More Amazing Learning Research: Spacing Learning Over Time .. 65

Chapter 25   More Amazing Learning Research: Simulating the Work Context . 67

Chapter 26   More Amazing Learning Research: Feedback for Learning........... 69

Section Five   The Performance Sciences and Behavior Triggers 71

Chapter 27   The Performance Sciences 73

Chapter 28   Performance Activation from Within the Work Context 75

Chapter 29   Prompting and Performance-Support Tools.................... 77

Section Six **Making Research Work for Your Learning Team** 79

Chapter 30 Research and Practice in Learning 81

Chapter 31 Separating Good Research from Bad 83

Chapter 32 Using A-B Testing in Learning 87

Section Seven **Fixing the Crap-Data Problem** 89

Chapter 33 Data Should Help People Make Decisions 91

Chapter 34 Learning Evaluation As Decision Support 93

Chapter 35 LTEM—The Learning-Transfer Evaluation Model 97

Chapter 36 Performance-Focused Learner Surveys 105

Section Eight **Advanced Topics** 107

Chapter 37 Customer Education 109

Chapter 38 Adding Learning to Leadership Development 113

Chapter 39 Integrating Values and Ideas Across Your Learning Efforts 117

Chapter 40 Training to Help Your Employees 119

Chapter 41 Compliance Training: Effectiveness and the Law 121

Chapter 42 Learning in the Workflow 123

Section Nine **Managing Your Learning Team** 127

Chapter 43 Your Learning Leader..129

Chapter 44 How to Tell If Your Learning Leader Is Doing a Good Job 133

Chapter 45 Your Learning Team Should Have a Strategy...........139

Chapter 46 A Full-Factor Learning Request Process 145

Chapter 47 Outsourcing Your Learning Team?........................151

Chapter 48 What If Your Learning Team Wins Awards? 153

Chapter 49 Learning Vendor Awards Are Just as Problematic......155

Chapter 50 Investing in Learning for a Competitive Advantage...................157

About the Author... Will Thalheimer, PhD, MBA 161

Chapter Notes Research, Evidence, Reflections...........................163

Index Of Critical Concepts and Names 247

Preface

This book is written for two audiences, organizational leaders, and learning professionals. Today's senior leaders fear for their organizations' viability. In a 2024 report from PricewaterhouseCoopers, 45% of CEO's say they are not confident their companies will survive more than 10 years on their current path. They say reinvention is critical, and they reported that a lack of skills in their company's workforce was a top barrier. The Conference Board asked C-Suite leaders what internal factors would most impact their businesses in the near future. Two of the top six barriers were focused on the talent and skills of employees.

We are clearly at a crossroads, where only the most competitive organizations will survive. Learning professionals would seem to be ideally situated to partner with senior leaders to drive talent development—to increase knowledge, innovation, productivity, and energy. But alas, learning-and-development teams are not as empowered as they need to be. Where learning professionals should be poised to create competitive advantages for their organizations and learners, they are hamstrung in multiple ways.

Two fundamental factors are crippling the effectiveness of learning teams. Senior leaders have fundamental misunderstandings about the work and potential of their learning teams—making it virtually impossible to manage learning to create a competitive advantage. Where learning teams need specific direction and support, only rarely do they get what they need to drive organizational success.

Second, learning professionals are too often mired in obsolete practices and constrained thinking—making it impossible for them to leverage their skills to full effect. While blame could be aimed at senior leaders for unreliable resourcing and direction, this would unfairly tell only half the story. The learning-and-development field itself must do more to upskill itself, utilize rigorous practices, and confidently assert standards of performance.

This book is written to enable senior leaders and learning professionals to engage in a healthy partnership—in more productive conversations and initiatives. The writing is bold, straightforward, honest, and compelling. For senior leaders, the ideas in the book will enable your organization to gain a competitive advantage. For learning professionals, the values, practices, and principles discussed will enable you to empower your teams to full effectiveness—producing competitive advantages for your organization and learners, and benefits beyond that to your communities, countries, and the environs.

Who Will Find Value
in This Book?

○ **<u>Senior Leaders</u>** — Chief Executive Officers, Executive Directors, Chief Operating Officers, Chief Financial Officers, Chief Information Officers, Chief Marketing Officers, Presidents, Chief Human Resource Officers, Chief Talent Officers, Chief People Officers, Chief Diversity Officers, Chief Organizational Development Officers—and other senior organizational leaders.

○ **<u>Learning-and-Performance Professionals</u>** — Chief Learning Officers, Chief Learning-and-Performance Officers, Directors of Learning and Development, Directors of Training, Training Managers, Learning-and-Performance Architects, Learning Architects, Learning Designers, Instructional Designers, Learning Experience Designers, Performance Experience Designers, eLearning Designers, Learning Developers, Learning Evaluators, Trainers—plus anyone who manages learning teams and anyone who has a job role or title in the learning-and-performance field not included above.

Acknowledgments

I would like to acknowledge all the people I have learned from: researchers, practitioners, book authors, article writers, podcasters, my clients, my social media supporters, my critics, my colleagues, my friends, my employers, the research-to-practice community, journalists, speakers, and my family.

I find myself, now 66 years of age, with a sense of deep gratitude for all those who have supported me and my work over many decades. In writing this book, my gratitude has swelled—sometimes so much that warmth rises through my body with a feeling of awe that so many brilliant people are willing to devote their time to this project.

I asked more than 30 people to give me feedback on various drafts of this book or on specific chapters when I needed targeted expertise. What an honor and privilege that so many people were willing to share their time! In the next paragraph, I list their names alphabetically by first name. They probably don't agree with everything I have written but they have improved the book dramatically!

Adam Neaman, Christina Reagle, Clark Quinn, Debbie Smith, Dick Clark, Donald Clark, Elham Arabi, Gale Stafford, Guy Wallace, Ilona Boomsma, Jack Phillips, Jane Bozarth, Jerry Hamburg, Jos Arets, Josh Cavalier, Julie Dirksen, Karl Kapp, Kellie Chamberlain, Lance Crow, Mark Nilles, Markus Bernhardt, Matt Richter, Megan Torrance, Michael Allen, Michelle Ockers, Nick Howe, Nikki Vassallo, Patti Phillips, Patti Shank, Paul Matthews, Rob Brinkerhoff, Roy Pollock, Ruth Clark, Sharon Castillo, Stella Lee, Steve Foreman, Thomas Harrell, Vince Han.

Thanks also to Neda Djavaherian for her inspired book cover design and for her patient counsel over many months of deliberations.

I also must thank my long-time editor, Ross Edwards (FreelanceScribe.com) who always improves my work immeasurably.

Most importantly, I thank my family—both my extended family of parents and siblings, and my immediate family, with special thanks to my wife and daughter who have borne the burden of the hours and efforts my work has entailed over many years.

Section One
Foundations to Get You Started

Welcome to the book! I've divided it into sections so you can focus on what's most important to you. Each section has a theme. In these section introductions, I'll tell you the theme and I'll outline the major points of each chapter before you read it.

Section One—Theme

Section One provides foundational information about the practice of learning and development. By understanding these foundations, you'll be better able to support your learning team as they work to create a competitive advantage for your organization.

Chapter 1—Introduction

I share a challenge with you—a wake-up call to get you thinking. Not everything is going well with your organization's learning-and-development practices. But you should have optimism that you and your learning team can partner to make things work.

Chapter 2—First Do No Harm

I describe the simplest of solutions: getting people—in this case, all the folks in your organization who impact learning and performance—to stop doing things that are counterproductive. I list things that can be cleaned up easily, but my overall message is that improvements can be made, and you have the leverage to help your organization utilize learning to create powerful advantages.

Chapter 3—Training and Development Related to Organizational Success

I provide you with scientific research—quite a lot of it—showing that training has been consistently related to organizational success. I caveat this a bit, saying that improvements can still be made and that you as CEO have a critical role to play.

Chapter 4—Weakness at the Heart of the Learning Field

I share a dark secret with you: that, despite the many skilled, knowledgeable, and dedicated learning-and-development professionals working today, many have also joined the field without adequate education or training. I will also show you how you can help.

Chapter 5—Remembering and Forgetting

I share a deep and fundamental insight about learning: that people forget, and that learning must be designed in specific ways to support learners in remembering. I share this insight for three reasons. First, to let you know there is scientific and practical wisdom behind the work of your learning team. Second, to hint that the most common training method—just sharing learning content—doesn't work, even though your learning team is too often asked to produce exactly that. Third, I share this information on remembering and forgetting to show how you can help.

Chapter 6—Author's Introduction

I introduce myself so you'll know what I'm trying to do and so you can get a sense of my sweet spots, my blind spots, and where my perspectives might come from.

Chapter 7—How to Use This Book

I suggest how you might use this book. Specifically, I say to read it, not just pass it along to your Chief Learning Officer. I ask you to make a small investment to see good returns. I also acknowledge that you don't need to read every chapter, and I point out where in the book to invest most of your time if your time is limited.

Important Note: Each chapter is written to be concise and short, filled only with the most essential information. At the end of the book, I've added many pages of chapter notes that add insights, share practical stories, or provide scientific research that supports the discussion in the chapters. There are over 350 research citations and over 80 pages of chapter notes!

Section One—Notes for Learning Professionals

We too must know the foundations of our work to be full partners in moving forward. We must embrace a do-no-harm mentality and clean up dubious practices. We must energetically work to educate ourselves, especially those new to the field. We must understand learning at a deep level so we can leverage its full potential. We must see that our work produces powerful benefits—and more if we continue to learn and grow.

Chapter 1
Introduction

You're the CEO. The sovereign leader. You get the glory, the paycheck, and the velvet perks of the leather throne. The rest of us look on with a mix of admiration and awe, worry and skepticism, hope and inspiration. Compared with us, you have the power. However, on many days you probably feel that your power is indirect, slow, and amorphous.

You may ask yourself, how can I do more? How can I, as the senior leader, enable everyone in the organization to perform more productively, to think more clearly or creatively, and to live more fully and effectively in their work?

You can't do it by yourself. You rely on managers throughout your organization to coach, support, align, and energize. You rely on your training-and-development professionals to oversee your organization's learning, development, and education efforts.

Here's what you may not know. Many CEOs (perhaps even you) have not done enough to leverage managers to enable learning and guide work performance. Many have not done enough to support and guide learning professionals. In short, too many organizations are failing to marshal learning to create a competitive advantage.

Here are some common issues:

- MANAGERS may not be motivated or may not know how to best onboard new employees, or coach their coworkers, or parlay training into action, or energize their teams to generate innovative ideas. All of these are failures of learning.

- TRAINERS and LEARNING ARCHITECTS (the designers of learning) are too often compelled to teach for knowledge, not for actionable performance. They are pushed to create learning events that induce employees to forget what they've learned. They are pressured to teach content that doesn't need to be taught. They don't have the time or budget to follow up with employees to support them in their work. They are dissuaded against innovating. They feel compelled to create outcome metrics that are meant to assuage senior leaders like you—or fool them—rather than enlighten.

Those of us in leadership roles have allowed this to happen. Many see training as an antibiotic—wrongly thinking that providing training cures the diseases of ignorance, incompetence, and apathy. We assign people who know nothing about learning to manage learning and development. We fail to require our organizations to use a robust planning process for learning, but instead leave our learning teams to take orders from managers who incorrectly diagnose work performance issues. We accept unimportant metrics as evidence of learning—compelling our learning teams to continue building ineffective learning events.

I know what you're thinking. *"Come on, Thalheimer! I know you're exaggerating to get my attention, but it can't be as bad as all this."* Let me be clear. The training-and-development ecosystem in almost all organizations is underperforming. Yes, there are many pockets of brilliance! Yes, there are dedicated professionals doing outstanding work. But overall, the way learning-and-development is managed and practiced is weaker than it should be—leaving organizations like yours to get poor returns on your investment.

The good news is the problems are fixable. A core problem is that the relationship you have with your learning team is tainted with misunderstandings, misconceptions, and misdirected priorities. One of the primary goals of this book is to help organizations like yours get out of this downward spiral.

What's the secret? *Learning!* Learning is more complex and confounding than rocket science—because human cognition is so complex. Learning is not easy; it's challenging for employees, coaches, managers, and learning professionals. Learning is not just tactical; it can also be profound in its life-changing, career-enhancing impact. Learning is nurtured through intentionally architected journeys, through deliberately designed work contexts, through self-motivation, and through compassionate coaching.

Today, too much of learning practice is based on folklore and tradition, not on what we know about human cognitive architecture, not on research, not on the best practices of experimentation, validated data, and improvement. If we learning professionals are adrift and not as effective as we want to be, senior leaders like you must certainly be perplexed. With this book, I hope to bring you insights on how to think about learning and performance—and how to partner with your learning team.

Decisions Enabling Learning to Provide a Competitive Advantage
On the following two pages, I provide examples of decisions that routinely confront you, your managers, and your learning team—decisions we'll discuss in the book. By knowing how to answer these questions, you and your learning team will be able to work together more effectively—aligned on a common goal, creating a competitive advantage for your organization and benefits for your employees, customers, investors, and other stakeholders.

- If your learning team succeeds in creating learning programs for 95% of the training requests they get, should you be happy that they are efficient or worried that they are not pushing back enough against a training-first mindset?

- If your learning team presents you with their findings that your new leadership program created a 110% return on investment, should you conclude that the leadership program is effective, or should you have doubts?

- Should you be glad your learning team is using its budget to demonstrate the impact of a training program, or should you be mortified that they are not using their limited evaluation budget to determine how to improve the program?

- Should your learning team move most of your organization's training programs online to save money, or should they keep most programs face to face in a meeting room to maintain effectiveness?

- Should your learning team utilize generative AI to reduce headcount, or will such a move create undue risks for your organization?

- Should your learning team seek periodic outside reviews from experts on human learning and instructional design or should they save money by relying on their own expertise?

- Should your learning team stop using after-course surveys as their primary method of evaluating your organization's training programs? Should they use them at all? Should they use some of their budget to improve their surveys?

- Should your learning team use more than surveys to evaluate their learning programs, or are learner surveys generally correlated with other important measures like work performance and business impact?

- Should your organization ditch your leadership-development program and start over by creating a program that is based on scientifically-sound recommendations, or should it maintain the current program to ensure continuity?

- Should your organization invest in a full repository of off-the-shelf courses, or should it be leery that these courses might be poorly designed, lacking in evaluation, or not fully aligned with your organization's strategic priorities? If not perfect, are they worth it anyway?

- Should your learning team be granted a larger budget to help your employees and managers perform better through other means—besides training?

- Should your learning team invest significantly more money in their own learning and development, or do they generally have the knowledge and skills to be effective in their roles?

- Is compliance training practically effective and legally acceptable when provided yearly, or should employees be reminded of safety, ethical, and regulatory issues more often?

- Do your managers need to be involved when their direct reports engage in training or other learning experiences, or is there scientific research that shows their involvement is largely a waste of time?

- Are your organization's training efforts aligned with your sustainability goals, or are your training programs unnecessarily polluting the environment? Should your learning team measure their environmental impact, or is that impact so minimal as to make this a waste of resources?

- Should your learning team utilize scientific research on learning to guide their learning design efforts, or is the research too uncertain to warrant confidence?

- If your learning team comes to you and tells you they've won a prestigious industry award, should you be glad they are doing exemplary work, or should you be suspicious that they've wasted time applying for awards?

- Should your organization do more to get benefits from customer education? Should you have a separate team devoted to customer education, or can customer education be managed by your regular learning team?

- Do you know what to look for in hiring your next Chief Learning Officer? Do you know how to evaluate the success of your learning team? Do you know how to guide your learning team to excellent performance?

The answers to these questions are practical and profound. This book is designed to help you navigate the complexities so you can support your learning team as they empower your employees and create a competitive advantage for your organization.

Chapter 2
First Do No Harm

If we could just stop people from doing stupid stuff, the world would be a whole lot better—even if we never even invested in positive improvements! It's the same in the learning field. There is a lot of stupid stuff that should be stopped immediately.

In this chapter, my goal is to get you thinking about this idea—the idea that stopping bad practices is a good place to start. I won't go into depth here on all the things that should *not* be done. I will weave warnings into the rest of the book as I also describe best practices. In this chapter, I just want you to see that significantly improving your organization's learning practices is not that hard—if you know what to do.

Teaching Too Much Content: One of the biggest problems in workplace learning is that we teach too much content. This is non-intuitive, so let me explain. When we try to teach too many topics, we just don't have enough time to reinforce the topics we *do* teach. People who are taught massive amounts of content end up remembering very little of it—essentially wasting their time and productivity for hardly any benefit.

Why does your learning team allow this to happen? Two reasons. Some of them don't know better. They don't understand the relentless push of the forgetting curve. Most of them know better but are either afraid to push back or are so marginalized in your organization that they just go along with directives to teach 100 things, when they know they should be teaching 25 concepts to full effectiveness.

Teaching Too Soon: We teach people things long before they need to use what they've learned in their work. People naturally forget more and more of what they learn as time goes by, so, when we teach them how to use new software a month before the software is available, we've set them up to fail.

Evaluation Based Only on Poor Learner Surveys: We evaluate training based on learners' feelings of satisfaction, how they liked their instructors, and whether they'd recommend the training to others. This may be the root of all evil in the training field as these types of learner surveys (aka smile sheets, happy sheets, reaction forms) give us faulty data—data that pushes your learning team to build training that makes people happy rather than training that is effective in building competence and skills.

Defaulting to Classroom Training: We default to classroom training when elearning can be just as effective, if not more effective. Indeed, there's scientific research on this point showing that elearning tends to be more effective because learning architects who build the elearning tend to engineer it using factors that actually work—compared with classroom training, when we often fail to use the most powerful learning approaches.

Failing to Support Application of Learning: We create training programs that don't support employees in using what they've learned in their work. We fail to prepare them for resistance to new methods. We fail to inoculate them against obstacles. We fail to give them job aids or other performance prompts. We don't provide coaching or follow-through. In short, we leave our employees with no support when learning's momentum is most fragile.

Suckers for Learning Myths: Our learning teams (and our managers too) are susceptible to myths and misconceptions in the learning field. You may have heard of the "learning styles" notion—the idea that, if we design learning to cater to people with different learning styles (for example, visual, auditory, kinesthetic), then learning outcomes will improve. Many people don't know that this myth has been scientifically debunked over many, many years. This is just one example. The problem is that, too often, we design our learning based on these myths rather than based on other more powerful learning factors—thus achieving negative results rather than positive benefits.

Focusing Only on Impact Measures: Your learning team has likely learned that providing you with data that shows "learning impact" is a way to win points with you—even though the data they are giving you is based on faulty and incomplete metrics.

Low Funding for Learning Evaluation: Very few resources are allocated for learning evaluation. This causes your learning team to go for the least costly evaluation methods—which, not too surprisingly, lack validity and produce the wrong kind of information.

Managers Not Leveraging Learning: Your managers are not taught about learning in your leadership-development programs. Their lack of knowledge causes them to coach poorly, to be slow in developing their people, and to fail to support the training process.

Focusing Only on Training: The focus on training pushes learning teams to ignore other points of leverage—including prompting mechanisms (like job aids and performance support), use of the performance sciences to nudge performance directly, and learning in the flow of work. Training is useful, but there are other tools in your organization's toolbox.

These are some of the biggest problems, but they are not the only problems. In some ways, though, these are the low-hanging fruit, readily available to provide significant improvement in your organization—if you can just stop these problematic practices.

Chapter 3
Training and Development
Related to Organizational Success

I want to clear up one thing right from the start. The work of learning-and-development professionals is consistently related to organizational performance. The training they build creates benefits for their organizations.

Decade after decade, researchers who study the impact of training have found that training is positively related to organizational performance. In a recent meta-analysis—a scientific study of many other scientific studies—the researchers reported the following:

> *"Our findings indicate that investment in training was associated with increased organizational performance. Specifically, a one standard deviation increase in training was associated with 0.25 standard deviation increase in organizational performance. This result indicates that organizations can achieve significant performance gains through investing in training."* (Garavan, et al., 2021).

While the above quote is from a recent scientific article, a decade ago a separate group of researchers echoed the same findings.

> *"Meta-analyses integrating a large number of empirical studies across various training topics from manager training to team training, cross-cultural training, and all forms of employee training consistently show that when training is designed systematically and based on the science of learning and training, it yields positive results."* (Salas, et al., 2012).

What this means to you as a CEO is that you can have comfort that your learning-and-development dollars are not wasted. Let me caveat this a bit because there is waste in all human endeavors. More precisely then, while some of your L&D investment is wasted in ineffective practices, overall, even now, training seems to be paying off in producing significant returns on your investment!

I've got more good news! The research shows that the learning-and-development field is getting better over time! Decade to decade, my fellow L&D compatriots are producing additional organizational impacts! As the most robust and recent review of research findings concluded:

> *"One of our significant and novel findings is that the*
> *strength of the relationship between training and*
> *organizational performance has increased year on year*
> *over the past three decades."* (Garavan, et al., 2021).

As a person who has dedicated his career to supporting learning-and-development professionals over the past three decades, I feel a sense of gratitude, even a feeling of accomplishment. As an industry, we are improving our craft—utilizing more and more learning methods aligned with the science of learning. We are improving our learning evaluation methods. We are improving the learning technologies we utilize.

At the same time, it's clear that my fellow learning professionals and I can be doing more; we can continue to professionalize our field and improve our practices.

There's also some skepticism deserved for the glowing results I reported above. The researchers themselves advocate for better research practices. They decry the large percentage of self-report data. They admit that, despite their efforts to temporalize the data—finding training data that comes before results data—the correlational nature of their analyses might leave us wondering what is causing what. Maybe (as we hope) training causes improved organizational results. But maybe the opposite is true. Maybe organizations that are doing well are more likely to spend money on training than organizations that are not doing well.

My perspective is this. Certainly, well-designed training leads to improvement in employees' knowledge, skills, and motivations. Overall, even given the current imperfect state of training practice, investments in training are likely to improve organizational performance and results—or at least break even. Further improvements in learning-and-development practices are likely to increasingly accelerate the power of training and other learning-related practices to support and enable organizational results. Indeed, the overall message of this book is that these improvements will lead to a competitive advantage for your organization and your employees.

My advice to you as CEO is to expect benefits but manage your learning team with rigor and care to accelerate the return on your learning-and-development investment! Again, this book is written to provide you with the practical wisdom to do just that.

Chapter 4

Weakness at the Heart of the Learning Field

I am honored to work with my fellow learning-and-performance professionals and humbled when I learn of their extraordinary efforts. They are a legion of dedicated, honorable people—almost always zealously passionate about helping people learn.

But I must tell you a dark secret. The workplace learning field is not nearly as professionalized as it should be. Organizational leaders like you are partly to blame! I'll explain why in a minute and tell you what you can do about it.

Here's the problem: Every year new people flood into the learning field without a background in learning. They work hard to get up to speed, but they can't possibly learn everything they need to know—at least not fast enough. You'd think there would be trade associations or a governing body to ensure some threshold level of competency, but you would be wrong. Indeed, the workplace learning field has a fragmented array of many trade associations, so there is no authority to enable and enforce professional standards. More troubling, some trade associations are still teaching debunked myths such as learning styles!

It's not a bad thing that subject-matter experts in our organizations move into training on a full-time basis. It's not a bad thing when people switch careers into learning and development. What's unforgiveable is that these good people are not given the rigorous training and education they need to be truly effective.

Sending them off to get a master's degree is helpful, but not always as helpful as you might think. There are many good graduate programs in the learning field, but too many produce graduates who have learned recipes for learning design, not principled wisdom about how people learn. Too many graduate programs teach academic theories that have very little usefulness. Too many graduate programs teach technology skills without teaching how to get employees to move through the learning-to-performance process. And sadly, too many graduate programs teach traditional instructional design concepts that have proven to be faulty. Higher education can be transformational, but not all programs are great. Providing tuition assistance is useful to the extent that the graduate program is good.

11

Where might CEOs have gone wrong? First, it seems quite often that senior leaders assume that anyone can do training, regardless of whether they have a background in it. Would you accept this of your legal team, your manufacturing team, your engineering team? Hell no! You wouldn't! Why is it okay for your learning team? This oversight pushes leaders to fail to provide the resources for a rigorous learning-to-performance education. Your learning team today, if you're lucky, might offer a week-long train-the-trainer program for subject-matter experts who will do standup training—but this is not nearly enough!

I've been consulting in the workplace learning field for over 30 years, and it's just weird how learning-and-development departments get the least technical training in the organization. Like the shoemaker's children who go shoeless, your learning team goes largely without learning and professional development.

And when they do get training, too often it is done with ineffective, feel-good training that energizes and motivates while teaching poor practices and wrongheaded principles. When your folks should be getting solid research-based learning recommendations, they get folklore and myths and pablum.

Your new learning folks need a long-term rigorous education schedule, something more akin to a yearlong process rather than a weeklong sheep dip. At the same time, your more experienced folks could benefit from the same sort of rigorous program to get everyone on the same page. In addition, your learning team should get periodic feedback from outside "learning auditors"—people who have a balance of practical knowledge and a strong background in the science of learning.

Let me give an example from my own work. The Navy SEAL learning team came to me and asked if they could get a research-based audit of their learning design, for their yearlong course for new SEAL candidates. They wanted to get a practical science-based perspective on the efficacy of their learning. I devised a program where we covered major learning principles and then together, over several days, we assessed the strengths and weaknesses of their yearlong training. The workshop involved the commanding officer, the SEAL and SWCC teams' instructors, and their learning architects. By the time I left, their teams had gotten feedback and had devised targets for improvement. By research-benchmarking their learning designs, the team had made time for reflection, had furthered their education about learning, and had made practical plans for improvement.

Learning is essential for excellence, even for your learning professionals! But this type of outside research-benchmarking is rarely seen in organizations like yours. To create a competitive advantage for your organization and employees, members of your learning team need rigorous training on a regular basis and occasional feedback from outside experts.

Chapter 5
Remembering and Forgetting

People naturally learn and forget. Forgetting is not necessarily bad. We tend to forget when other things are more important to remember. For example, if you switched from a computer running Windows to one running Apple's macOS, you would begin to forget how to use Windows and would remember more and more about how to use macOS. Nothing wrong with forgetting in this case.

However, think of the flip side. If we are training or educating people on how to use their new macOS computer, our hope is that they would (1) remember what they needed to remember, and/or (2) remember how to look up what they didn't need to remember.

Note this very important point: We not only want our learners to understand what they're learning; we also want them to be able to remember!

Why is this distinction—between understanding and remembering—so critical? Because we can design learning that only helps people understand, but that fails to help them remember! You may recall from your schooling that, when you crammed for an exam, you did okay on the test, but a week or two later, you had forgotten virtually everything. You used a learning method that was good for supporting understanding, but poor in supporting your remembering. Sadly, most training is designed to support understanding but not remembering! Think now of all the wasted learning in your organization! Your employees learn, but soon forget—so we've wasted their time and untold resources to build and deliver training that didn't fully work.

There is good news! There are specific learning designs we can use to help people remember. I will go into these in more depth later, but there is still more to learn about remembering and forgetting.

People forget over time, but they tend to forget more information at first—gradually losing a diminishing amount as time goes on. This is a general trend. If you hear that people forget 90% in a week, 50% in a day, or any specific percentage, you are being bamboozled. The rate of the forgetting curve depends on many factors. There is no set timeframe for forgetting! Indeed, some things we never forget! You will never forget how this book changed your perspective on learning, for example!

Given that forgetting is natural, learning architects have at least six options for creating solutions that support performance—and these can be used in combination.

1. Provide learning events close in time to when they are needed.

2. Reinforce learning to minimize the forgetting curve.

3. Set up contextual triggers during learning to support spontaneous remembering later.

4. Forget about using learning as the primary performance vehicle; use prompting tools (like job aids, checklists, performance-support systems, signage, etc.) to directly support performance.

5. Prime employees' personal motivation to learn, help them establish habits of learning, and set up conditions where they may succeed in learning.

6. Place learners in nurturing apprenticeship-like work situations, where they are learning while working under the direction of experienced workers who are skilled in the work and competent to act as coaches.

The options above will be described later, so don't worry if they don't make sense yet.

What I hope you will understand now (and remember for later) is that using learning to support performance is a lot more complicated than we might think. Because it's more complicated, you as the leader of your organization will do well to ensure you have a strong learning team and managers who are managing their people in a way that aligns with how learning and forgetting actually work!

Also, you'll want to enable your learning team to utilize more than just traditional training. One-time training sessions can be useful, but maybe you could support your learning team when they suggest that learning spread over time might be more effective at supporting remembering. When your learning team suggests that training isn't actually necessary in all cases—that they'd prefer using performance support in some situations—maybe you could give them cover when your senior managers complain they want a good old-fashioned training course. When your learning team designs training that challenges your employees with rigorous practice, maybe you could stand up for them when your employees trained in that way rate the training lower than previous trainings—even when the training is clearly superior in supporting their job performance.

There is lots you can do, and we'll explore more ideas as we continue.

Chapter 6
Author's Introduction

OMG. Some of these first chapters are so over-the-top that you must be thinking, "*Who the hell is this guy? Can I trust him?*" You have a right to know, so let me share a bit about myself. Toward the end of the book, I provide more detail, but here I share who I am.

I'm Will Thalheimer. I'm a veteran in workplace learning, with over 35 years in the workplace learning field. I've been a consultant, leadership trainer, instructional designer, simulation architect, learning evaluator, research translator, workshop facilitator, conference speaker, keynoter, writer, and advocate.

I've worked with hundreds of organizations. Large companies like Walgreens, Bloomberg, ADP, Boeing, Genentech, Microsoft, AMD, Novartis, Kaiser Permanente, Liberty Mutual, Colgate, Procter & Gamble, McKinsey. Government entities like the Navy SEALs, the Centers for Disease Control and Prevention, the Defense Intelligence Agency, the National Park Service, and the US Postal Service. Universities like Tufts, UMBC, and MIT. Mission-driven organizations like Oxfam, the Gates Foundation, the World Bank, and the United Nations. Also, many small to midsized elearning and training companies.

I have taught or developed instruction on a variety of subjects, including leadership, business strategy, change management, conflict resolution, coaching, business acumen, presentation skills, learning, elearning design, research-based learning, the spacing effect, and simulation design. I've also helped others build learning interventions for manufacturing safety, coaching, sales training, call-center performance, onboarding, military boot camp, leadership, diversity and inclusion, and farm business management.

Since the 2016 publication of my book on learning evaluation, I've helped hundreds of organizations build more effective learner surveys. I've been very active in debunking myths and misconceptions in learning. I've been writing research-to-practice reports, articles, and posts on learning—and giving them away for free for several decades.

And I guess I should add that, earlier in my life, I had a series of lower-level jobs, so I've seen workplaces from the ground floor up. I processed health-insurance claims in a room that stretched longer than a football field, sweated through shifts as a short-order cook, worked with mental health clients in three separate institutions, drove a van, sold suits and menswear at a large retailer, and sold vacuum cleaners.

What I promise to do in this book is to distill what I have learned over my many varied experiences into a useful guide to achieve organizational and personal improvement through learning. I also promise to tell you the truth.

Some people are going to be angry about the ideas and recommendations in this book. I will tell hard truths, criticize practices that seem to work but don't, debunk myths, and make recommendations that will disrupt and overturn years of tradition and stagnation.

On the other hand, this book will make many people extremely happy. You will be one of the happy ones. I'll give you enough deep understanding of the learning-to-excellence process that you'll see how to leverage it for competitive advantage—but I won't overload you with the jargon of the learning field (well, there may be a little).

There are two other groups that will be happy—the best and the brightest in the learning field and the most dedicated and honest vendors in the learning industry. You and your organization will benefit from their ascendency as well.

In every field of endeavor there are superstars. Much of the time, they are rewarded and recognized for their excellence, but this is not always true; and, in some fields, it is less true. In the workplace learning field, the best and brightest are sometimes overlooked. This book will help you see who they are, and they will be happy to finally get the credit they deserve. Notably, they will be even happier to finally get the green light to make learning the killer practice it should be.

Your organization almost certainly hires vendors in the learning-and-development field. Too often you've hired mediocre vendors—some who sold your organization on some snake-oil dream that did more harm than good. This book will help you hire effective, honest vendors, and they will be happy to get the business they have earned.

Your organization is likely investing poorly in learning and development. In the final chapter of the book, I'll tell you how to spend your L&D money; where to spend less and where to spend more. I can provide such guidance because I've been around for a damn long time, and I've worked with hundreds of organizations that invest in learning.

Two more things about me. I'm a learning-and-performance expert and I have some hard-earned business savvy; however, I'm not a skilled business leader like you are, nor do I know your industry like you do. Where my recommendations seem to go beyond learning-and-performance practices, you should use your own counsel.

One final thing about me, which you've probably already guessed: I write differently than most. I'm going to attempt, to the best of my ability, to talk directly to you—as if we were in a conversation focused on getting things done. I will certainly be heard by others, but it is you I want to reach, because you are the one who can accelerate learning effectiveness and work performance most quickly. Thank you for joining me on this journey!

Chapter 7
How to Use This Book

Read it! Don't just pass this on to your learning people! You've learned as a leader that you must make an investment to get returns! Do it for learning too! But don't feel you have to read every chapter all at once! I will point you to what is most important.

If you treat your learning team as a silo—throwing this book over the wall to them—you'll only get 5% of what you could get. Indeed, this has been one of the fundamental problems over the years. Training departments are treated as commodity producers, not as true partners. Would you treat your marketing team as a commodity? Your operations team? Of course not! Your employees are fundamental to your organization's success. So first learn the basics; then, you'll know how to partner with your learning team to leverage the learning-to-excellence process—to leverage your employees and their productivity and passion. It truly does begin with you!

If you like the ideas and recommendations I share with you, get this book into the hands of all your learning people—not just your Chief Learning Officer (aka Chief Talent Officer, Chief People Officer). Later, you'll see why this is so critical. And whatever you do, don't just delegate this to your Director of Human Resources. That would be a mistake! I'll explain why later.

This book may hold value for other senior managers. You'll be able to make decisions about that as you read, but here's my best guess as to how it might benefit your team. They will all benefit as managers, being able to unleash learning to the benefit of their teams, but they will also find advantages in their specific roles as well.

- Your Chief Financial Officer (CFO) will benefit in understanding how learning resources are investments, how your organization can save money in the long run.

- Your Chief Operations Officer (COO) will benefit by seeing how tiny investments in time by line management can produce sizable improvements in productivity, quality, and motivation.

- Your Chief Information or Technology Officer (CIO or CTO)—or whoever is running the learning tech stack—will benefit from seeing how learning is not just about training, but about personal journeys employees take. Also, by understanding learning's potential, your CIO/CTO will see how your Learning Management System (LMS) may be limiting your learning team and failing your organization.

- Your Chief Product Officer (CPO) and Chief Marketing Officer (CMO) will benefit in seeing how learning can improve creativity and boost innovation.

- Your General Counsel will benefit by seeing the legal risks.

- Your Chief Human Resource Officer (CHRO) will benefit by seeing how timidity and risk-aversion have harmed your learning-and-development practices.

After you've developed a new partnership with your learning team, review the book when you need a reality check, when you want to remember how to hold your learning team and managers accountable, and when you're looking for new innovations in learning.

I've designed the book to make things easy: chunked it into short chapters, written it plainly and directly, and provided an extensive index where you can search for what you need. I hope these design efforts maximize the benefits you and your organization gain from reading, studying, and applying what you learn. If I can do anything else, please contact me at https://www.worklearning.com/contact/.

If you're severely constrained for time, I recommend the following five sections as must-reads for you as a senior leader:

- Section One on Foundations to Get You Started (you're here now)

- Section Two on Fundamentals of Training Practice

- Section Three on Learning and Technology

- Section Seven on Fixing the Crap-Data Problem

- Section Nine on Managing Your Learning Team

I recommend skimming the other chapters as well and reading all the section introductions, as they provide an overview of the main points.

Finally, pay specific attention to the last chapter, where I suggest in which learning-and-development practices to invest less and in which to invest more.

Section Two
Fundamentals of Training Practice

Section Two—Theme

Section Two shares fundamental insights about current practices in learning and development and illuminates why change is necessary. These chapters will help you think clearly about the work your learning team is doing—and will serve as a foundation for decisions you can take as you manage your organization's learning practices.

Chapter 8—Learning Data Is Often Crap Data

In this chapter I tell you how most learning teams gather data and how these practices produce data that is not only meaningless but is likely to push them—and you and your senior team—to advocate for poor learning designs. Poor learning data is arguably the biggest problem in the practice of learning and development.

Chapter 9—Other Learning Evaluation Failures

Here I highlight additional issues in learning evaluation. I talk of the limitations of the learning industry's traditional 1950s-era evaluation model: the Kirkpatrick-Katzell Four-Level Model. I share how we in L&D float businessy-sounding terms to appear credible, even though our overall evaluation efforts are too often flawed.

Chapter 10—Training Is NOT Always the Answer

Here I tell you about a common problem in organizations: Too many managers think that training alone can solve their problems. They don't consider that training might be the wrong solution, or that training will not work if other changes aren't made, or that training works best when it's part of a larger learning-to-performance initiative.

Chapter 11—Training Does NOT Work Alone

In this chapter I highlight how training requires after-training support to ensure that learners—your employees—can transfer their learning back to their work.

Chapter 12—Your Learners Don't Always Know Learning

Tons of research, which I outline in the chapter notes, shows that learners regularly make poor learning decisions. The implication is that your organization should not rely solely on the reputation of a learning program or on the survey data gathered from learners.

Chapter 13—Why Your Experts Aren't Always Great at Teaching

There are three major reasons why experts should not be designing training courses. Their skills are needed for work. They have so much in-depth knowledge that they have difficulties communicating with novices. They have poor intuitions about what good learning design looks like.

Chapter 14—Avoiding Myths and Misconceptions

In this chapter, which is longer than most of the chapters, I share a dozen learning myths that are likely to be influencing your learning team and managers and harming your organization's learning practices. I share these so you'll see the depth of the problem.

Chapter 15—Managers and Learning

Acknowledging the importance of managers, I show how their effectiveness is based largely on how they leverage learning. I list 11 ways managers can better utilize learning to improve the knowledge, productivity, and morale of their direct reports.

Chapter 16—Managers' Performance Checklist

Here I provide a checklist that managers can use to support their direct reports in learning and performance—and thus fulfill their organizational role as force multipliers.

Chapter 17—Stop Your Managers from Demanding Stupid Stuff

In this chapter I show how well-meaning managers can push your learning team into using poor learning designs and faulty tools and approaches.

Section Two—Notes for Learning Professionals

The fundamentals described above apply to us as well. We must begin to invest more in learning evaluation—using better learner surveys but also measuring constructs like decision competence, skills, and behavior change. We must upskill our teams to avoid myths and use research-inspired practices. We must support our organizations' managers by helping them leverage learning. We must assert ourselves constructively in a healthy partnership with managers.

Chapter 8
Learning Data Is Often Crap Data

OMG. You're going to hate this! As CEO, you know the importance of data—and you also know that some data is more important than other data. Most importantly, you know that some data is valid and some data is crap data!

In the learning field, most of the data used by learning teams to make decisions is crap data! Let me repeat. Most of the data used by learning teams (likely including your learning team) is crap data! This is a huge problem because "what gets measured gets managed" even if what gets measured is meaningless, trivial, or misleading.

In the excellent book *The Tyranny of Metrics,* Jerry Muller admits to the benefits of data but shows case after case where data pushes organizations and industries toward poor decisions. He shows that, when we rely on data that is *easy* to collect rather than data that is *meaningful* to collect, we head for trouble.

As an MBA student I learned of the classic salesperson problem: collecting data on the amount of revenues a salesperson brings in but forgetting to measure the amount of profit the salesperson generates. By measuring one and not the other, we reward sales while hoping for profits. Would it be rude of me to point out that your compensation is likely tied to some things that are easier to measure (like current profits or stock price) in lieu of other things that are important to measure (like the strength and innovation of your R&D team)? The bottom line is that the bottom line is not always the only metric that matters.

Crap data manifests itself in the learning field in so many ways. What are the two top ways organizations like yours measure learning? Do you measure comprehension, remembering, or ability to apply skills on the job? No! Not often. Do you measure the benefits of training to your organization? Not really! You'll see what I mean in a minute.

The two most popular methods of measuring learning are learner perceptions of learning and learner attendance. When your Chief Learning Officer (CLO) reports on your year-end results, he or she tells you how many people were trained or how many hours of training were delivered, right? Your CLO (or VP of Talent, Head of Training, or whatever you call them) also reports on your learner-survey ratings, correct? Learner surveys (aka smile sheets, happy sheets, reaction forms) are surveys of learners, usually reported on a five-point scale. *"This year, our evaluation results averaged 4.35 on a 5-point scale, up from 4.29 last year, so things are looking good."*

Ha! This is the biggest lie your learning leaders are telling you! I wrote the definitive book on how to make these learner surveys better, but even I don't believe they should be your primary tool to evaluate success. They have several problems. First, they can be easily gamed. Trainers can do things to create happy participants, even when making them happy hurts learning. Second, learning that really makes a difference—maybe we could call this "transformational learning"—is often difficult. People don't always like things that are difficult, so they rate challenging training lower. Third, there's a ton of scientific research on learner surveys. In two meta-analyses on workplace training—reviewing over 150 scientific studies—the correlation between smile-sheet ratings and learning results was 0.09 (virtually no correlation at all)! Statisticians tell us that any correlation below 0.30 is weak. And this is a general phenomenon in learning. Even in universities, the correlation is 0.20. The finding that traditional smile sheets provide poor data is universal.

What this means from a practical standpoint is that, if your learning team gets high marks on their learner surveys, they could be producing excellent training; however, it's almost equally likely that these high marks mean they are producing poor training. And the same is true about low marks on learner surveys. With traditional smile sheets, you just can't tell!

Later, I'll talk about how your learning team can create much better learner surveys—Performance-Focused Learner Surveys—but still, these should not be your learning team's sole source of valid data on learning success.

There are other problems with learning data—and we'll go into depth later—but briefly here are some specific problems: (1) too many evaluations rely only on subjective data, (2) too many evaluations don't control for extraneous causal factors, and (3) too much of what is reported to you has been cherry-picked to "prove" that training works.

Here is the MOST IMPORTANT POINT: If your learning team is getting data that has no relationship to learning outcomes, they are freaking in the dark! They have no way of knowing what to keep doing and what to change! They are committing learning malpractice right under your nose.

You could blame them, of course, or you could blame the learning industry. Being a pragmatic CEO, though, you're probably better off looking forward—thinking about what you can do to get this fixed. Later, I'll show you how.

Chapter 9
Other Learning Evaluation Failures

Here in the beginning, I'm emphasizing learning measurement because it is the root of all evil in the learning field. I repeat this phrase because it is so important, not just because of its poetry and power.

I was doing some learning-evaluation consulting in one of the world's most prestigious consulting firms, when something happened that woke me up to a huge problem. I tell this story as a warning.

I gave a short presentation on some new concepts in evaluation and then sat off to the side of the room as the organization's learning analytics team gave a presentation on their new approach to displaying their data. I had NOT gotten a preview of their new reporting tool, but I had learned how they collected their data. What the team unveiled was a beautiful visualization system for learning evaluation, complete with gorgeous graphics and the ability to click on the data and drill down to its constituent details. I kept quiet as they rolled out a demonstration of the proposed new dashboard.

At the end of their presentation, the head of the learning unit stood up and said, *"This is fantastic! This is exactly where we need to go in learning evaluation!"*

I was stunned, horrified, and amused. The system did look beautiful, but the data was based on poorly constructed smile-sheet questions, so the data had no meaning. Indeed, if the learning team relied on data from the beautiful dashboard, they would be induced to make bad decisions about their learning designs. If business leaders relied on the data, they would reward and promote the wrong people on the learning team! It was a major clusterfog, but everyone was all smiles.

Later, when I had a chance to work with that same learning-evaluation team, I kindly (but forcefully) described the problem. By that time, however, it was too late: The momentum for rollout could not be stopped. Once again, there had been a rush to judgment because they had taken the wrong factors into consideration. And this was happening at one of the world's most prestigious consulting companies! It could happen anywhere! Maybe even in your organization.

Fancy dashboards and visualizations are not the only gilded diversions in learning evaluation. Another major problem is the bullshitification of learning-evaluation terminology. We learning folks use terms like return on investment (ROI), learning analytics, big data, return on expectations (ROE), and predictive analytics. Because these terms sound authoritative, they are more likely to be accepted as valid and useful—regardless of their actual benefits.

My colleagues and I in the learning field are suckers for using businesslike terminology. We think it will help us "get a seat at the table" in talking to you. Vendors and consultants in the learning field tell us that we should use business terminology because that's what will resonate. This is, of course, good advice in some ways. We want our work to align with your concerns as the leader of the organization. We want learning to be aligned with business results. The bad part is that we think mimicking your terminology guarantees that we are being clear and forceful—when too often we are bastardizing business concepts and rendering them meaningless. For example, our ROI calculations are often based on employees' wild guesses about how much a training program will increase revenues and/or reduce costs, as if the employees had such wisdom.

Another learning-evaluation pitfall is the Kirkpatrick Four-Level Model of evaluation. It has dominated the learning-and-development field for half a century, but its flaws are legendary. One group of training researchers reported that the Kirkpatrick Model *"is antithetical to nearly 40 years of research on human learning, leads to a checklist approach to evaluation... and, by ignoring the actual purpose for evaluation, risks providing no information of value to stakeholders..."* Other researchers wrote: *"Kirkpatrick's framework is not grounded in theory and the assumptions of the model have been repeatedly disproven over the past 25 years."* And yet, there are almost certainly people in your organization who are using the Kirkpatrick Model today. This model, born in the 1950s—before the cognitive revolution in learning science—has no place in your organization.

While most often called the "Kirkpatrick Model," you may hear it called the "Kirkpatrick-Katzell Model." I have been advocating for this because Raymond Katzell originated the four-level idea and Donald Kirkpatrick labeled the four levels and popularized the model.

For all the problems with our current learning evaluation methods, there are solutions. Later, I will help you discern good learning data from bad learning data. I'll tell you which terms are useful and which are just eye candy. I'll detail a new learning evaluation model, LTEM (the Learning-Transfer Evaluation Model). Full disclosure: I created LTEM in 2018—with feedback from experts in learning science and evaluation—to help overcome the deficiencies in the Kirkpatrick-Katzell Four-Level Model.

We will come back to learning evaluation—over and over—because it is so important.

Chapter 10
Training Is NOT Always the Answer

One of the biggest complaints learning professionals have about working in an organization like yours is that senior leaders like you—and almost every manager in your organization—believes too strongly in the power of training. It is used like a magic potion, good for whatever ails the organization.

Sales are down; let's train the salespeople. We need everyone to be more emotionally intelligent; let's train everyone on EQ. Call center times are rising; let's train the reps to shorten their calls. Safety incidents in manufacturing are above industry averages; let's train everyone on lockout-tagout. We need managers to become leaders; let's train them on servant leadership. Blockchain is the next big thing; let's train all our developers. A new software app will soon be rolled out; let's train everyone before it arrives.

I was called into a large meat manufacturing company to fix their safety training. Their safety record was a disaster. After asking a variety of their people a bunch of questions, I told them I'd have to see how the sausage was made before I could make recommendations. Remarkably, they agreed. I say "remarkably" because, too often, organizations don't look beyond training once training is targeted in the causal spotlight. I spent a week talking to their trainers, walking around their factories, sitting in line meetings, and interviewing people who had a good record on safety and people who had screwed up. They did have training issues, but training wasn't their only problem. Their managers did a terrible job in helping their teams be safety conscious. In pre-shift meetings they would spout useless phrases like "10 fingers 10 toes" to remind people to follow safety procedures. Safety numbers weren't posted, but speed of production was—sending a message that speed was the most important goal.

I told them they could improve the training—and I described how to do it—but I also told them that training was not the only problem they had. Like many organizations, they had somehow thought that training could work magic without examining other factors that were causing problems.

Let me describe how training programs are born. Most often, your learning-and-development folks receive training requests. "Hey, Sam, we need a course on coaching; can we sit down and plan how to get that done?" The second most popular method—one that is more proactive—has your learning team surveying or interviewing employees/managers about training needs. Okay, as a CEO you're likely a very observant person: What is the focus of both methods? More importantly, what is left out? I'll give you just a moment to think about it. I'm serious; go ahead—do this thought experiment before moving ahead.

Simple, really. What comes into focus is training.

What fails to come into focus can be a bit harder, but here are some questions to ask:

- If training can help, what other supports will also help?
- Should learners' managers be involved in some way?
- Will learners need coaching, support, guidance?
- Will they need extra time in their schedules to work on their new skills?
- What obstacles might learners face? How can these be overcome?
- Do rewards or incentives need to be re-aligned?
- Do people have the resources they need?
- Will they need reinforcement or occasional retraining?
- Will learners benefit from job aids, performance support, or other prompting tools?

And the list of learning-support questions could go on.

But all that ASSUMES training can help. What if training can't really help at all? What if the real problem was with incentives, or non-intuitive software, or bad management, or turf wars, or lack of resources, or poor equipment? OMG! So many things can go wrong when we assume training is the answer!

So why are your managers treating your learning folks like order-takers at a fast-food restaurant? I'll tell you why: It's easier. It's tradition. "The damn department creates training, doesn't it?" and managers figure they've already diagnosed the problem and they don't see what they don't see.

Learning departments—or whatever you call yours—should really be learning-to-performance departments. They can't know everything your line managers know, but they can help your line managers think through the most common causes of performance failure and the most common opportunities for performance improvement.

Later, I'll describe two practices you can use to expand your organization's lens beyond training. One practice involves a radical shift in your organization's training-request process—and it's quite simple. I'll provide a series of questions your learning team can ask when they get a training request. The second practice involves performance diagnosis, a checklist your managers can use to think about their performance issues.

Chapter 11
Training Does NOT Work Alone

I hinted at this in the previous chapter, but it's critical to be forceful on this point. Providing training alone is guaranteed not to succeed as well as training that is supported with other resources and practices.

There's a ton of research on learning transfer. Transfer occurs when training is used later in work situations. The scientific research is clear on one very important point: Relying on training alone is just damn foolish.

Think about it. When your organization builds a kick-ass training program, you've invested time and money in (1) investigating training needs, (2) networking a team of stakeholders, (3) building preliminary plans, (4) vetting these plans with subject-matter experts, legal, learning, and maybe marketing too, (5) creating training, (6) perhaps piloting the training or aspects of new learning designs, (7) getting final sign-offs, (8) rolling out the training, (9) evaluating it, (10) improving it, (11) sharing results, and (12) monitoring it. And, of course, that doesn't include the time and lost productivity of dragging people away from their jobs and into training!

With all these costs, you really *oughta wanna* invest a little bit more to ensure that training produces maximum benefits. You invest in motor oil on top of the cost for your car. You invest in software over and above the cost of your computers. You don't just send your kids to school; you also encourage them to read, help them with homework, and love and nurture them in ways that support them as they grow up to live independently in the real world.

What does the research say about enabling training transfer? There are two ways to enable transfer. First, the learning must be well designed based on science-of-learning best practices. Second, and this is where we are focusing here: Learning must be supported after training with a focus on applying what was learned.

To provide after-training support, we can get learners' managers involved before and after training; ensure learners can apply what they learned soon after training; prepare learners to stay motivated even in the face of work pressures, obstacles, and distractions; monitor and support learner progress in applying what they learned; remind learners of learning concepts and their goals for application; provide learners with time and resources; and enable early successes in applying the learning to the work.

Four sets of stakeholders can support these after-training interventions. Learners can sometimes support each other, either through preplanned alliances or through technology-enabled communities of practice. For example, pairs or groups of people can agree to meet once a week for two months to support each other and hold each other accountable. They can share lessons learned and encourage each other. Similarly, online communities can be formed to facilitate after-training communication and support.

Trainers can expand their role beyond the original training events. They can check in with employees as they work to implement what they've learned. They can form and facilitate the communities of practice mentioned above. They can remind employees of key concepts, milestones, and goals. They can make themselves visible and available to employees to help them overcome obstacles.

Managers of learners can set expectations for training and the application of the training, they can coach and support, they can provide resources and time, they can troubleshoot obstacles and confusions, and, generally, they can set a climate where learning is encouraged.

Senior managers—including you as CEO—can role-model the manager-as-a-learner role, can set the expectation that managers should be involved in training support, and can ensure your learning team has the resources and political cover to be more than just producers of training events.

I am focusing here on after-training support because it is so critical, but the most effective training is also supported prior to training—not just in designing and planning for training delivery but also in building relationships with managers and the organizational units targeted by the training. Enrolling support and resources is critical.

Yes! All this training support adds a little time and cost, but it's well worth it.

To go back to the car analogy: Training support is like the fuel that runs your car—it's an extra cost, but you're not going anywhere without it!

Chapter 12

Your Learners
Don't Always Know Learning

You and your fellow CEOs are rarely interviewed about training (we know you rightfully have other things on your mind). However, when you were surveyed about a decade ago by IBM and ASTD (the largest workplace trade association in the world), you said something I'll never forget, because it scared the hell out of me. In those interviews, CEOs and other C-suite executives said they didn't really care that much about measured learning outcomes; what they really cared about was what they were hearing about the training from their business unit and line leaders. It was the reputation of the training that mattered as it filtered up from employees to their managers to executives like you.

The logic seems to be this: Learners can distinguish between good and bad learning events and can accurately translate this to their managers, who can accurately convey this to executives. Unfortunately, this logic is built on a dangerously faulty foundation: Learners are notoriously unreliable judges of learning effectiveness! If we rely on learner perceptions, we are almost certainly going to make bad decisions about what works.

There is a ton of scientific research on the problems learners have in making good decisions about their own learning. For example, learners are overly optimistic about their ability to remember, so they fail to give themselves enough repetitions to solidify new concepts. Learners fail to provide themselves with practice to support long-term remembering. Learners can't always shake off their incorrect prior knowledge. Learners often fail to properly use examples to foster deeper learning. Learners sometimes falsely believe that, if they can remember something easily, then they will be able to remember it easily in the future. These scientific findings don't mean that learners are always wrong about their own learning, but the results do show that learners are often inaccurate.

You might even be more shocked to know that educators—and I will include trainers, learning architects, and elearning developers—can also be unreliable in their judgments of what works in learning. The human mind is brilliant in many ways, including in its ability to make us think we understand something when we don't. You may have heard of the Dunning-Kruger effect: the finding that people who don't know very much are often the most confident. If learning professionals can be fooled, and learners themselves have blind spots, what makes us think that people with no background in learning—say, managers and executives—can make assessments about learning simply by talking to learners? It's absurd!

Here's the bottom line: As CEO, you should not rely on the say-so of your line managers, or anecdotal reports from your employee learners, or even sophisticated surveys or interviews of those learners. Human learning is too complex to be gauged by subjective opinions alone!

Are there other implications of this learners-don't-always-know reality? Yes! Unfortunately, an overwhelming majority of your organization's training programs are measured using ONLY learner perceptions (in addition to measuring attendance). This means your learning team is relying on unreliable data to make all its improvement and maintenance decisions!

Yes! I mentioned this problem earlier when I talked about crap data. I mention it again, not only to warn you about the learning data you're hearing about as CEO, but also to remind you that the crap-data problem is at the heart of what needs to be fixed in your organization's learning efforts. It is the root of all evil in the learning field, and, if you can fix this, you will unleash a juggernaut of learning and job-performance improvement!

OMG. There's more! What other implications can you imagine from the reality that people don't always know how best to learn? Well, you probably can't rely on people to learn on their own. Maybe they'll learn, but more slowly and ineffectively than we'd like. You probably can't rely on your managers to know how to coach and support the learning and development of their direct reports—at least not without some additional guidance.

Let's be real. Some learning inefficiencies are fine! There are inefficiencies everywhere in all human endeavors! But the bottom line for you as a CEO is that it's probably worth the investment to have your learning team work to (1) design effective training, (2) nudge and support your employees after training to help them apply what they've learned, (3) train your managers to facilitate on-the-job learning, and (4) directly enable workflow learning and creativity within your employee teams. It is the organizations that do this that will gain a competitive advantage.

Chapter 13

Why Your Experts Aren't Always Great at Teaching

As CEO you might wonder why you need learning-and-development folks. Maybe you could cut costs by transferring responsibilities to your operational units. You might ask your chief learning officer, "Why don't we just get our experts in operations, finance, marketing, research, technology, legal, and so forth, to teach what they know? We could give them training and support in how to craft good presentations. Seriously, why do we need so many instructional designers and trainers, so many learning experience designers, learning architects—or whatever you call them? Can't we rely on our experts to teach?"

No! No! No! You can't! Let me explain why. First, your experts are busy doing work. Certainly, they can make time for coaching other experts and sharing what they know, but creating effective training is very time consuming. Most estimates suggest that, to create one hour of training, it takes somewhere from 30 to 70 hours of preparation. To create a one-day (six-hour) course, it might require one of your experts to spend 300 hours. Is that really what you want your most knowledgeable employees to be doing?

But it gets worse. There are two other major problems with the presumption that your subject-matter experts can develop and teach your courses. First, experts are often poor teachers. Not always, but very often! Indeed, if we consider human cognition, we'd see it's natural that experts have trouble teaching. Experts have deep knowledge structures. They are so experienced in their own areas of expertise that they have forgotten what it's like to think like a novice. Their knowledge is automated. That is, they use it without thinking about how they're using it. So, when they try to explain what they're doing—to help novices make sense of the content—they often omit important foundational concepts and/or critical steps in a work sequence.

Researchers have studied this extensively. They call it *"the curse of knowledge."* Experts simply aren't very good at explaining concepts to non-experts. Have you as CEO always been successful as you try to explain things to your senior staff? To your employees? To your teenagers? Do they always understand your meaning? If you thought they were ignoring you or that they were just daft, maybe the problem was the curse of knowledge.

Or maybe you were momentarily delusional. You thought they understood you. Ha! This too is a problem. When we communicate, we have a tendency to believe we've been successful even when the recipients of our communications are confused. There's research on this too! See the chapter notes for an extensive list of research citations.

When we make presentations, we overestimate how successful we are in communicating. When we speak to other people, we tend to overestimate what they have understood. This can be especially problematic for people in authority—like CEOs and managers and experts. We tend not to encourage our listeners to share what they understand, and people in subordinate positions are unlikely to feel comfortable to voice confusions or ask questions.

Your experts—those who you might expect to teach your organization's courses—suffer from another huge limitation. They simply don't know what good learning looks like. They tend to lecture. They don't check their learners' comprehension. They teach too much content, overloading their learners. They don't provide enough realistic practice. They too often teach principles devoid of situational context. They don't provide meaningful repetitions. When they do provide repetitions, they don't vary repetitions to keep learners engaged and attentive. They don't space repetitions or practice activities over time to support long-term remembering. They don't inoculate learners to the obstacles they'll face when they attempt to apply what they've learned to the job. They don't provide sufficient feedback early on to help learners build correct mental models. They don't provide delayed feedback later, to support employees in remembering. They don't provide job aids or performance supports. They don't stay in touch with learners after their courses, to provide coaching and reminders, or to see what worked and what didn't. In short, your subject-matter experts tend to produce courses that are highly ineffective.

To summarize this chapter, there are three reasons your experts should not be relied upon to build your training courses:

- First, it takes a ton of time to create effective training, and your experts are almost always more useful to your organization as experts, not as trainers.
- Second, experts tend to be bad teachers, and there is no quick fix.
- Third, experts are not good at learning design. They don't have the knowledge, and their tendencies are all wrong.

As CEO, your primary role here is to discourage your managers from assigning experts to build courses. Instead, encourage the practice of having your experts partner with your learning team. You also might draw wisdom from this chapter for your own practices in communicating. Watch out for your own curse of knowledge. Encourage those who receive your messages to share their understandings. Seek feedback. Fine tune. Repeat.

Chapter 14
Avoiding Myths and Misconceptions

Every field has its myths and misconceptions, but I think the learning field has more than most. As I've mentioned before, the problem is that learning measurement is underfunded, suffers from moribund traditional practices, and CEOs like you haven't yet asked for better practices. Also, it's very hard to measure learning outcomes—even without the frictions currently slowing your learning team. Because we learning professionals have done a bad job in evaluating learning, most of us can't track what works and what doesn't. Where cause and effect swim in muddy waters, myths and superstitions thrive and persist. Elsewhere in this book I show how we can measure to create more accurate feedback loops, but today we need to proactively inoculate ourselves from learning myths. For this reason, I'm going to provide a long list of the 12 most dangerous learning myths and misconceptions—ones that have almost certainly infected your organization already. Remember: We must first do no harm!

A note: This chapter is longer than most. You may start reading and wonder why I'm sharing all these learning myths with you. You might think, "I'm a senior leader; I don't need to know this." You're right: You don't need to know the details, but you do need to know that your learning team is under attack from misinformation. They need your support in having the resources and encouragement to train themselves on evidence-based practices and to get periodic audits of their learning programs and designs from outside experts in research-aligned learning-and-performance improvement.

I share the details with you so you'll have a sense of the depth of the problem. Here are just some of the learning myths that make it difficult for your learning team and your managers to think productively about learning.

Myth 1: Learning Styles

The learning styles myth is ubiquitous in the workplace learning field—and in education as well. There are many forms of learning styles, but the most common argues that training should be designed to support different types of learners: those who are primarily visual, or auditory, or kinesthetic. The believers in this myth say that visual learners should be given visual content, auditory learners should be given audio content, and kinesthetic learners should use their hands or bodies in a learn-by-doing mode.

Unfortunately, it's just not true. It's not true that designing learning to cater to people's learning styles works. Dozens of research reviews of this practice—hundreds of scientific studies—have shown that it just doesn't work. Worse yet, when your learning team focuses on designing learning based on learning styles, it is wasting time and resources that could be better used to focus on the research-based learning factors that do work. If your people are using the learning-styles idea, they are wasting your organization's time and money!

Myth 2: Microlearning and Attention-Span Workarounds

There is a belief floating around today that everyone's attention spans are shorter and that our modern learner just can't handle long learning events anymore. This is malarkey! Human beings' cognitive machinery hasn't changed that much over the past 10,000 years, even as far back to when the word "malarkey" was invented. We are all more distracted today, but that doesn't mean we should necessarily give our learners shorter learning events. In fact, it might be argued that the opposite is the case. Research has discovered that, when people switch from one task to another, there is an attentional cost to the switching. Given this, it might make sense to get our employees away from their distractions so they can focus better—instead of trying to shoehorn microlearning events into their generally cacophonous work environments.

I'm not suggesting the opposite, however. I don't necessarily endorse a seven-hour training day! I've often called day-long trainings "barbaric" because they overtax people's attentional energy reserves. Even the world's best chess players have trouble concentrating beyond three or four hours or so. Even the world's most accomplished writers tend not to write more than four hours a day. Cognitive work is tiring work—and learning is hard! But let's not overreact either; day-long trainings can be designed to maintain cognitive energy, even if they are often less efficient because we add mental breaks and tangential activities, thus diluting the learning.

I'm also not suggesting that periodic short learning events can't be helpful. They can be extremely helpful, especially in providing spaced repetitions and reminders. The point I want to emphasize is that there is no magic need to shorten all your learning events into 10-minute increments. The big-picture takeaway here is that learning is complicated, and overly simplistic solutions are just going to cause problems! And again, this is another reason your learning team and the people who manage them need to have a strong background in research-based knowledge about learning.

Myth 3: eLearning Is Less Effective Than Classroom Training

Later I will share a whole chapter on this, but it's worth repeating here in our list of learning myths. If it is well designed, elearning can be just as effective as classroom training. In fact, in practice, when training is created as elearning, it tends to be slightly more effective than standard classroom training.

But keep this in mind, too: Both elearning and classroom training can be significantly improved by using research-based science-of-learning wisdom!

Myth 4: Training Is NOT Effective

There is a group of people (running around like their heads have been cut off) who claim that training is not effective. This is simply false. Some of them are trying to sell performance-support applications or workflow-learning applications, etc., while others have noticed that training doesn't *always* work, or it doesn't always work as well as it should, or training doesn't work by itself but requires other organizational actions to be effective.

There is overwhelming evidence that people can learn through training and education, that they can use what they've learned, and that training benefits learners and their organizations. See the chapter notes for Chapter 3 on the impact of training.

Training is effective if it is well designed, if learners get after-training support, if the organizational culture is structured to enable learning application, etc.

Myth 5: Training Is ALREADY Effective Enough

There is another group of people running around with heads disconnected from reality. This group believes that most trainings are generally effective. They don't see much reason to change how training is designed. Indeed, they often point to learner-survey ratings to show that learners think training is effective.

Here's the truth. The standard training design is badly flawed and ineffective! This is true for elearning, classroom training, and most educational settings as well, including at the university level.

And the kicker is that improvements are not hard to make. Providing less content and reinforcing the critical content with realistic practice, feedback, spaced repetitions, after-training support, and other science-based methods can create learning events that are much more effective.

Myth 6: The Learning Pyramid

There are literally thousands of versions of a pyramid-shaped graphic floating around cyberspace, incorporated into train-the-trainer trainings, and published in magazines. Sometimes the levels differ. Quite often the numbers differ. Different people and organizations are cited as the original source. They all say something like this: *"People remember 10% of what they read, 20% of what they hear, 30% of what they see, 50% of what they see and hear, and 80% of what they do."* NONE of this has any basis in science, yet people continue to share this nonsense widely even despite vigorous efforts spanning decades debunking this mythical pyramid.

Here are some telltale signs that this is bogus. First, the numbers all end in zeros or fives. Humans are too variable to produce data like that! Second, note that reading and seeing are separate categories, but how can one read without seeing? Third, what measure of learning is being used? None of the diagrams explain. Fourth, and most importantly, these numbers cannot be traced back to any actual science. Once, on my own, I tracked the numbers back to an employee of the Mobil Oil Company in 1967. Later, when a group of academic researchers asked me to join them in a deeper exploration, other members of our team traced the numbers back to 1913 and 1922. Interestingly, sometime after 1947—when educational theorist Edgar Dale created a cone-like diagram—someone took these numbers and mashed them together into the pyramid shape.

Regardless of whether the numbers are presented in a list or in a pyramid, they are complete baloney and send faulty signals to trainers and educators. Your learning team would do better if it focused on other research-based learning methods.

Myth 7: Brain Science

Neuroscience is all the rage the world over—and much of neuroscience's popularity is deserved. We are learning more and more about the brain and how it functions. However, neuroscience alone tells us very little about how to design learning. Even most neuroscientists admit this! What they tell us is that neuroscience must work hand-in-glove with behavioral science. And that's the key: We already have a ton of behavioral science—most commonly cognitive science—we can rely on.

Here's the problem: Neuroscience is so sexy that learning professionals like me can't resist alluding to it. When a vendor, consultant, or author says their work is based on neuroscience—or when they show us a pretty picture of the brain—we salivate and wait to hear what the neuroscience gods have extolled. This leads us to waste time exploring these so-called neuroscience solutions—almost all of which include little or no neuroscience!

Bogus neuroscience claims fall into two categories. Some share "neuroscience" findings that are based not on neuroimaging but on behavioral science. This isn't as problematic as the second type of bogus claim because at least they are sharing solid research-aligned recommendations. It is still harmful, however, because the neuroscience shine can focus learning professionals to wrongly prioritize what is most important. Rarely do these neuroscience proselytizers do a rigorous exploration of the research to find the most important learning factors. Rather, they grab interesting findings and share those—pushing their readers toward a random assortment of recommendations that are not usually the most important learning factors.

The second sort of bogus neuroscience claims are especially problematic. In these, people share neuroscience findings and make a magic leap to learning implications. *"When the amygdala is hijacked, no learning can take place."* These claims sound important but push learning professionals to focus on the wrong things. For example, rarely in training is anyone's amygdala hijacked. Plus, raising the stakes in training is sometimes exactly what we need to do!

All these neuroscience sleight-of-hand allusions are harmful. They trick learning professionals to focus on tangential points of focus when they could focus on proven behavioral-science research. The neuroscience-for-learning fad costs organizations like yours time and money because you buy products and services in the learning space that just aren't that effective—and your learning team buys into ideas that deflect from what they should really focus on.

Neuroscience seems like it ought to help us create better learning, but it just doesn't. Maybe someday, but rarely now!

Myth 8: Bloom's Taxonomy

Bloom's Taxonomy, published originally starting in 1956, and updated by different sets of authors in the early 2000s, was originally designed as a guide for developing learning objectives and assessments.

There are numerous problems with the original taxonomy. First, since it was developed before the cognitive revolution in psychology, the original version is outdated. Second, the original structure of the taxonomy was divided into the cognitive, affective, and psychomotor domains—but people only use the cognitive taxonomy. Third, the taxonomy was based on how educators assessed learning at the time (assessed from 1949 to 1953), and thus it conveyed *what was*, not *what should be*.

There have been two notable efforts in rejiggering Bloom's Taxonomy, but neither resolved the original issue. Indeed, both are too complex to utilize. Each is offered in book form—one over 200 pages long and one over 350 pages.

But the biggest problem with Bloom's Taxonomy—both the original and the new—is that it is assessment centric, not performance centric. They offer levels that do not provide a good guide to learning design or to learning evaluation. Learning professionals need models that are more actionable and clearer. I have offered several models over the years that provided guidance to learning professionals. For example, the Learning Maximizers Model presents eight clear goals for learning design. The Decisive Dozen outlines 12 key learning factors. LTEM (the Learning-Transfer Evaluation Model) presents eight tiers for learning evaluation.

The Performance Activation Model (a work created with Jerry Hamburg) outlines both learning- and performance-improvement factors. These are just some of my examples; there are also the 4C/ID-Model from researchers Jeroen van Merriënboer, Richard E. Clark, Marcel de Croock—most recently detailed in Jeroen van Merriënboer and Paul Kirschner's book *Ten Steps to Complex Learning*. There is David Merrill's *First Principles of Instruction*. There are also excellent books on learning design by research-to-practice experts Julie Dirksen, Patti Shank, Clark Quinn, and Donald Clark.

The bottom line is that your learning team should use guidance other than Bloom's Taxonomy when designing learning or learning objectives.

Myth 9: 70-20-10

The 70-20-10 model claims that 70% of employee learning is done experientially: by working. It claims that 20% of learning is social learning: learning from others. And 10% is formal learning: learning in the form of training or other intention learning events.

The research on which the model was based was poorly designed and relied on people's subjective assessments of their learning. You might remember that people are not good at assessing their own learning. Also, the respondents were managers, not representative of all employees. Also, other studies produced a wide variety of numeric breakdowns, so the numbers varied from 70-20-10.

Only one scientific study on 70-20-10 has been published utilizing 70-20-10 in a real organization, and the results were not good. The researchers concluded that the 70-20-10 framework *"is failing to deliver desired learning transfer results."* The failures were attributed to (1) unrealistic assumptions that unstructured experiential learning will automatically lead to performance improvement, (2) an unfounded belief that social learning was separate rather than an important element across all three learning modalities, (3) an expectation that managers trained in 70-20-10 would seamlessly be able to implement it without further support, and (4) a failure to intentionally design and support the integration of the three learning modalities.

The only good thing about the 70-20-10 framework is that it reminds us that training isn't the only way learning happens. Did we need a bogus numeric model to tell us that? No! We. Did. Not.

Let me add that some of the strongest advocates for the 70-20-10 model deserve our admiration. After they learned about the weak research backing for the numbers—through public debunking and private conversations—they turned away from the numbers and worked hard to develop effective practices around workplace learning.

Myth 10: Different Generations Must Be Taught Differently

There is a faulty belief that different generations must be taught (and managed) differently than other generations. There are two popular versions of this. The first says that, for example, Gen Zs (for Generation Z) learn differently than Millennials (Gen Y), who learn differently than Generation X, and Boomers, etc. The second perspective says that people who grew up using computers—so-called "digital natives"—have a fundamentally different way of approaching computers, web browsing, smart phones, and other digital technologies.

Neither of these things is fundamentally true. People's human cognitive architecture has not really changed in the past 10,000 years, so it's certainly not true that there are generational differences in our cognitive functioning. Also, while older people do experience some slight cognitive declines, they actually improve and compensate in other ways. Also, it's not true that young people are always better at using computers—or that they think about them differently. There are more differences within age cohorts than outside them.

The fundamentals either don't differ much across generations or they are too variable within generations to matter in comparing one generation to another. This isn't to suggest that age cohorts don't have different interests or preferences or aren't attentive to different types of visuals, stories, or characters. Surely, they do have different proclivities. But gross generalizations—like "younger learners need shorter training or more video"—are unlikely to provide good guidelines for effective learning designs. Similarly, we should not assume that older learners will not benefit from podcast-like audio or mobile learning. Finally, silly notions like "young people require more job-relevant training" are just BS. Older employees prefer job-relevant training as well.

On the other hand, this doesn't mean we should ignore learner characteristics. For example, we know from research that all people are inclined to be persuaded more by people who are similar to them than by people who are different from them. So, if we're trying to encourage young new-hires to make an effort to proactively network during the first year of employment, we might ask a few relatively new employees—say, people who have worked for the company one year—to act as spokespeople in our onboarding training, to tell stories of their networking successes and failures perhaps.

The bottom line is that, as CEO, you should discourage your learning team from wasting their time creating generationally specific training, or hiring vendors who claim to use generational learning designs, etc.

Myth 11: Training Is Not Needed; People Can Look Up What They Need

This is a big one; I hear it quite regularly. People who believe this myth say things like, *"Training is not needed anymore because people can just look up the information they need on*

Google, or YouTube, or Wikipedia, or ChatGPT." This may sound reasonable at first hearing, but it's one of the stupidest ideas of the Internet Age.

Here are the gaps. First, let's think about what this myth conveys. It assumes that people know when they need to know something. Maybe that's true sometimes, but not every time! This is why we have coaches and mentors; they give us feedback when we're doing things wrong. This is why we track performance, so we can let people know when they are succeeding and when they're not. This is why managers benefit from diagnostic feedback from their direct reports: because, otherwise, they might not know what they are doing well and poorly.

Second, it's a luxury to have time to look things up. Sometimes, when we work, we have time to stop and look things up. Very often, however, we move from one action to another without enough time to search for info, reflect on it, search for second opinions, etc.

Third, very often it would just be completely inappropriate to stop in the middle of an activity to look up information. Imagine a salesperson talking with a customer, stopping every 30 seconds to look up how to handle each objection. Imagine a manager running a meeting, looking at their phone to access their good-leader cheat sheet every minute to remind them how to respond to various issues that come up.

Fourth, being productive is not just about knowledge recall. It's also about noticing the situational cues that are critical to performance. It's about acting authentically, naturally, consistently in the presence of others. It's about habits of action engaged in fluently.

Fifth, lots of performance requires practice and repetitions to achieve competence and fluency. Looking up information provides zero practice.

Note that this myth has several downsides. It suggests that we don't need training, coaching, and management. It suggests that large repositories of information are sufficient. It suggests that access to short video explainers is all we need. This mistaken idea also gives rise to the myth that performance tools—like job aids, checklists, and performance support systems—can replace training. All these ideas are dangerous, leaving employees unprepared to notice key situations and unable to act fluently when it matters most—in the flow of their everyday work.

Myth 12: Learning Events Should Be Easy and Comfortable

By its very nature, learning is transformational; it moves us, as learners, from one mental state to another. Sometimes this transformation is easy. When I learn that the produce code for organic bananas is 94011, that is a small transformation. When I learn that sugar is unhealthy even if I'm not overweight—that it leads directly to heart disease, liver disease, cancer, stroke, diabetes, leptin resistance, breakdown in the brain's dopamine system—this is a huge mental transformation, and overwhelmingly gigantic when I begin to try and follow through to cut most sugars out of my diet.

Here's a whole list of large transformations: Recently hired salespeople trying to become fluent in responding to customer objections. People learning a new complicated software app. Managers looking to improve their coaching behaviors. Lawyers getting up to speed on a new area of law. Electricians learning how to deal with Wi-Fi dead zones. Nurses and doctors learning a new surgical technique. Pilots learning a new airplane. Journalists learning to write for social media. Speakers learning how to craft podcasts. Workers learning how to be better stewards in preventing sexual harassment.

Almost everything important we learn requires a large transformation—and large transformations don't just happen! They require intensive learning and practice and a long-term journey to proficiency.

What do learners like? They like easy! We all like easy! So, what do trainers tend to provide? Easy, fun, enjoyable activities. What do trainers tend to avoid? Challenging learners, providing them with significant practice, staying with learners through the journey. And again, why do we allow this to happen? It's the damned idea that learning should be fun and easy—and we reinforce this damaging practice because we primarily measure learner satisfaction. It's a self-reinforcing system that pushes everybody to deliver fun and easy training, leaving learners unprepared.

Enough Is Enough!

These dozen myths are representative of many more. There are hundreds of such myths outlined in excellent books like Clark Quinn's *Millennials, Goldfish & Other Training Misconceptions*, and Pedro de Bruyckere, Paul Kirschner, and Carl Hulshof's two books on *Urban Myths about Learning and Education*.

Here's the thing: If we can educate and persuade your learning team and their key stakeholders to stop building learning based on these myths, they will cause less harm and build more effective learning! *First do no harm* is good advice in medicine and it's good advice in learning. It quickly reduces damaging practices, and it frees up your learning professionals to focus on more effective learning methods.

Chapter 15
Managers and Learning

Managers are indispensable. They are the glue that enables organizations like yours to function. Bad managers are toxic—and there are too many bad managers in our organizations. Great managers balance competing priorities. They get things done, they make the workplace worthy of human habitation, they enable employees to develop and thrive, they energize innovation, they drive ethical behaviors. All these things require learning! Teams must learn to coordinate, overcome obstacles, get along, inspire each other's performance. People don't always know how to learn on their own—or they fail to prioritize their learning and development. Managers can help. In addition, innovation doesn't happen in a vacuum; it must be nurtured and learned.

Unfortunately, managers—like everyone else—don't really understand learning, at least not its intricacies. Even in coaching, managers aren't very good. In my work doing learning audits, I've watched how managers coach others. They tend to make some fundamental errors. They too quickly do tasks for their rookies, they don't provide enough practice with feedback, they don't take the time to understand why their direct reports are making mistakes before correcting them. The upshot of this—this lack of learning wisdom—is that managers could benefit from learning how learning can help them as managers.

Here's how managers can support learning:

- Guide their direct reports toward training that is appropriate and timely, and away from training they don't currently need.

- Set expectations for training and the application of learning.

- Support after-training application with encouragement, monitoring, feedback, and guidance for further development. Create a psychologically safe environment where people can fail safely.

- Give direct reports roles, situations, and tasks that will accelerate their learning of critical knowledge, skills, values, and motivations.

- Run meetings that invite curiosity, teamwork, and learning from each other. Regularly ask, "What can we do better for next time?"

- Create a team culture where a learning focus predominates over a just-do-it attitude. Regularly do after-action reviews, focusing on what went well, what didn't go well, and what we can do better.

- Create better presentations, aiming for the four essential presentation goals: ECRA! Engagement, Comprehension, Remembering, and Action. (I developed this for my workshop called Presentation Science.)

- Enable creativity by following science-based findings about how to support idea generation and follow-through to innovation. Creativity and innovation are a form of learning!

- Provide performance feedback on a regular basis, rather than waiting for an annual performance review or arbitrary milestone.

- Enable a culture of curiosity and experimentation. Be willing to try things out and see how they actually work—as opposed to making final decisions based on assumptions of how things will turn out.

- When providing guidance, don't just stop after showing people what to do. Provide supervised practice with immediate feedback. Then, monitor and be available when people have questions.

I'm touching the surface here, but it's easy to see how learning and leadership go hand in hand. Great managers do a zillion things to support their direct reports in learning. Typical leadership training hints at some of these things, but a more comprehensive learning-centric leadership approach is worth considering.

This is where you set the tone for the whole organization. If you do a great job in supporting the people who report to you—specifically, accelerating their learning—they will be more likely to role-model these behaviors to their folks, creating a ripple effect throughout your organization.

Learning is a competitive advantage. It creates virtuous cycles of improvement. When your employees learn, they do better and they can learn more, and so forth.

And one more thing: People are said to leave their managers, not their organizations. Because one of the most highly prized perks of employment today is learning new things and developing new skills, helping your managers be more sensitive to learning is probably a really good investment in keeping great people in your organization!

Chapter 16
Managers' Performance Checklist

In this chapter, I share a checklist your managers can use to help them reflect on their teammates' performance—and their own performance. This list is inspired by social science research and my experience as an organizational citizen.

1. ***Trust and Comfort***

    Do employees trust their leaders and coworkers to be honest and trustworthy? Do they feel confident that they will be treated fairly and with respect? Do they believe that someone is watching out for their best interests? Is the work situation stable enough so employees need not be distracted with worry, stress, or confusion? Has employee trust been reviewed or considered recently?

2. ***Resources, Tools, and Time***

    Do employees have the resources and tools they need to be effective and productive? Do they have enough time to meet their work goals while also having time to learn, reflect, network, engage in productive social interactions, and restore their mental and physical energy? Has an audit of resources, tools, and time been conducted recently?

3. ***Basic Needs***

    Do employees have enough of their basic needs met that they can focus and bring effort to their work? Are they healthy enough to do good work? Are their financial situations sufficient so they don't need to do side work to earn money and they aren't likely to ruminate and get distracted about money troubles? Is their mental health good enough to bring their full selves to work—their creativity, energy, problem solving, and caring for others? Has an audit or review of employees' basic needs been undertaken recently?

4. ***Obstacles***

    Are employees' work situations set up to enable their good work or are there obstacles that make productive work more difficult? Are there toxic leaders or coworkers who create dysfunction? Are there too many unnecessary steps, procedures, or rules that get in the way? Are there too many layers of management or approval that unnecessarily slow down decision making? Are there work-

45

culture expectations that demotivate, disincentivize, or dominate the thinking of the group? Has a friction audit been done recently to surface issues that are mucking up employee performance?

5. *Incentives*

Are workplace incentives encouraging good behaviors or bad? Are incentives encouraging or discouraging collaboration? Are they creating healthy or unhealthy competition? Are they creating unhelpful stress or invigorating challenges? Are they encouraging or stifling creativity and experimentation? Has an incentive audit been done recently to bring the power and perils of incentives into focus?

6. *Knowledge, Skills, Attitudes*

Do employees have the knowledge they need to be fully effective in their work? Are their skills sharp, up to date, and well-practiced? Are they motivated to do good work? Are they inspired to keep learning and growing? Are they willing and active in supporting others in learning? Are they willing and energized to try new practices, consider new ideas, and challenge their own thinking? Are they given ample opportunities and time to learn? Are meetings run to encourage learning, productive dialogue, and openness to new approaches? Has an employee learning audit been done recently?

7. *Action and Thinking Prompts*

Are prompts used to nudge thinking and action? Do employees have access to well-designed prompting tools like job aids, checklists, and performance supports? Are the prompts they do encounter useful or counterproductive? Are key ideas—such as values, principles, and best practices—kept highly accessible in employees' long-term memories? Have individual and team habits been integrated into the workflow such that they automatically encourage beneficial thinking and action? Has an audit been conducted recently to determine how effectively prompting is being used?

There are myriad factors that influence individual and team performance. The list above is foundational but certainly not exhaustive. For our purposes here, the most important takeaway is that training can only solve for a small percentage of these performance leverage points. As CEO, you can help by reminding your managers of the wide range of performance-improvement opportunities they have at their disposal. You can communicate that training should not be the primary go-to solution, and that, even when training is chosen, it should be augmented with these other leverage points.

Chapter 17

Stop Your Managers from Demanding Stupid Stuff

Here's a problem you should know about. Some of your smartest managers—those who go out of their way to learn things outside their areas of expertise—create some of the biggest headaches for your learning professionals. These zealous managers are well meaning but cause untold damage to your organization when they demand stupid stuff from your learning team. I've seen untold examples of this.

Suggesting Bogus Tools: Alex, who is a CTO (Chief Technology Officer), reads a *Harvard Business Review* article that describes the Myers-Briggs Type Indicator (MBTI) and asks that the MBTI be utilized in the next round of the IT department's project management training—even though the MBTI is not scientifically valid and its use distracts from the main topic (project management) and it also tends to exacerbate gender bias (which makes it particularly toxic in a department that is 80% male).

Beautiful But Weak Data: Jenny, who is a CFO (Chief Financial Officer), learns about big data and insists on having the business's largest trusted vendor, Big Consulting, Inc., analyze how big data can be used to support the learning team. They overwhelm key stakeholders with dreams of beautiful graphics and implement a system that focuses on all the wrong learning metrics—capturing data that's easy to measure (like attendance and completion rates) while completely ignoring learning factors that really matter—like challenging practice, spaced repetitions, motivation to implement, and manager support.

Not Measuring Learning Factors: Albert, who is Head of Sales, learns about the four-level Kirkpatrick learning evaluation model and decides that his most important training for new hires should measure Kirkpatrick Level 4 Results, and specifically sales revenues, while ignoring learning factors. The learning department obliges, spending a ton of money (over $50,000) doing a rigorous exploration using randomized comparisons. They find that the new sales training design does not improve sales significantly, but, because they only measured sales results, they can't tell what went wrong or right in terms of learning.

Poorly Designed Subjective Measures: Tabitha, who is a CEO, wants everything measured in ROI. She directs the learning team to measure the ROI of every training course.

After hearing the seven-figure price tag, she balks, but asks, "Isn't there some other way to measure the return we are getting from training?" Her learning-evaluation team concocts a plan to survey learners by asking them to estimate how much the training will increase revenue or reduce costs. This is ridiculous, of course—people are not good at estimating these things; but, to compensate, the learning team plans to ask people how confident they are in their answers, from 0% confident to 100% confident. Each answer is multiplied as follows. If an employee says the coaching course will increase revenues by $10,000 and are 40% confident, then the estimate is $4,000. Eventually, Tabitha gets the results and is satisfied. But sadly, the results are practically meaningless and misleading, and the money could have been better spent by your learning team elsewhere. They could, for example, focus on key courses and examine learning factors that are under their control. For example, they might have measured whether providing two more practice sessions in sales training was worth the investment in time and sales hours.

All these examples—and similar requests that happen every day—show the waste and misdirection that powerful, well-meaning managers can cause when they dictate or even suggest ideas to your learning team.

You will do your organization a world of good if you can get your managers to use a respectful and inquisitive approach with your learning team. "Hey, Akeem, I was reading about this new LTEM learning-evaluation model and was wondering what you thought about maybe measuring our new coaching program at Tier 4 and 5 instead of just at Tier 3? I know you guys in learning are the experts, but I thought you could explain to me the pluses and minuses, the costs and benefits of doing more than just surveying learners."

If you could nudge your managers to utter a few sentences like that, you would do four things: (1) waste less time and money on dubious projects, (2) build up the fluency of your organization around learning, (3) induce your learning team to swoon to their knees, crying tears of joy for being asked for their expertise, and (4) be much more likely to keep your best and brightest learning people—because they would be able to do their best work and maximize their impact in helping your organization.

Your learning team must step up too. They must be more assertive in turning wayward requests into productive conversations. I'm sure you have some wicked-smart people on your learning team who can give practical, research-informed advice about learning. If not, you should find some immediately—or temporarily hire a consultant with a background in research-based learning design and practical experience to act as a sounding board.

Overall advice: You can help by expecting and enabling your learning team to assert their expertise and by encouraging your managers to work with your learning team as equal partners in performance improvement.

Section Three
Learning and Technology

Section Three—Theme

Section Three covers several critical issues in learning and technology. More than ever before, technology is critical for your learning team, with new learning technologies available all the time. Still, the overarching message from these chapters is that technology should not be used for the sake of the technology; learning and performance-improvement factors are still paramount. This section touches on elearning, course repositories, generative AI, and technology's role in environmental sustainability.

Chapter 18—Technology and Learning

Here I warn you about a common problem that might infect the practice of learning in your organization: the overzealous excitement about new technologies. Most learning professionals know it's not the technology that creates learning outcomes; it's the learning method that matters. And there's a ton of scientific research to back this up. Still, it's critical to keep this warning top-of-mind because it's easy to slide into a downward, technology-first spiral.

Chapter 19—Classroom Training vs. eLearning

In this chapter I share wisdom from the research showing that elearning often outperforms classroom training, except when the learning methods are held constant across both—and then they both produce equal benefits. There are subtleties, of course, and I describe those as well. I specifically advocate for not oversimplifying your decision-making around in-person vs. online learning. Encourage your learning team to embrace elearning while also giving them the authority to use their wisdom to experiment and decide which is most appropriate.

Chapter 20—Large Course Repositories: Be Very Careful

In this chapter I list all the problems and limitations of using large course repositories, and I advise that you don't use these as your primary learning delivery system.

Chapter 21—Generative AI: How Learning Can Help

Here I share some insights on how your learning team can support your organization's effort to prepare itself for the generative AI revolution. I also share wisdom from AI experts on the trajectory and critical issues involving how to organize your teams to deal with the changes coming from ChatGPT and other generative AI tools.

Chapter 22—When Training Pollutes

Here I share some insights on how your learning team can support your organization's efforts to utilize sustainable practices. Three efforts are particularly important. First, we should consider how to integrate ideas about sustainable practices across our learning interventions, not only in a few targeted courses. Second, travel to training should be limited to times when in-person experience is crucial, because of the large amounts of pollution that travel requires. Third, we ought to begin to measure the environmental impact of our training programs.

Section Three—Notes for Learning Professionals

As learning professionals, we know that technology is critical to our work, with new learning technologies appearing every month. Hopefully by now we know that technologies are enablers and that we should first decide what we want to accomplish in learning—and only afterward determine which technologies will be most effective. We must put aside the old notion that classroom training is always better than elearning. eLearning has proven itself to generally be at least as effective as classroom training. We must be cautious about using large course repositories as a primary method of providing our employees with learning, as they have many downsides. We must accelerate our knowledge of generative AI and support our organizations in how to utilize GenAI tools to our advantage, while minimizing the risks. We must consider how to support our organizations' efforts in being good stewards of the environment, and we must reduce training travel.

Chapter 18
Technology and Learning

We live in a massive womb of technology in almost everything we do. The workplace is no different. Until recently, most of us as everyday citizens thought technology was great. Love my smartphone, one-day deliveries, clicking for a taxi, my playlist, video games, half-driving cars, video everywhere! Recently, however, a backlash has begun. Facebook/Meta is stealing elections; Google and Amazon, and almost everybody, has all our information, including our health records, our naked pics, our angry outbursts, our mental-health tendencies, our youthful indiscretions.

But still, so far, our insatiable love of technology is outcompeting our technology worries. Big data, artificial intelligence, neuroscience, automation—whatever! There's an app for that! While some of us, some of the time, are techno-skeptics, more of us are driven—relentlessly driven—toward technology as the root to our salvation.

You guessed it! It's the same in the learning field! It's endemic! Let me share with you some of what's passed for salvation over the past few years. Neuroscience has grabbed headlines and eyeballs—even though there is SCANT evidence that it has anything practical to add to the practice of learning. Big data is seen as salvation—even though the data we currently collect in learning isn't big but small, from limited data sets with limited numbers of people. Learning evaluation systems are hailed as essential when they let organizations benchmark their results against other companies even though the data used for benchmarking is based on poorly constructed smile sheets.

There's good news here, however! Lots of your learning professionals now understand this mantra: "It's NOT the technology; it's the learning methods that enable learning!"

Still, vendors and consultants and trade associations find value in advertising their products and services with a technology-first framing. Recently in the learning field, we've been told that everything must be "microlearning"—short learning segments—instead of our traditionally longer learning programs. This is crazily wrong, but it makes sense to most of us because we keep hearing headlines of how our devices are distracting us, how attention spans are shorter, how young adults want everything to arrive on their smartphones. Microlearning has its place, but it's not a panacea.

We in the learning field are also suckers for neuroscience! You should see all the vendors and consultants in the space touting their neuroscience credentials. One guy I've seen boosts his consulting and product business by claiming he's a neuroscientist, even though neither his doctorate, nor his research, nor even his consulting has anything to do with neuroscience! It's a mad gold rush toward neuroscience nirvana, and I'm almost certain it has infected your organization already!

Artificial intelligence is all the rage as well. Vendors create projects with a tiny bit of AI—for example, maybe they use AI to get a chatbot to respond with reasonably-sounding phrases—but then tout their learning program as being built on AI, when in fact AI comprised less than 1% of the design. Worse, vendors are using regular old algorithms beneath fancy graphics and calling their product AI-enabled when in fact there is zero AI under the hood. Generative AI has potential (and we'll talk about it later in this section), but right now there's a mad rush to label everything AI. Let your learning team beware!

We in the learning profession are not the only people who are dupes when it comes to technology. It's happening in almost every industry in the world. More importantly, I'm certain your most thoughtful learning people know better than to jump on these new-technology bandwagons. Unfortunately, there are forces both in your organization and outside that push these shiny objects on us all.

Once again, we are helped by science to see reality. There have been a ton of scientific studies over the years that show it's not the technology that matters most in learning; it's the learning method used. If you show a video in a classroom, or show it in elearning, or show it on someone's tablet, people will learn the same amount regardless of the technology. It's the same with a visually stunning animation. Regardless of the technology used, if the animation is the same, the learning will be the same. True also of any learning method! It's the method that matters, not the technology!

There is a subtle caveat here. Some technologies enable some additional learning methods. It's hard to animate an image on a whiteboard. You can do it, but a digital interface probably makes it easier.

Technology also enables learning opportunities for those who might not otherwise get access—whether they can't get budget or permission, or are deemed unworthy of the opportunity, or have physical or cognitive challenges that make learning difficult without technological assistance, or whether they face language or cultural barriers.

We'll come back to all these technology decisions later. For now, I hope you remember this: Your organization's learning efforts should NOT be driven by technology; they should be driven first by your learning needs and learning design considerations! Keep your people skeptical of technology-based panaceas.

Chapter 19
Classroom Training vs. eLearning

One of the major decisions your learning team must make is whether to provide training in the classroom or online. Traditionalists say that only classroom training can be truly effective. eLearning advocates point to cost savings and logistics benefits for online learning approaches. These considerations are mostly wrong. Let me get straight to the truth. Warning: You're going to have to pay close attention here because of the subtleties involved.

When a learning method is used in one of these modalities—classroom or elearning—it can generally be used with equal effectiveness in the other modality. If you use a short video in elearning it will be equally effective if it is used in the classroom. Same with animations, discussions, worksheets, etc.

On the other hand, sometimes one learning modality will offer an easier, more natural, or more powerful way to implement a learning method. So, for example, if you're teaching engine maintenance, you can teach some general concepts online, but you can't give people the hands-on experience they will need to be fully skilled. If you're teaching data visualization, you can show examples in the classroom, but you can't give people experience building a dashboard unless they have data-visualization software.

Here's a very interesting finding from the research: When a typical elearning program is compared with a typical classroom training program, elearning tends to outperform the classroom. But be careful; don't under-interpret this! First, elearning does only a little better, not a lot better. Second, and more importantly, elearning outperforms classroom training only because our classroom training designs tend to be weak.

Recently, we've all gone through the COVID epidemic. Most workers around the world were sent home. In an instant, training went from the classroom to Zoom and Teams and other online meeting platforms. It worked! It worked even though the learning profession was still learning how to teach online. It worked even though vendors were just beginning to create innovative tools to support online learning.

Even I, working all by myself, was able to create excellent online learning experiences. One of my learners said my online "Presentation Science Bootcamp" self-study workshop was the best online course they'd ever taken! I'm bragging partly to make a point! My workshop was good, and I know I can keep making it better! My point here is to emphasize that, first, online learning is already outperforming classroom training and, second, we in the learning field are now getting new tools and learning new research-inspired approaches that will enable us to be even more effective.

Let me debunk further. You may have heard that online learning for kids was a disaster during COVID, and that's completely true for many students (though not all)! That was partly because teachers had poor tools and no time to reinvent their teaching methods. But also, younger kids just don't have the brain structures and extensive practice required to stay focused through a single medium. So don't make decisions based on this schooling-during-COVID evidence. The truth is that online learning can be effective even for deep and complex topics—and this has been proven with adult learners!

The research on this is complicated, so let me reiterate. When elearning and classroom use the same methods, they are equally effective. However, they tend not to use the same methods, though elearning tends to use better (though not always the best) methods. The reason neither elearning nor classroom use the best methods is because research-inspired methods are not utilized, because the learning evaluation methods we are using can't find differences even when they exist, and because senior management (people like you and other senior managers) don't give your learning team the permission, time, and resources they need to build truly effective learning interventions.

You and other managers cause problems for your learning team when you dictate global proclamations like, "Within five years all of our learning should be elearning!" Yeah, maybe not you, but some of your counterparts make decisions that should be delegated to people who know learning. Would you tell your civil engineers, "Within two years, I want all our geomembrane testing to be conducted under 10 degrees Celsius?" No! You wouldn't dictate where you had no expertise!

Some more information for you. Switching to elearning can save money for learning departments, but budgets usually stay the same. Don't assume you can save a ton of money just by switching to elearning! On the other hand, where employees must travel to training, you certainly can save on travel costs, reduce pollution, and avoid lost work hours. Also, note that it's not easy to switch to elearning. Some people think, "Oh, gee, we can take the PowerPoints we used in the classroom training and put them online." One of the worst ideas ever! You're taking poorly designed classroom courses and smashing them into elearning.

The bottom line is that both classroom training and elearning can be effective—and both can be made much more effective if they are designed with research-aligned practices and good feedback from evaluations and testing.

One final reminder. eLearning and classroom training are not the only options for supporting learning and development. I highlighted the debate because it is so prevalent.

Chapter 20
Large Course Repositories:
Be Very Careful

Many organizations are tempted to purchase a large batch of online courses, sometimes paying millions upon millions of dollars, euros, pounds, yen, or rupees for the privilege. The thinking is that having courses on almost every imaginable topic will save money and time—and will generally be more efficient than having your learning team develop and deliver training. But this is not true—and if we think about this from a learning standpoint, the reasons will be clear.

There are lots of options these days, from LinkedIn Learning to Skillsoft to Udemy to Coursera—and many others. There are course repositories with a wide array of topics and ones that focus on a specific niche: for example, computer programming.

There are many inherent problems in using course repositories.

- Some courses are well designed; others are poorly designed. Some instructors are effective; others are not.

- Content might conflict or not be reinforced across courses. Individual employees might get mixed messages or differing priorities—causing confusion, loss of enthusiasm, or cynicism.

- Teammates may take different courses on the same topic and not develop a common vocabulary or a skillset of reinforcing goals.

- Learners may learn useful knowledge and skills, but, because their managers can't possibly track the wide range of courses taken by their direct reports, learners will get no support, coaching, or monitoring of their follow-through efforts.

- Unmonitored courses often have very low completion rates, often as low as 5-10%.

- Even if the courses have an instructor (many self-study online courses do not), rarely is there after-training instructor support.

- Courses from generic repositories often cannot provide contextual realism for the situations your employees will face in their work.

- Generic courses do not reinforce organizational values and goals.

- Evaluating repositories of courses almost always devolves to the easiest, least meaningful evaluation metrics: completions and poorly constructed learner surveys. This leaves your organization with no means to determine the value of the learning, if any.

Let's consider the factors required to ensure learning programs are effective. Learning initiatives need content that is valid, credible, and aligned with organizational values. They need to help learners comprehend concepts clearly and see their relevance. They need to motivate learners to apply those concepts and be prepared for workplace-specific obstacles and resistance. Learning programs must provide lots of relevant realistic practice to support remembering. They must also be supported with after-learning reinforcement, reminders, coaching, and monitoring. They must be evaluated so improvements can be made.

Generic course repositories simply aren't very good at doing these things. Even the best courses from these repositories are unlikely to provide context-relevant content, reinforce organizational values, or provide after-training follow-up.

I recently was involved in a research study investigating an after-learning intervention on employee learning. We provided a post-training intervention for some learners, but not all. Unfortunately, we had to end the study because learners just didn't engage fully in the learning; they had been provided with a large repository of courses from a well-known company. They had been given good guidance, instructions, and goals. Still, most of the employees sampled only one or two courses; most courses were left uncompleted. I've heard this story dozens of times. It's the most common outcome.

On the surface, course repositories seem sensible since they provide employees access to lots of ready-made courses. But course repositories should not be used as your primary solution. As an augmentation, yes. As an employee perk for your most self-driven employees, yes! But, if you make them your go-to learning strategy, you will not get the results you need. In short, use large course repositories only if you have a clear need for them.

Chapter 21

Generative AI:
How Learning Can Help

Generative AI is here! We all know this. Unfortunately, right now we tend to view it simplistically. Some see salvation; others know that the apocalypse is coming. AI will either increase everyone's productivity and free us all from the boredom of the mundane or it will take our jobs, lower our wages, and destroy the institutional fabric of society.

Let's get a few things straight:

1. Generative AI is not coming; it is already here, making itself useful.
2. As history shows, useful general-purpose technologies never get stopped.
3. There will be both benefits and harms. At first, we will use GenAI poorly, get poor results, cause some harm, and waste a ton of money, resources, and time.
4. Generative AI will produce winners and losers. It can help provide your organization with a competitive advantage; it can also do the opposite.
5. Most importantly, generative AI will have moral and ethical consequences. It will impact your employees, customers, communities, and nation—and you and your organization, of course.

Your organization has likely begun developing strategies around generative AI. Your learning team has two responsibilities here. First, it can help your employees learn about AI. Second, it can use AI itself in its own work.

Before we get into the practical, it's critical to lay out the real-world context involved in AI work. Here I list some of the wisdom coming from AI experts:

- User trust and confidence in AI systems is critical for adoption and organizational risk. Such trust depends on many factors, including the quality and the level of certainty associated with the AI output, the extent of human autonomy as users interact with AI systems, and transparency (who is involved, who has control, where does the data come from, how did the AI decide, etc.).

- Teams working with AI must be multidisciplinary. Generative AI is not just about data and information technologies. It involves human motivation, cognition, and productivity. It impacts customer loyalty, branding, employee behavior, finance, and the environment.

- Diverse sets of stakeholders must be brought into decision-making to ensure AI systems meet and balance the needs of all your organization's critical stakeholders.

- There is a severe dearth of expertise in AI throughout almost all organizations today. And recent research shows that almost all corporate boards have completely ignored AI, and it may be even more of a blind spot in the nonprofit sector.

So, what should your organization and learning team be doing? First, know that, early on, as your employees look to use GenAI, they will likely take a technology-first approach—trying it out to see what it can do. It's useful to encourage experimentation, but this must be balanced with time and costs. Soon, your organization should pivot to a problem- or opportunity-first approach: for example, listing and prioritizing major marketing, operations, and financial issues and working backwards from there to see if GenAI can help.

Your learning team has several special competencies that can be leveraged. First, it can build a strategy and approach to upskilling your workforce in AI. They can start right away teaching "prompt engineering": the art and practice of communicating with AI tools to constrain and optimize the AI output so it's beneficial. Your learning team can also insert short GenAI projects into non-GenAI courses. With a variety of touchpoints, your employees will deepen their AI skills, giving your organization a competitive advantage.

Your learning team can and should invest substantial efforts in evaluating the first wave of the AI training they produce or purchase, so they can utilize lessons learned as you move forward with advanced training and learning practices to integrate AI.

Also, encourage your learning team to partner with AI experts to conduct a learning needs assessment to determine the knowledge, skills, and sensitivities that need to be taught and reinforced in your organization. Your learning team must quickly upskill itself in AI. If you teach AI smarter than your competitors, you'll have an advantage.

As CEO, you're going to have to spend money here and hire some real AI expertise, whether as employees or trusted advisors. Your learning team can help your organization be prudent—maximizing benefits and minimizing risks by supporting and organizing the many teams in your organization that are evolving your generative AI practices.

Chapter 22
When Training Pollutes

As CEO you're certainly concerned about your organization's reputation. You're also likely to be concerned about the environmental impact your operations are having. Sometimes these two things combine. Companies that utilize more sustainable practices can gain advantages through customer interest and loyalty, employee motivation and loyalty, talent recruitment, cost savings, and stock price. Also, what's good for your organization may also help your children and grandchildren avoid the perils of severe climate disruption.

Is your organization using training to reinforce your sustainable-practices goals? If you are interested in making this happen, let me suggest that, rather than just having one or two courses focused on sustainable practices, it would be better to integrate messaging over a number of courses, particularly in courses to your managers—as they are your force multipliers. Too often, most of our training courses are silent on major organizational initiatives. We wrongly expect that adding a course or two will create learning and behavioral change. But human cognition doesn't work that way. We humans often need multiple touch points to be persuaded, to remember, to organize ourselves to action.

It may not be easy to set up such a learning-multiplier strategy—to integrate themes across learning events and manager activities—but difficult efforts can be the best way to create competitive advantages, because competitors are less likely to marshal the will and resources to make the same investment.

Another opportunity for sustainability is in reducing training travel. Travel is a necessity for most of today's enterprises. For large or global operations, air travel is a requirement. Yet the pollution caused by travel is huge! Ten roundtrip flights, say from New York to San Francisco and back, produce the same amount of carbon-dioxide pollution as an average four-person family produces in a single year! One roundtrip flight—just one—over the same distance produces one-third of the pollution a Honda CR-V produces in a whole year. It is not true that jet contrails contain only water vaper; that is bogus information. Air travel is damaging, but also somewhat easy to leverage for change.

And note that air travel pollutants aren't just composed of carbon dioxide, which is catastrophically harmful on its own. Airplane exhaust includes pollutants like carbon monoxide, sulfur dioxide, and lead.

If your organization is flying employees all over the place to get to training, their travel produces lots of pollution. When employees drive long distances to your trainings, you're not doing the environment any favors. Indeed, one major initiative to reduce automobile pollution is to let employees work from home—as much as possible. After the COVID pandemic, we've seen that having employees work from home is a sustainable strategy.

If you can encourage your learning team to reduce training travel, you'll be lending a hand toward your organization's sustainability goals. And remember, as we've already seen, learning online can be just as effective—or even more effective—than standard classroom training for most topics.

As a senior leader, how specifically can you help? By simply advocating for more online learning and less training travel. You're the boss; they may listen. You can also insist that your learning team begin to measure their impact on the environment. They are not likely to be doing it now, but there's no reason they can't estimate the environmental impact of your learning efforts. This probably doesn't need to be an ongoing activity, but an occasional spot check might be beneficial to nudge sustainability into consciousness.

As an aside, traveling first class has about a four-fold pollution footprint compared to flying economy, and business class has almost a three-fold disadvantage.

Let me be clear that I don't recommend you outlaw face-to-face learning events, which have some advantages you may not be able to reproduce online. On the other hand, maybe you could challenge your learning team to come up with creative ways to use technology to get the same benefits as in-person interactions. Where your organization's learning activities do require training travel, there are ways to make amends and sanction yourself—for example, by buying carbon offsets. These transfer payments should probably be a last resort, because transferring dirty laundry to another organization doesn't solve the underlying problem, and it fails to role-model the beneficial behaviors you might hope to induce in our team and organization.

Reducing travel associated with training also substantially reduces your overall training costs: the cost of airfare, hotels, taxis, and meals, but so much more. Think of the time wasted in traveling and in making travel arrangements. And don't forget the wear and tear that travel takes on your employees and their families.

Traveling for training should be saved for unique circumstances.

Section Four

The Powerful Practicality
of the Learning Sciences

Section Four—Theme

Section Four introduces important findings from the learning sciences. As CEO, you don't need to know the details—although they are interesting and can be parlayed to your personal advantage to support your own ability to learn. The main thing you should take away from this section is that there is a massive database of rigorous scientific findings that can be parlayed to great advantage if your learning team is resourced and organized to learn, implement, and build learning-science wisdom into their learning strategies and everyday practices. Most importantly, using the learning sciences creates a competitive advantage for your organization.

Chapter 23—The Amazing Power of Learning Research: Retrieval Practice

The first golden nugget I will share is retrieval practice ("retrieval" is a fancy word that researchers use for remembering). When we use what we've learned, we are retrieving information from long-term memory. The best way to support our learners in doing their work is to give them practice in retrieving information from memory. The best way to do this is to give them lots of realistic practice that mirrors the actual decisions and tasks we are training them to do. Too many of our learning interventions just broadcast information. Retrieval practice reliably produces learning improvements of 25%, and sometimes even doubles learning results—enabling 100% improvements!

Chapter 24—More Amazing Research: Spacing Learning Over Time

The spacing effect is one of the most studied phenomena in the learning sciences—and is quite fascinating as a human cognitive phenomenon. We know that repeating information—as long as it's not done in a boring way—helps learners comprehend ideas and learn them more fully. The spacing effect shows that repeating things after a delay or after teaching another topic increases long-term remembering. Many learning programs do the exact opposite. They organize content into chapters and never revisit the information. They design learning to fit into one session when it would be better to repeat things in a second or third session later. Spacing repetitions over time reliably produces learning improvements of 35-150%.

Chapter 25—More Amazing Research: Simulating the Work Context

We humans are consciously and subconsciously influenced every second by the contexts we inhabit. Good learning designers know this and build learning activities based on the work contexts where their learners will use what they've learned. They provide many real-world examples, focus discussions toward real work situations, and give their learners plenty of challenging realistic practice. This is backed up by a ton of scientific research. Researchers who study context often compare how well people remember in the context where they learned versus some other context. When people are asked to remember in the same context, they typically remember somewhere between 10% and 50% more than they do in other contexts.

Chapter 26—More Amazing Research: Feedback for Learning

Feedback is critical during learning. It helps people correct their misconceptions, motivates them to keep going when learning gets difficult, and helps them calibrate what they know and what they still need to learn. The research shows that feedback improves learning results by 15-50%—and, for learner misconceptions, 25-100% or more.

Section Four—Notes for Learning Professionals

The learning research has really solidified over the past 10, 15, or 20 years. We now have very strong recommendations we can use when we design learning. As the four chapters in this section show, we learning professionals must provide our learners with significant amounts of realistic practice and provide helpful feedback as our learners work through these practice opportunities. Early in learning, we should provide immediate feedback to ensure learners are comprehending correctly. Later in learning our learners may benefit from delayed feedback, which helps people remember. Finally, we ought to space repetitions over time or intersperse them with other content. Again, such spacing enables long-term remembering. These four chapters represent only a small fraction of the learning sciences. We as learning professionals must learn broadly and continuously revisit what we have learned—providing ourselves with spaced repetitions—and keeping these powerful learning factors top of mind.

Chapter 23
The Amazing Power of Learning Research: Retrieval Practice

This book might seem like it's filled with bad news: our poor learning practices, trapdoors to ineffective training, and mistakes many senior leaders are making. But here's some good news to help comfort you on this arduous (but beneficial) journey.

There's a ton of scientific research on learning, available from over a century of work by thousands and thousands of scientists who have made it their life's work to study learning, memory, instruction, training, elearning, coaching, leadership, and more. No single research study is perfect, but the scientific enterprise moves inexorably toward more perfect recommendations. We now live in a time where the science of learning has coalesced around some very strong findings.

Let me share one of these learning factors with you. It is called "retrieval practice," and it is one of three critical elements of "realistic practice" as I will explain over the next chapters.

Do you have a driver's license or a son or daughter you helped nurture through the learning-to-drive years? Think about how we learn to drive. We can study a handbook or take a course, but the most important thing we can do is get lots of realistic practice driving a car. Practice doesn't always make perfect, but deliberate practice in realistic conditions is almost always the most powerful way to learn. Learning researchers know why.

There are three major components of realistic practice, all of which have been studied extensively by scientists: Retrieval practice, context alignment, and feedback. I'll describe the second two in later chapters.

When a person gets "retrieval practice"—just as the name says—they get practice retrieving concepts or skills from memory. Specifically, they are retrieving information from long-term memory and moving it into working memory, where it can be utilized for action. Consider a person learning to drive. As she takes her parents' 2009 Subaru Outback on a ride, she is retrieving all kinds of information. When she sees a stop sign, she retrieves the meaning of a stop sign and the idea that she should stop. When she notices it's starting to rain, she retrieves the idea from memory that rain makes roads slippery and she'd better slow down. Because driving is such a complex skill, new drivers go into retrieval overdrive, retrieving lots of information all at once. Only when they've practiced these retrieval routes through memory many times, do new drivers begin to automate their actions—that is, carry them out fluently and with few mistakes.

When people answer questions or take tests or do tasks, they are retrieving information. Indeed, researchers used to call retrieval practice the "testing effect"—until they realized that testing was not the only way to practice retrieval.

So how powerful is retrieval practice in helping people learn? There are hundreds of scientific studies on this, and they almost always show very strong benefits. Typically, the research compares learners who are given retrieval practice to those who get extra time to study what they've learned. The research isolates retrieval from the additional benefits that might be gained from other learning factors such as context alignment, repetition, spacing, and feedback.

How much benefit do you think this retrieval practice creates on its own? Take a guess. Do those getting retrieval practice learn 5%, 10%, or 20% more than people who don't? Let's put this in perspective. If your company outcompetes your nearest competitor by 10% on customer satisfaction, or has 10% lower manufacturing costs, or you have salespeople who have 10% more sales than your competitors, you are almost guaranteed to be on your way to market success. Your organization's learning results are not nearly as important as your most critical organizational metrics, but they can be a leading indicator of how well you are resourcing your organization to reach your ultimate goals.

If your learning team utilizes retrieval practice, they can increase learning results by up to 100% or more, with almost certain improvements of 25%! Results will vary, of course, but these numbers are based on conservative estimates because scientists are comparing retrieval practice used alone to the benefits learners accrue by getting extra study time. In real-world situations, your learning team would utilize additional learning factors to produce additional learning benefits—and the comparison would not be to learners who do extra study but to learners who are listening passively to presentations.

If one learning factor can produce 25% improvements all by itself—or sometimes up to 100% improvement—imagine what your learning team can do if you make sure it's resourced and tasked to use a full regimen of research-based learning factors!

Chapter 24
More Amazing Learning Research: Spacing Learning Over Time

When asked, learners almost always say that intensive learning is more effective than learning that is spaced over time. Teachers and trainers often believe the same thing. This is kind of weird, because most of us admit that the cramming we did to prepare for exams in our university days and in school really didn't work that well. So, what does the research say? Is there research on this?

There is a ton of research on spaced learning—more than 400 well-designed scientific studies have been done with all types of learners and all types of content. Indeed, the "spacing effect" may be the most studied phenomenon in all of learning and memory. So, what is this spacing effect? Well, there are several varieties of spacing, but the essential elements are the same. When concepts or skill practice are repeated, they create greater long-term learning results if the repetitions are repeated after a delay rather than repeated immediately. So, for example, if you as CEO want to reinforce your organization's values to your senior team—in hopes that they will remember and act on them—you would do better to have a second discussion of the values after a couple of days rather than revisiting them within the same 90-minute meeting.

The magic of spacing also occurs when delays between repetitions are longer than if they are shorter. So repeating learning content after four days will create better remembering than repeating content after two days. Repeating content after two hours is better than repeating it after one hour, and 20 minutes is better than 10 minutes.

Spacing benefits are also created through interleaving. If we teach Topic A fully, that is not as good as teaching Topic A partially, then teaching Topic B, and then teaching Topic A again. When we interleave topics or separate topics with activities interspersed between, we create the benefits of spacing.

Finally, we can create benefits by delaying feedback we give to learners—but we must be careful because sometimes delayed feedback is better and sometimes immediate feedback is better. I'll explain this subtlety later when I go into depth about providing feedback.

We can all see the spacing effect at work. If we avoid cramming and instead space our study sessions, we won't forget everything soon after our exams. We can still ride a bike even a decade after last riding one because we spent so much time—over many years—riding a bike as a kid, over hundreds or thousands of spaced repetitions. We can remember our grandparents' house even long after they've died because we visited them over many years, each event repeated and spaced out over time.

Unfortunately, most training courses go out of their way to avoid spacing. Instead, we "chapterize" our courses, covering Topic A and then moving on to Topic B and never coming back to Topic A. We have half-day trainings or 90-minute elearnings—never to visit the content again. These chapterized, single-event trainings may be useful in helping people understand content and skills, but they are suboptimal in supporting remembering.

Why do we persist in these poor learning designs? Largely, it's tradition. Most educators and workplace learning professionals went through schooling that was chapterized and unspaced. Trainers and teachers and learning designers began their careers before the spacing effect was widely known. Fortunately, the spacing effect has become more established over the past 15 years; unfortunately, our traditions still push against it.

But there's another reason spacing has not been embraced as much as it should be. Spaced repetitions can feel more difficult for learners, so—because progress seems slower—learners like them less. Trainers and learning architects need to push themselves to integrate spacing where chapterized content is easier to organize and develop. And finally, logistics can be more difficult, especially when we try to space learning over a day or more.

On the other hand, digital technologies now make spacing repetitions easier than ever. Even after a classroom workshop, online practice or reinforcement or coaching can be provided—all of which provide spaced repetitions.

What kind of benefits can spacing provide? With spacing, learners are getting two benefits: repetition and spacing. Repetitions, of course, are better if they are not rote or verbatim, but rather if they are varied and designed to be engaging, relevant, and challenging. Repetitions routinely produce learning benefits of 25-110% or more. Spacing those repetitions produces an additional 10-40% or more. That's 35-150% improvements in learning, or more!

There are many ways your learning team and your managers can utilize the benefits of spaced learning, but they will have to be creative, be open to using technology, and be supported by you and other senior managers when they face resistance from those still pushing for traditional non-spaced practices.

Chapter 25
More Amazing Learning Research: Simulating the Work Context

We learn everything within a specific context. If next Saturday you have to fix your toilet, you're likely to find yourself in your bathroom, taking the lid off the back of the toilet, futzing around in there a bit, noticing the objects therein—the bulb, the pipe, the lever, the chain, the water—trying a few things, then deciding you need to learn more.

What situation are you in? Which contextual stimuli are most salient in this situation? What can you do to learn how to fix the damned toilet? You whip out your phone, go to YouTube, and find some videos on how to fix a toilet. On the eighth video, you have a eureka moment. You see a loose chain, and the lady in the video shows you how to fix it. You reach into the back of your toilet and fix the chain just the way she showed you. You wash your hands and feel a sense of accomplishment.

A year later, after your mind has gone on to other things, your toilet stops working again. You can't remember much about the earlier toilet-fixing episode. You vaguely remember fixing the toilet before, but you don't remember how. You have zero recollection of the YouTube woman. Still, you take the top off the toilet. You persevere. When you look inside, you see the dangling chain and instantly remember how to fix it. It's almost like magic. Once you saw the dangling chain, you knew what to do.

What happened to you? Why did your brain work this way? The secret is context. When you learned how to fix the toilet the first time, you noticed certain contextual cues—the bulb, the pipe, the lever, the water, and, most importantly, you remembered the dangling chain. The dangling chain—a great name for a band, I think—triggered your memory for the toilet fix. This contextual cue enabled you to remember and to act successfully.

When we act, it's usually because we are triggered to action. We are not as proactive as we'd like to think. How many times have you forgotten your bank PIN until you see the bank keypad? The keypad triggers your memory. Or you can't remember much about high school until you see pictures in your yearbook. The pictures trigger your memory, helping you remember a flood of detail. It's the same when we intentionally try to learn. You're a CEO. You know how to use a spreadsheet. So, take a moment to explain to me how to take the contents of a cell—say the cell contains the number $2,222—and copy that number to the next 10 cells toward the right. Do you remember how to do that? If that's too easy—if you're a more advanced user—tell me the formula for doing a logical test. Suppose you want to know whether a particular cell is greater than $2,000; what's the formula you'd put in that cell? Do you remember?

If these questions are difficult for you to answer, I'll bet good money that, if you opened Excel, you'd be more likely to remember. You'd be more likely to remember that grabbing the $2,222 cell and the 10 cells to the right, then hitting CTRL-R, will copy $2,222 into all those cells. You'll also be more likely to remember that the formula is =IF(logical_test, [value_if_true], [value_if_false]).

The best and brightest members of your learning team know all about the power of context. Simulating realistic work situations helps employees learn and remember. When employees practice new skills in their actual work contexts, they learn better. The key is context—simulating the right context! And practice, and feedback, and repetition.

To help our employees perform better, we want to create for them spontaneous remembering. When they encounter certain work situations—work contexts—we want the stimuli in those contexts to trigger useful memories. Just like the dangling chain might trigger your toilet-fixing skills, we want our employees to be prepared with appropriate memory triggers.

Let's reflect. When we give a lecture, we are not simulating. When we teach content devoid of context, we are not preparing our learners to remember or act.

What kind of benefits can simulating the work context provide? When researchers provide learning in Context A and later test learners in either Context A or Context B, the learners tested in Context A remember roughly 10-50% more! And these figures don't include the benefits of retrieval practice or spacing or feedback, all of which multiply the power of context.

You might worry that giving people real or simulated practice would be too difficult or maybe even dangerous. This is true sometimes but is generally not a barrier. At a minimum, you can simulate the decision-making required in taking action if you can't fully simulate the action. The bottom line is this: If you want to prepare your employees to perform, your learning team and managers must enable context-relevant practice—whether simulated or situated in real work!

Chapter 26

More Amazing Learning Research: Feedback for Learning

Feedback is the lifeblood of learning—and for successful living as well. Without feedback, we'd all keep doing what we've always done. Imagine trying to learn to golf without being able to see where the ball goes when we hit it. Difficult to get better! Imagine trying to learn multiplication tables without getting feedback. Seven times seven is 51. Four times four is 24. Without feedback, we wouldn't know we needed to make a change.

Nobody learns without some sort of feedback, because feedback is information. But it's more than information. Feedback is information that is relevant to our current actions and thoughts. It corrects us when we're wrong; it reinforces us when we are not sure.

Feedback comes in many forms. There is didactic feedback—for example, from a friend or teacher. "Jimmy, as you presented that graph to us, you could have been clearer by describing the meaning of each bar and showing each bar one at a time." There is feedback we get from the consequences of our actions. "Damn, when I presented that graph, I noticed that people looked confused." "Ugh, this algebra problem. The answer key says I got it wrong." There is also feedback we get from our reflections. "Hmmm. It's funny, I used to think I was good at marketing, but the evidence is clear now. Over the past few years, only a few of my marketing initiatives have worked."

Feedback can come from ourselves, from others, from consequences of our actions (or seeing the consequences of others' actions), from comparing our results to a standard, or from a rigorous diagnostic. We can seek feedback or shy away from it. We can take feedback seriously or ignore it. We can be brave to feedback or fearful. Those who learn the most are those who bravely seek feedback and take action to improve themselves. My colleagues where I used to work often repeated this statement: "Feedback is a gift."

Feedback is not just the job of your learning team. It's the job of managers, coworkers, and employees themselves.

Feedback is tricky too! When it is punitive, oppressive, or unnecessarily negative, people can turn away from the benefits it can provide. When feedback praises behavior at the wrong time or combines feedback with rewards, it can also cause problems—pushing people to focus on the rewards instead of the intrinsic value they are getting.

For now, let's focus on the feedback we give learners when they engage in training or online learning—feedback on questions they've been asked. There's a ton of research on this type of feedback. The science shows that giving people feedback when they get an answer wrong is more important than giving people feedback when they get an answer right. Corrective feedback is better than just telling people whether their answer is right or wrong. The research also shows that, when learners are struggling to comprehend a complex concept, giving them immediate feedback is better than waiting later to give them feedback. But the research shows the opposite as well: after people have fully comprehended a concept, delayed feedback can support long-term remembering better than immediate feedback.

Most importantly, despite all the subtleties, the science tells us that feedback is critical in enabling learning. By using feedback, your learning team can improve learning results by 15-50% overall—and, for incorrect answers, 25-100% or more. Indeed, one study shows feedback on incorrect answers improved learning by 474%. Another study showed improvements of 380%. These improvements are beyond the normal range of what we can expect, but I share them here to show how powerful feedback is in correcting the misconceptions that learners often have.

Finally, let me add that feedback never works alone. To utilize feedback, you must first have some sort of learner action—either answering questions, making decisions, or performing tasks. If your learning team is giving feedback at all, that means they are likely using methods beyond ineffective lectures and information dumps. So, at a minimum, if you're combining retrieval practice and feedback, you're likely getting learning improvement from 50-200% or more!

Again, my percentage estimates are best guesses from looking at a sample of the scientific literature. They are not to be carved in stone! Still, I'm confident that they are reasonable and are representative of the learning improvements your learning team can garner from good learning designs. I share them not to connote a certain level of improvement but to convey the power and potential of research-inspired learning design.

The four chapters in this section presented lots of details you as CEO don't need to know. I share the research with you to show you that (1) learning is deeply complex, (2) designing learning programs is not as easy as it looks, and finally and most importantly, (3) the best learning teams bring a ton of rigor and well-earned knowledge to their work. As a senior leader, you can help by taking learning seriously, by being willing to make investments in learning, and by ensuring your learning team has the resources to keep developing their knowledge of how best to design and deploy learning.

Section Five

The Performance Sciences and Behavior Triggers

Section Five—Theme

Section Five moves away from training and learning and focuses on how thoughts and actions can be more directly enabled. The three chapters in this section arise from new ideas in the performance sciences and timeless ideas born in ancient practices. Learning matters, but so do the objects and stimuli that employees encounter in their work. By considering the recent research coming from the performance sciences as well as proven practices like job aids and performance support, your learning team can directly nudge performance. And, because most organizations are only weakly utilizing these approaches, you'll be creating a competitive advantage. As CEO, you don't need to know the details (although the performance sciences certainly apply to you and your team—and can bring you personal benefits) but you should know that there are powerful ideas your learning team and organization can leverage that go beyond training.

Chapter 27—The Performance Sciences

In this chapter I share many examples of how recent strands of research are illuminating human behavior and giving us new tools to support employees in doing their best work. I describe how fully 40% of our daily functioning is based on habits and how the science of habits can be parlayed into individual and team performance. I talk about the behavioral-economic notion of nudging and how nudges and performance triggers can be utilized to improve behavior. I show how your employees and teams can be more creative—and thus more innovative.

Chapter 28—Performance Activation from Within the Work Context

Here I introduce a radical new idea for learning-and-performance practice. The performance activation approach is based on the indisputable observation that we humans are influenced by the stimuli in our environment—and, more specifically, in our work context. Some of these influences are obvious and we are influenced by them consciously: for example, when a sign warns us of a safety hazard. However, most of the stimuli that influence us do so subconsciously, without our awareness: for example, having a window that looks out on trees is more likely to lower our blood pressure, make us feel healthier, and enable our creativity than having a window that looks out at a brick wall, without us even realizing it. The main point of this chapter is that the work-performance context can be designed to promote more productive and healthier work practices—and your learning team should be able to support such initiatives.

Chapter 29—Prompting and Performance-Support Tools

In this chapter I talk about how prompting tools can be utilized to support desirable behaviors, both consciously and unconsciously. I emphasize how prompting tools can sometimes replace or augment training. I describe how some prompting tools—some job aids, for example—need to be taught and practiced in training to produce their maximum benefits.

Section Five—Notes for Learning Professionals

In this section I highlight something we already know: that training can sometimes be replaced by prompting tools such as job aids, checklists, or more complex performance-support systems. I also describe how such prompting tools can support (and be supported by) training. In addition to describing these well-worn pathways, I also introduce two new major concepts: the performance sciences and performance activation. The performance sciences include things like nudges, habits, performance triggering, network science, persuasion, and creativity. To maximize our impact, we should study the performance sciences and figure out how to use them to directly support employees in their work. Performance activation is based on the idea that work contexts influence thinking and action—sometimes consciously but usually subconsciously. Again, we as learning-and-performance professionals should figure out how to leverage the work context to improve work performance.

Chapter 27
The Performance Sciences

Throughout this book, I've dedicated a large amount of space to some of the most important findings from the learning sciences—and their implications. Now it's time to talk about the "performance sciences."

Learning is one way to support performance. People learn and then later they use what they've learned in doing their work. But performance can be elicited or improved through other means as well. We'll soon talk about prompting tools—items such as checklists that are utilized in a person's work-performance context to guide actions. But this is just the tip of the hidden iceberg that is the performance sciences.

It's likely you've heard about the behavioral-economic notion of nudging: using contextual stimuli to trigger action. Putting healthy food at eye level in the cafeteria nudges more people to select healthy food items. Using default meeting times that end at five or ten minutes before the hour (or half-hour) nudges people to take short breaks. Placing printers far away from cubicles nudges people to print fewer documents. Richard Thaler and Cass Sunstein are famous for popularizing this line of research through their book *Nudge,* but there are hundreds of researchers focused on nudging.

If you ask your learning team to be responsible for performance improvement—not just cranking out training programs—perhaps they will utilize performance sciences like nudging to give your organization a competitive advantage.

Other performance sciences cover concepts such as habits, contextual triggering, creativity, persuasion, wellness, and more. Let's peek at some of these.

Habit science researchers like Wendy Wood and B.J. Fogg have shown that habits are foundational to human behavior. Wendy Wood has reported that nearly 43% of our daily behavior is under the control of our habits. That's close to half! Certainly, your employees' performance is governed by their habits—not just their individual habits but also their team habits and your organization's cultural habits as well. Habits are particularly powerful because good habits tend to persevere, and bad habits are hard to change. Perhaps your learning team might leverage the research on habits to support performance improvement directly and integrate habit ideas into the various trainings they produce. Consider leadership development as an example. New leaders often come up through the technical ranks—and shifting to a leadership role requires them to learn a critical set of new habits while disengaging from habits that don't suit the role of management.

Another performance science opportunity is found in team creativity. One of the recent focuses of senior leaders like you is innovation—for which creativity sows the seeds—but your managers likely don't know how to brainstorm creative ideas with their teams. I'll bet they think group brainstorming generates the best ideas. They are wrong! Having people generate ideas on their own creates a higher quality and more diverse set of ideas. And that's just one subtlety from the creativity research.

What about open office space? You may know that scientists have studied open offices and found that they generally create more stress, hurt productivity, and distract your employees so they can't fully concentrate on their tasks.

How many key roles in your organization require persuasion? You as CEO must persuade your board, the public, shareholders, and employees. All your hundreds of managers must persuade their teams—and often other teams. Your salespeople must persuade your clients and customers. Your R&D staff have to persuade... okay, you get my point. Persuasion is critical, and there is great science behind it—packaged into powerful books by folks like Robert Cialdini, David McRaney, Jonah Berger, Loran Nordgren, David Schonthal, and Jane Austen (okay, for Jane Austen, I tried to make a novel joke).

Many of the new performance sciences are founded on the discovery that much of human performance is triggered by contextual cues—and critically, we as humans don't even know that our thoughts and actions are under these unconscious influences. Did you know that, if you're about to make a decision, you could be nudged to make a riskier decision if a woman touches you on the shoulder? If you hold a warm mug of liquid, you're likely to become more gregarious in the moment. If you go into a negotiation after thinking about the number of miles/kilometers from the Earth to the Sun (a big number) you'll be more likely to offer someone a higher salary than if, prior to the negotiations, you were thinking about the number of planets in our solar system (a small number). Your behavior will be influenced, but you won't even know it.

The performance sciences have blossomed over the past two decades. We in the learning-and-performance profession are just beginning to develop practices on how to parlay these findings into workable practices. You could help by charging us with the responsibility to explore these new opportunities. You could help also by seeing your learning team as performance-improvement professionals, not just course creators.

And here's the thing: If your organization innovates in using the performance sciences, you gain a competitive advantage.

Chapter 28
Performance Activation from Within the Work Context

In this chapter, I promote a radical new idea for learning and development. You can champion this "performance activation" idea if you think it has value for your organization. Here's the idea, derived from patterns of research in the learning-and-performance sciences which clearly demonstrate the power of contextual influences on our behavior. All of us employees, including you as CEO, do our work within a context that is constantly and forcefully nudging, triggering, and influencing us toward some thoughts and actions and thus away from other thoughts and actions.

Let me use a nautical metaphor. It is as if we humans exist as sailboats on the ocean. We know consciously that the wind is pushing us around, but we hardly notice the tides, which are equally powerful. We see the results of the tide when we're near the shore—the water is higher or lower—but we don't feel how the tide exerts influence on our keel, rudder, and hull. The tide's influence is below the surface of the water, monstrous and sublime.

Here is the point: Our work contexts are filled with stimuli that influence our thinking and actions minute by minute, day by day. Because of this elemental behavioral mechanism, the truth of human behavior is clear: Situational context is the primary irresistible instigator of human thought and action. Those of us who care about employee performance must know that work performance is activated from within the work-performance context.

To be clear, employees bring cognitive and behavioral tendencies with them into their work-performance contexts, but only some of their tendencies are activated by the stimuli in their work-performance contexts; others remain unutilized. Your learning team can (and should) influence these tendencies through training and other learning opportunities, but they can also bring the power of performance activators into the work-performance context. Some of this they do already with prompting tools like job aids, performance-support tools, and contextual help systems, but they can now do more by dipping into the vast sea of wisdom from the performance sciences.

I'm still exploring the deeper implications of the performance-activation idea, but so far, I see six categories of performance activators.

1. ***Context Triggering***

   Context triggering occurs when people encounter contextual cues within their work contexts—triggering thoughts and actions. Examples include cue-triggered memories, reminders, nudges, signs/signage, intuitive cues built into tools, and contextual support.

2. ***Memory Accessibility***

   When ideas or concepts are highly accessible from memory—when they are either top-of-mind (consciously retrievable from memory) or triggerable (readily available from memory to exert unconscious influence)—they can significantly influence what people think and what they are inclined to do.

3. ***Behavioral Guidance***

   People in their work contexts can be guided by other people or by objects they consult for guidance. Examples include job aids, performance tools, guidelines, coaching and feedback, demonstrations, role models—plus statements of goals, visions, missions, and values.

4. ***Proactive Behaviors***

   People at work are not just buffeted by circumstances; they regularly act proactively to do their work and improve their performance. They seek knowledge and they reflect, problem solve, brainstorm, use tools, observe, learn and study, and set triggers for themselves.

5. ***Personal States***

   As humans, we are influenced by a wide variety of personal states. Some are within our control; some are not. Our work performance can be impacted by our physiological and psychological states, our family situations, our financial circumstances, our feelings of belonging/safety, by our goal orientations.

6. ***Enablers and Obstacles***

   As employees, we are beholden to structural forces integral to our work situations, including such things as the physical space we work in; the resources, tools, and time we have; the rules, practices, expectations, and norms in our work teams; the espoused mission, vision, and values; and incentives.

You can help unleash the power of performance activation by giving permission and resources to enable your learning team to use the work context to directly drive behaviors. Because the performance-activation idea will be new in most organizations, being out in front provides another opportunity to gain a competitive advantage.

Chapter 29
Prompting and Performance-Support Tools

Prompting tools directly elicit employee performance. Checklists, job aids, performance-support systems, signs and signage, embedded help, user manuals, and instructions are all prompting tools. Human beings have used these tools for millennia because they work better than the alternative: trying to remember everything. We saw earlier that forgetting is not only normal; it is relentless. Prompting tools do two things at once. They help us overcome one of our fundamental weaknesses: forgetting. At the same time, they utilize one of our most important cognitive strengths: associative triggering. Humans are more reactive than proactive. We constantly and subconsciously filter the stimuli in our environment. When walking on the savannah, if we see a tiger, our thoughts are automatically triggered for danger and escape. This is a very good thing, and we are deeply wired for it.

When we see prompts, we are triggered to thoughts and actions. Prompts can be used intentionally: for example, when we use a checklist to assemble a piece of equipment. Prompts can also be set as triggers, placed in a context, waiting for us to notice and be nudged by them. For example, traffic signs and road designs prompt our behavior, often subconsciously if we are experienced drivers. Narrower lanes and traffic circles nudge us to slow down with little conscious recognition, while speed limit signs may require us to consciously process messages from both the sign itself and our speedometer.

Prompts work because they set our minds in motion. If we hide our cookie jar in a drawer, we are less likely to be prompted to eat a cookie when we enter the kitchen—compared to having the cookie jar looming prominently on the counter, which prompts us to think about grabbing a fat-imbued sugary treat. This associative triggering is a fundamental aspect of human cognition, so we should use it in our organizations where and when it can do the most good.

Once again, you might notice a theme: that training may not always be needed. Well-designed prompting tools can sometimes replace lengthy trainings. More often, prompting mechanisms and training can work as an integrated package. Where memory is likely to fail or a prompting tool is simple and easy to utilize, prompting may be the way to go. Where subconscious nudging won't work and deliberate use of a prompting tool would be slow or socially awkward to use, then training for remembering will be needed. Finally, sometimes training is needed to support the use of a prompting tool. Learners may need practice in using the tool to be motivated or comfortable in using it. They may need practice using the tools so that later, back on the job, they'll remember that the tool exists and can be used in the current situation.

Let me emphasize again that there are two types of prompting tools.

The first kind relies on employees' conscious intentions. We give them a checklist and they intentionally use it as they carry out a task. For this type of prompting tool, it is best that your employees get significant practice using the tool during training or coaching sessions! Too often, job aids are mentioned during training and distributed to employees under the dubious assumption that they will be used. Unfortunately, people are likely to forget that they have the tools available, they forget how to use them, or they forget their motivations for using them. Giving people practice in using prompting tools helps employees remember. A second benefit, too little discussed, is that prompting tools used on the job can remind learners of what they learned. By reviewing a pre-meeting checklist focused on meeting efficiency, a manager may remember that the training also emphasized valuing input from direct reports—even if the checklist doesn't mention it.

The second type of prompting tool relies on unconscious triggering. When employees encounter cues (stimuli) in their work environment, they may be nudged to think or act differently than if they hadn't encountered those cues. As described earlier, prompting tools are just one way we can utilize performance activation to drive improved performance.

Why should you, as CEO, care about these prompting tools? The answer is probably obvious: They can save your organization money, reduce stress on your workforce, and eliminate or reduce time spent in training!

Should you actively advocate for their use? Probably not. Leave this to your Chief Learning Officer. However, you can help by reminding your managers that training is not always the answer and that other tools exist to support successful performance.

You can also make a huge difference by demanding that your learning team have a full-factor training request process in place that forces all your stakeholders—both your learning team and your line managers—to investigate all the possible factors involved in the current problem situation (or opportunity situation) before jumping to conclusions about solutions. You'll also have to allow your learning team a bit more time and resources to do a reasonable learning-needs analysis so they can think beyond training and consider other opportunities to improve work performance.

I will talk about how to craft a full-factor training request process in Chapter 46.

Section Six
Making Research Work
for Your Learning Team

Section Six—Theme

Section Six describes how your learning team can utilize research to maximize their effectiveness. This section also has a wider message—showing how your organization can better use research wisdom to get a competitive advantage. I balance my advocacy for research with warnings about how difficult it is for your learning team to use research wisely because they are buffeted by waves of off-target research that are difficult to decipher. These discussions about how to get the most from research are critical because your learning team makes decisions and takes actions based on what they glean from the research they do encounter. Too many learning teams are not adequately prepared to think about research. If yours is one of them, your voice as CEO is critical to nudge them to maximum performance.

Chapter 30—Research and Practice in Learning

In this chapter, I describe how research (particularly scientific research) provides unique benefits. These benefits accrue mostly because, when we look to the work of scientists, we are looking at the work of people who have studied topics in more depth and with more rigor than is possible for those of us doing other work. I share the power and potential of research related to the learning field, but I also remind us that not all scientific recommendations are useful—that we must use the research with our practical wisdom to guide us. I end the chapter showing how you, as a senior leader, can support your learning team in using good research wisely.

Chapter 31—Separating Good Research from Bad

I start this chapter on a high note. I give examples of other strains of scientific research—beyond those directly related to learning—that would greatly benefit your organization. For example, organizations can parlay research on leadership, creativity, office design, onboarding, brainstorming, *ad infinitum* into a competitive advantage. Also in this chapter I critique a common L&D practice. I tell you how your learning team might have gone off the tracks in using research. I talk about how industry surveys encourage your learning team to benchmark their work against mediocre practices, thus harming your organization with uninspired learning-and-development work. I talk about the strengths and weaknesses of this industry research and describe how to vet it—and how to avoid spending big bucks for faulty research. I share an alarming truth about using internet research and generative-AI research—specifically for researching learning-and-development best practices. Both are filled with poor learning advice. Finally, I make recommendations for how you can partner with your CLO to support your learning team in using research wisely—and thus boost organizational performance.

Chapter 32—Using A-B Testing in Learning

In this chapter, I talk about the benefits for your learning team in using A-B testing—testing one learning design against another. Not only can this help your learning team select the best learning designs, but, even more importantly, it can inspire them to be curious, to be creative, and to engage all members in thoughtful deliberations.

Section Six—Notes for Learning Professionals

Research is not the only source of wisdom we can use in being good learning-and-performance professionals, but it has unique advantages. To be most effective in our work, we need to know how to access and interpret research insights. We must be careful not to be swayed by industry research based on surveys of our contemporaries. If we don't deeply understand the limitations of industry research, we will push our organizations to align with mediocre practices across the industry. We don't need to read the scientific research ourselves—indeed, this would not be a good use of our limited time—but instead, we can seek out research translations and get periodic reviews of our work from research-to-practice experts.

Chapter 30
Research and Practice in Learning

Your learning team almost certainly utilizes research in their decision-making and strategic planning. Unfortunately, too few know how to make sense of research. Even worse, some of the research they rely on—which you are paying for—isn't very good. Over the three chapters in this section, I share insights so that, when it comes time for you to review your learning team's budget, you'll know which research efforts to fund and which to cut.

I'm going to talk about four kinds of research: scientific research, industry survey research, internet search research, and A-B testing. Research, of course, is not the only way for professionals to guide their work. They can also rely on their own experiences, on wisdom from others, on rigorous evaluations of their efforts, and from models and frameworks that are imbued with evidence-based wisdom.

Still, rigorous research provides unique advantages. Let's start with scientific research, as it is foundational. I dedicated four of the previous chapters to powerful learning-science factors to show you that your organization's training-and-development work can be based on rigorous proven practices. I shared only a small fraction of an immense body of research on learning, memory, and instruction—research that has been building for a century.

Scientific research has advantages over our personal observations and experience. Scientists look to find the true causes of outcomes. They test their hypotheses. They try to rule out alternative explanations and avoid interpreting correlated events as causal unless some set of factors really causes an outcome. They work hard to avoid confirmatory bias—a common scourge in human thinking. Researchers try to disprove other researchers' conclusions and find boundary conditions. In this way, science is self-perfecting over time. Research conclusions are not always right in the moment, but—because of the rigor of the scientific method—they usually have an advantage over our anecdotal observations.

The scientific research on learning is not without some flaws. I have spent close to 20,000 hours studying, compiling, and reporting on the learning research. For over 23 years, I've led my consulting practice—Work-Learning Research—based on translating learning research into practical recommendations. I have helped organizations build more effective learning interventions based on the wisdom from the research. Working directly with organizations like the US Navy SEALs, Harvard Business School Publishing, Walgreens, Liberty Mutual,

Kaiser Permanente, the CDC, Bloomberg, and the Gates Foundation, I have learned that research must be compiled with practical wisdom to be useful.

Recent scientific research on learning is very good and continues to improve, but too often in the past researchers didn't test learning in real-world settings. Too often they relied solely on university students in controlled laboratory conditions. Until about 25 years ago, most learning researchers didn't test learning after a delay—making it impossible for them to know whether learning would be remembered. It's only been in the past two decades that learning researchers have tested their results on "far-transfer" tasks—tests of performance that demonstrate generalizable results, not just mechanical stimulus-response retrieval.

Still, even with these deficiencies, scientific research is vital to maximizing your learning team's effectiveness. If you add up the percentage learning improvements from representative research on retrieval practice, spaced repetitions, simulating the work context, and providing feedback—the four areas of research I reviewed for you earlier—your learning team can more than double its effectiveness! More than double!

As a leader—whether you are in a business, nonprofit, government agency, the military, or in education—what would you be willing to do to double your revenues, double the citizens you serve, double the percentage of battles won, double the number of students who move from proficient to advanced? You'd invest a ton to double your results! But here's the thing: Your learning team doesn't have to make major investments; they just have to stop using ineffective methods and start using more research-inspired practices.

What can you do as CEO? Rather than have your whole learning team read the science themselves, ensure they have access to research translations, which are available from the learning field's research-to-practice experts and available from rigorously written nonfiction books, articles, and research-to-practice reports. Some of your learning team—those with extensive experience doing scientific research—will benefit from reading the scientific journals. Most will find more advantages in translated research.

In addition to reading research or research translations, your learning team will also benefit by using models and frameworks that are imbued with practical research wisdom.

I can't possibly provide a full list in this limited space, but here are some of the workplace-learning research translators your folks should look for: Ruth Clark, Julie Dirksen, Clark Quinn, Patti Shank, Mirjam Neelen, Karl Kapp, Jane Bozarth, Guy Wallace, and Donald Clark. And here are some other learning experts worth following: Paul Kirschner, Pedro De Bruyckere, Richard E. Clark, K. Anders Ericsson, Henry Roediger, Mark McDaniel, Jeroen van Merriënboer, Gary Klein, Ulrich Boser, and Richard Mayer. These lists are not exhaustive, and I have certainly missed important people—to whom I apologize.

Chapter 31
Separating Good Research from Bad

In this chapter, I describe how some members of your learning team have been fooled by "research" into following mediocre practices—benchmarking themselves against industry averages and following pied pipers toward new and unproven technologies and learning methods. They are wasting time and your organization's money and are building inadequate practices, thus eroding your organization's effectiveness. You might share the chapters in this section with your CLO to encourage a small investment in developing research wisdom and using research more thoughtfully.

We've talked already about scientific research on learning. But scientific research exists on many other areas relating to organizational functioning—coaching, managing, onboarding, creativity, habits, human-technology interface design, embodied cognition, office design, leadership, and much, much more—that can also be utilized to design training, elearning, and workflow learning interventions.

Without the benefits of this research, your organization's managers and teams are likely to make suboptimal decisions. For example, most people think that brainstorming in groups is better than brainstorming as individuals, when the science is clear that the opposite is true. Most organizations focus on conveying information during onboarding, when research shows that creating personal connections for new hires is much more important to employee success and loyalty. These are just a few examples of how well-translated scientific research can improve your organization's success.

Indeed, if you're running a well-funded organization, you might consider hiring a half-dozen people whose sole job is to index your organization's needs and search for and translate scientific research into practical recommendations based on those needs. Yes! It's an extra cost but it's a relatively small cost for a competitive advantage.

Organizations typically underutilize scientific research—at least in relation to learning and employee performance—and rely on vendors and consultants who underutilize it as well. As we might expect, this underutilization leads to ineffective learning, development, and workplace practices.

Why do learning teams underutilize scientific research? Primarily because L&D measurement practices don't capture what's effective and what's not. With poor measurement, we just can't tell an effective program from an ineffective one. Measurement blindness allows other forces to fill the vacuum. Vendors tend to convey information and market their products in ways that get sales—routinely ignoring what works.

Also, consultants and vendors know that "research" brings credibility, so some of them look for the quickest, cheapest way that can earn research credibility. They often turn to industry research, one of the most hidden-in-plain-sight problems in the learning field.

Let's now switch away from scientific research. Lots of people everywhere, in every field, hear regularly about other types of research, including survey research and qualitative research. These methods have important contributions to make, but they can be dangerous when not understood for what they are. Indeed, a major problem in the learning field—certainly elsewhere as well—is that many of us who are practitioners see the word "research" and assume all research is cut from the same cloth. It is not!

Industry research uses surveys (and sometimes focus groups or interviews) to compile opinions from people in the learning field. The biggest strength of industry research is that most people find the results very compelling. When we see that 70% of organizations are using microlearning videos, we can't help but think that maybe we should be using microlearning videos as well. Again, if we had access to scientific research or A-B testing, we would know that microlearning videos used alone are unlikely to be effective. However, since we don't have this data (and our managers don't have this data), we tend to follow the crowd over the cliff— utilizing practices that are not very effective.

It's absurd to blindly trust survey research in the learning industry when so many people join the field without education and experience, when so many fads float through the ether, when so little good measurement is getting done that would provide guidance on what works! Many who complete these industry surveys are likely to have incomplete knowledge on at least some of the questions asked. Yet organizations like yours fall for industry survey research over and over.

Your organization almost certainly pays good money to industry analysts or trade associations who make recommendations based on the "research" surveys they do. They survey, survey, and survey on different topics to bring forth new reports and new analyses— and learning professionals like me keep paying for this "research" because we fear we might be missing out on some new secret technology, method, or practice.

I am not saying that well-done industry research is worthless. Some very thoughtful industry research analysts are doing great work, and their findings can give us great insights into where learning professionals see the field. What I am saying is that, too often, problems creep into this work and in the interpretation of the data.

I have done industry research myself at Work-Learning Research and when I worked in a team at TiER1 Performance on the annual Learning Trends survey. Given these experiences, I know intimately about the strengths and limitations of industry survey research as well as how to maximize the benefits and limit the dangers.

What are the dangers? There are many. The biggest problem is mediocrity. How will your learning team get a competitive advantage by aspiring to industry averages? Worse, what will they learn from industry averages in a learning-and-development field where the constraints on professionals have too often hampered best practices? They will learn to aspire to mediocre practices!

The mediocrity problem is compounded by the designs of most industry surveys. The questions asked on the surveys accentuate people's tendency toward current practices and shiny new objects of faddish affection. Where surveys present a list of practices for respondents to choose from, they include too many popular but dubious practices. They too often omit research-inspired models and frameworks. Also, in the false hope that open-ended responding will provide a truer view of the industry, they fail to realize that people's top-of-mind thinking is more likely to prompt thoughts of traditional practices and exciting new technologies rather than foundational proven practices.

Remember too that learning evaluation is so bereft and broken in the learning field that people in the field—those responding on industry surveys—have likely gotten their sense of what works and what doesn't from poorly-designed smile sheets and lazy platitudes circulating in the industry.

In addition to the mediocrity problem, industry survey research almost always suffers from sampling bias. The surveyors (me included) don't have the resources to do the difficult work of ensuring a truly representative sample. Surveys are blasted out to anyone who is willing to take them. This isn't a fatal flaw, because demographic data can be used to get a sense of the population that was sampled and the reports generated can communicate important characteristics of the audience who was surveyed. However, report writers often don't caveat their findings based on their respondent samples. Also, report readers don't often notice who took the survey; they just look at the data and assume it is a fair snapshot of the industry in general.

The mediocrity problem and the representation problem are bad enough. What's worse is that, when people in the field think "research," they too often don't distinguish between scientific research and industry survey research. This leaves folks on your learning team thinking they are following science-based best practices, when in fact they are following survey-based mediocre practices.

And, of course, there are vendors, suppliers, and consultants who exacerbate the problem exponentially because they use the industry-survey research to bolster their claims and their credibility. Vendors amplify the noise, and your learning team hears messages of mediocrity over and over again.

The best industry analysts use survey research with wisdom, bringing in other sources of information and expertise to make sense of the survey data—even highlighting when industry perceptions are out of whack with evidence-based best practices. They also work hard to ensure that casual readers of their reports can't misinterpret their data.

Again, this doesn't prevent vendors and consultants from picking and choosing from these research reports, decontextualizing the data to send their preferred messages.

Another practice that harms your learning team's performance is web searching or GenAI searching for learning best practices—even when searching for research-based practices. The internet is filled with poor recommendations for the practice of learning. When your learning team searches for research-based learning practices, they're liable to run across bogus information that looks credible. Similarly, large language models like ChatGPT were trained on the internet and their results can also be faulty. The bottom line is that these types of casual searches are no replacement for expertise.

Given all these problems with your learning team's common practices in using research, what can you do as CEO? Probably, you're not going to want to get down into the weeds on this, but, when the annual budget gets discussed, your organization should ensure your learning team spends its research money wisely—not making strategic decisions based primarily on industry research. It should only use industry survey research that (1) is specifically designed to lessen the siren song of mediocrity, (2) caveats findings based on the respondent sample, (3) communicates clearly about those caveats, and (4) connects survey findings to scientific recommendations.

Your learning team should have access and be encouraged to use scientific research and research translators to help make sense of the evidence. If there is any doubt about the quality of the industry data your learning team is paying for, those who negotiate your learning team's budget might consider dropping your industry-research subscription—and often it is a very expensive subscription—until your learning team can do their due diligence to ensure the quality of the data and its strategic usefulness.

You can also fund and encourage your learning team to bring in outside unbiased help in interpreting industry data—enabling them to hire trusted advisors on an occasional basis or on a retainer, or by getting an outside audit of their learning practices. By bringing in experts with a research background in learning and in learning practices, your learning team will get clearer insights from the data.

Chapter 32
Using A-B Testing in Learning

Your learning team is extremely unlikely to be using A-B testing. Thus, they are missing a golden opportunity to create virtuous cycles of continuous improvement. In this chapter, I describe why A-B testing is important and how to make it happen.

Your marketing team uses A-B testing all the time. They create five versions of an internet advertisement and then observe what happens. They look at click-through rates, cost per clicks, and conversion rates. Based on results, they delete some ads, prioritize others, and create new versions. A-B tests are experiments to see what actually works. Your marketing team is always experimenting to get information to help them make good decisions.

Why do they do this? Why don't they just get their smartest people in the room and decide in advance—with no testing—which ad will be most effective? They A-B test because they know that human beings are unpredictable and that even experts aren't always right about human behavior. Experts will likely create better advertisements than rookies, but even their best attempts will not create the most effective advertisements.

A quick digression. As CEO, there are issues in your organization that revolve around amazing complex entities we call human beings. Because we humans are so multifaceted and unpredictable, a two phase approach is required when we hope to maximize their performance. First, we find experts who can make evidence-informed recommendations. Second, we A-B test and refine those recommendations to determine what works in the situations and contexts we're targeting for effectiveness. This idea is so important it deserves a name. Let's call it TRACT decision-making. We should "Translate Research And Comparison Test" to enable our human-performance decision making.

What about your learning team? Is their work focused on human performance? Of course it is! Should they be TRACTing their decisions? Of course. Are they? Not many are, but more and more learning teams (still too few) are utilizing science-based recommendations—but hardly any learning teams are doing A-B comparison tests. Even more troubling, hardly any learning-industry vendors are using A-B testing. Hardly any! And this is odd because you'd think they'd want to gain a competitive advantage by distinguishing their products with credible research. You might think they'd want to do research to improve their products. By now, you know why they don't—because the learning industry does not measure properly, so it's hard to tell good learning programs from bad, and therefore there is no incentive for vendors to create maximally effective learning interventions.

As CEO, you can help by nudging your learning team to seek vendors who are TRACTing their programs. Also, your learning team's Requests for Proposal (RFPs) should directly query potential suppliers on (1) how their solutions were developed based on science, (2) how they have used comparison tests over the years to refine and improve their products/services, and (3) how they will TRACT the intervention they will provide to you. Because many will not have done any of this, for the foreseeable future you will need to ask them how they are planning to use a TRACT process. Finally, if you don't have research-to-practice experts on your learning team, you should contract with a research translator to help you vet potential vendors and their efforts in TRACTing.

Can your learning team carry out its own A-B testing? Absolutely! They may need some outside support at first, but this is eminently doable. How might this work? First, and most importantly, we should only test when we have a decision to make or a potential opportunity to grab. Here's a common one. Your subject-matter experts tend to want to teach a ton of content, while your learning folks may want to teach less content and reinforce the material that is taught. So, create two versions of a training—one that teaches 50 concepts and one that teaches and reinforces 25—and use rigorous and valid metrics (not just learner opinions) to test what happens. Similarly, you might test two vendors' programs against each other, or test a new training design against a current training program, or test what happens when you replace an old learning practice with a new one.

The benefits of using A-B comparison testing go beyond what you will learn from the actual results. When you A-B test, you unleash creativity and break down knowledge blockades. Testing creates a mindset and culture that encourages independent thought, truth-seeking behavior, and creativity. Without a testing mindset, people's opinions clash but issues get resolved based not on effectiveness, but on authority or expediency. Bad decisions get made, and then the organization or team gets stuck, unable to move away from these bad decisions. Also, your best people leave in frustration.

As CEO, you should expect your learning team to do some A-B comparison testing, but not go hog-wild and test everything. And again, you'll want your learning team to hire vendors who are doing comparison testing as well.

Finally, it's important to remember that comparison testing should come after the first part of TRACT: translated research recommendations. Your team should rely heavily on translated scientific research—and generally avoid industry research, except perhaps as a place to generate hypotheses to be fully vetted through science and comparison testing.

Section Seven
Fixing the Crap-Data Problem

Section Seven—Theme

Section Seven focuses on learning evaluation. As I said earlier in the book, poor learning evaluation is probably the number one thing hurting organizations like yours as they attempt to leverage learning to improve performance. Without good measurement your learning team can't build continuous cycles of improvement. They end up lost in debate rather than improving the effectiveness of your learning programs. This section provides a clear-eyed prescription for improving learning evaluation. Learning evaluation is very complex, but we can do better.

Chapter 33—Data Should Help People Make Decisions

In this chapter I make an impassioned argument that we gather data to make decisions. That's a no-brainer, of course, but there are subtleties. Each of us in our job role has certain data—or evidence or information—that we should pay attention to, while paying less attention to data that isn't relevant to us. I make this argument—irrefutable as it is—because there are folks in the learning field who have been hoodwinked into focusing on the wrong data. By focusing primarily on business impact, they forget to focus on leverage points they have the most control over. I list seven learning leverage points that your learning team can use to guide their learning-evaluation work.

Chapter 34—Learning Evaluation As Decision Support

Here I introduce the LEADS framework, which stands for Learning Evaluation As Decision Support. The basic idea is that learning teams should first figure out what their most important decisions are, and then develop a learning-evaluation plan that helps them gather data they can use to support them in their decision-making. I provide a list of 14 points of focus for learning-team decision making. I then go in-depth on each of these, guiding learning teams to consider what they might measure to support them in their key decisions.

Chapter 35—LTEM—The Learning-Transfer Evaluation Model

I introduce the Learning-Transfer Evaluation Model (LTEM) and show how its eight tiers can be utilized to guide learning teams in thinking broadly about learning evaluation and learning design. I describe how LTEM integrates wisdom from the learning research, and I recommend that LTEM replace the Kirkpatrick-Katzell Four-Level Model—previously the dominant evaluation model in L&D—because it does not align with what we know about human learning.

Chapter 36—Performance-Focused Learner Surveys

In the final chapter in this section on learning evaluation I recommend that your organization utilize performance-focused learner surveys. I contrast them with traditional smile sheets, which focus on the satisfaction and reputation of the learning program—and which have been shown to be uncorrelated with learning results. I make the case that improved learner surveys are a good way to get started in improving your learning evaluation efforts. They should not be all your learning team does, but they do create momentum to do more rigorous evaluations.

Section Seven—Notes for Learning Professionals

In this section I make a passionate case for learning evaluation, and I argue that we learning professionals are mostly doing a terrible job in evaluating our learning programs. We must do better. By measuring better, we will know better what to do. By using more rigorous learning evaluation approaches, we're likely to be seen as more credible by senior leaders in our organizations. To get started, we must further educate ourselves about the fundamentals and intricacies of learning evaluation. Every time we are asked why we are not able to do the learning measurement we want to do, we say we don't have the knowledge. We can start by using better learner surveys—performance-focused learner surveys. But we must do more: measuring decision-making competence, task competence, and on-the-job behavior change. We also ought to replace the Kirkpatrick-Katzell Four-Level Model with LTEM, the Learning-Transfer Evaluation Model. Finally, we ought to consider LEADS, a new framework for thinking about learning evaluation. By thinking about Learning Evaluation As Decision Support, we open up a world of new learning-evaluation opportunities.

Chapter 33
Data Should Help People Make Decisions

You're the CEO. You know data! Your Board uses data to evaluate your performance. They use things like your organization's share price, profits, market share, revenues—and projections of these metrics into the future. If the data, taken as a whole, points to a rocky future for your organization, your board will MAKE A DECISION to fire you.

Does this mean everyone in your organization should focus on market share and revenues? Of course not! Should the custodians who clean your bathrooms focus on market share? Should they utilize their work time analyzing the competitive landscape—or would they be more effective IN THEIR OWN DECISION-MAKING if they focused on bacterial counts related to cleanliness? The answer is obvious.

What about your company's software developers? Do you want them spending their time tracking your company's stock price or would you rather have them thinking about their team's current sprint cycle?

Performance requires focus. When employees spend a lot of time looking beyond their focal horizons, their productivity drops. Sure, they and their teams may find motivation in keeping the ultimate goals in mind, but spending time strategizing and planning for things largely outside of their control is a big fat waste of time and effort.

For your employee teams to be successful, they must do one thing really well: Figure out what their most important decisions are and then make good decisions on those priorities. As CEO, you can help by determining (1) whether your teams are prioritizing the right decisions, (2) whether they are collecting reasonable data or evidence to enable themselves to make those decisions, (3) whether they are making good decisions based on that data/evidence, and (4) whether they are following through effectively in implementing those decisions in their work.

Let's bring this back to learning. Should your learning team be looking at meta "businessy" numbers like sales revenue, market share, and R&D costs? Yes, sometimes, but not all the time! If your learning team helps design a new sales training program, then it makes sense that they track whether the new training helped increase sales numbers better than the old program. Even better, your learning team might test three training designs and their impact on sales revenues before selecting the most effective option.

But should these businessy numbers be all your learning team looks at? Of course not! You would hope that they'd look at data and indicators relevant to learning as well—metrics that enable them to make good decisions about their work. Your learning team should ALSO be tracking the following, as they relate to what was taught or learned:

- Whether learners COMPREHEND key concepts and skills.

- Whether learners REMEMBER key concepts and skills.

- Whether learners are MOTIVATED TO APPLY the learning.

- Whether learners can MAKE WORK-REALISTIC DECISIONS.

- Whether learners can PERFORM WORK-REALISTIC TASKS.

- Whether learners ATTEMPT TO PERFORM the newly learned skills IN THEIR WORK.

- Whether, and to what extent, learners are SUCCESSFUL in using their newly learned skills IN THEIR WORK.

Your learning team doesn't need to measure each of these for every learning intervention. That would be much too costly. But they should measure a representative sample of their learning programs. They should also periodically measure impact and often measure learner perceptions focused on learning effectiveness, not just on general satisfaction or the reputation of the instruction or instructors.

Here's how you can help. Tell your learning team you want them to focus where they have the most leverage—on measuring the learning outcomes listed above. Provide them with time and resources and monitor them to see how well they are doing. Recognize that your learning team has almost certainly been browbeaten to think that measuring business impact is all that matters. When they come to you with a plan to measure impact alone, be skeptical! Coach them to measure things that directly inform their effectiveness. Counsel them to use the LTEM framework, which helps learning teams focus on leverageable learning factors. Fire those who remain undisciplined in wanting to measure only business impact. You are needed here to knock sense into those who want to pander!

Because most organizations do a terrible job in learning evaluation—and because good learning evaluation creates so many benefits—if you do better evaluation, you'll create a competitive advantage. If you do excellent learning evaluation—which is hard to do and thereby provides a kind of *barrier to entry* for competitors—you'll create the best kind of competitive advantage—one that is sustainable, energizing to your team, and admired.

Chapter 34
Learning Evaluation As Decision Support

In the previous chapter, I recommended that learning-related data should be aimed directly at the decisions your learning team makes. In this chapter, we dig deeper—examining specifically each of the major decisions your learning team must make and then looking at the options they have for gathering data related to those decisions. As CEO, you don't need to get into the weeds here. Instead, direct your CLO to rebuild your organization's learning-evaluation strategy from the ground up—building learning-evaluation practices that help your learning team make its most important decisions.

What I'm suggesting here is new to the learning field. Where, typically, we in learning have been taught to focus first and foremost on measuring the outcomes of learning, I'm recommending we focus first on the decisions that must be made related to learning and then devise measures that enable these decisions to be made.

Because it may help to have a name for this approach, let's call it LEADS (Learning Evaluation As Decision Support) pronounceable as "Leeds," as in, "We do learning evaluation to get leads to help us make decisions." The benefit of LEADS compared to the traditional approach is that traditionally we would gather a bunch of data and not always know what to do with it. Indeed, as I've talked with thousands of learning professionals over the past few decades, many have told me that their organizations collect learning data but do not even look at it! With LEADS we are specifically starting with the decisions that must be made, and then working backwards. We are collecting data we can actually use!

Here's a warning before you read this. This section is augmented with a ton of detail in the chapter notes—detail that is dense and complicated. As CEO you don't need to know the specifics. What I hope you'll understand from this chapter is that your learning team can go beyond traditional ways of measuring learning by focusing first on the decisions they have to make. You will also find advantage in knowing that the decisions they make should not just be focused on training design or training impact but should also include such things as support for remembering, enlisting managers to enable learning in the workflow, and designing the work context to nudge performance.

Let me also add that learning is too complex for me to include all the types of decisions your learning team must make. Still, by focusing on the 14 items here, your learning team will significantly improve their learning-and-performance measurement.

The Central Decisions That Learning Teams Must Make:

- **Outcome Targeting**

  For each learning or performance-improvement initiative, are important outcomes being targeted? Are clear goals outlined for each program? Are these goals important for the organization, for work performance, and for key constituencies?

- **Outcome Evaluation**

  How successful were we in achieving our program goals? And how appropriate, meaningful, useful, and cost-effective were our evaluation practices? Did we use our evaluation findings to improve our practices?

- **Behavior Targeting**

  Which behaviors are most critical for a particular job? And what are the most leverageable ways to upskill people to perform those behaviors?

- **Motivational Targeting**

  Which motivations are most critical for a particular job? And what are the most effective ways to motivate attention and perseverance?

- **Solution Selection**

  Which learning and performance-improvement tactics, tools, and technologies are likely to be effective and workable given the behavior improvement targets?

- **Management Enlistment**

  Are employee managers on board and prepared to provide encouragement, guidance, monitoring, and feedback?

- **Support Enlistment**

  What additional supports and resources are needed to augment the selected solutions?

- **Content Vetting**

  Is learning content accurate, backed by science or evidence, and credible to the targeted learners? Are the tools that learners are being trained to use backed by science/evidence, and workable in practice?

- **Engagement Design**

  Which learning (or performance) designs will entice and keep the attention of employees as they learn and perform their work?

- **Comprehension Design**

  Which learning (or performance) designs will enable employees to comprehend key concepts and skills?

- **Remembering Design**

  Which learning (or performance) designs will support employees in remembering the concepts and skills they learn?

- **Action Design**

  Which learning (or performance) designs will enable and energize employees to take action based on what they've learned?

- **Prompting Tool Design**

  Which prompting tool designs (e.g., job aids, performance supports) will work to nudge employees to take specific actions?

- **Work-Context Performance Activators**

  Which contextual stimuli in people's work-performance contexts can be leveraged to trigger thoughts and actions?

These decision categories are among the most important that learning teams must consider. When taking a LEADS approach, your learning team will look at these decision areas and determine how to get data and evidence to support their strategic and tactical decision-making. Without using this list, your learning team will likely do what it's always done: missing key leverage points and failing to improve its decisions and practices.

So how will your learning team know what to focus on? I've included almost 10 pages of specifics in the chapter notes. As CEO, you don't need to know these specifics, but let me cover some guidelines for this work and an example to make sense of it.

Here is a key point—one that is not often discussed in learning and development. There are two types of data we can use to make decisions: data gathered *before* we make a decision and data gathered *after* we've made a decision. For clarity, I will call these "input data" and "output data." We gather input data before we make decisions. We evaluate the results of our decisions by gathering output data. Of course, there is a subtlety here: Output data can, and should, become input data for subsequent decisions.

Why is this distinction between "input data" and "output data" so critical in learning evaluation? Because both provide unique insights. More pointedly, looking at "output data" only—as all learning-evaluation approaches have done up till now—is simply not sufficient.

Here's the problem with "output data": The results of any effort depend not only on the original decisions that were made, but also on luck, on random noise, on the level of risk that was taken, and on good or bad execution. Also problematic is that outcomes depend on many factors—and outcome data examines them as a whole, essentially ignoring the impact of the individual factors. As Jacob Bernoulli, famous Swiss mathematician, once said: *"One must not decide about the value of human actions from their outcomes."*

Measuring results alone—as some evaluation gurus recommend—is problematic because we want to know which learning approaches to keep and which to improve. We should still measure our results, but we must understand that outcome data are hiding insights of the kind we need to make good decisions. As Olivier Sibony wrote in his excellent book on cognitive biases in business decision-making, *"In many circumstances, there's a lot to be said for the simplicity of focusing on results and the accountability it creates. But the price we pay for this simplicity is steep."*

Let's use leadership development as an example of a situation where it would be irresponsible to only measure learning results. One of the decisions your learning team must make in their leadership-development work is what gets taught. As researchers Scott Tannenbaum and Eduardo Salas have written: *"A great deal has been written about leadership, and most of it is unsupported advice written by leadership gurus."* Because dubious leadership advice is a known problem, your learning team would do better to look at the inputs rather than the outputs. That is, instead of using a common leadership curriculum and later evaluating the results of the program to determine whether the content was well chosen, it would be better to evaluate the topics selected before the program is rolled out.

My gentle recommendation about all of this is to encourage your learning team to consider the LEADS approach described here, starting with the decisions they must make and then determining the data they might gather. Then, they should determine whether cost-benefit considerations make gathering the data worth the investment.

LEADS is brand-new and complex, but its underlying logic is sound and powerful. LEADS practices will evolve with time, but organizations that want a competitive advantage will start exploring LEADS right away. Next, we turn to another innovation in learning evaluation: LTEM (the Learning-Transfer Evaluation Model).

Chapter 35
LTEM—The Learning-Transfer Evaluation Model

When we evaluate a learning intervention, we do it with the expectation that evaluating will help us make better decisions and take more useful actions. Evaluation costs us time and money. It is an investment we should get a return on! Unfortunately, as I detailed earlier, the learning-and-performance field too often uses poor evaluation methods, leaving learning teams in the dark about the true effectiveness of their methods.

In the previous chapter, I described a new way of thinking about learning evaluation, called LEADS—Learning Evaluation As Decision Support. As a reminder, LEADS argues that learning professionals should first determine the decisions they need to make and only then should they design their evaluation methods to surface data and information to support those targeted decisions.

In this chapter, I share with you an evaluation model—LTEM, pronounced "L-tem"—that helps guide us to outcome measures that are aligned with many of the key decisions learning professionals must make—decisions that impact learning transfer.

Learning transfer is one of the most important goals of training. It's the process whereby learning enables and motivates a person to use what they've learned in their work. To get to learning transfer, a learning intervention must embody numerous learning-design elements that support learning. For example, effective learning programs guide and inspire learner attention, enable comprehension, support remembering and minimize forgetting, motivate learners to apply what they've learned, marshal after-learning support, and prepare learners to overcome obstacles in applying what they've learned.

LTEM focuses on the outcomes expected from these learning-design elements. For example, LTEM encourages us to determine whether learners can make work-realistic decisions (LTEM Tier-5) and/or carry out work-relevant tasks (LTEM Tier-6). If we evaluate these with rigor, we will find out whether learners comprehended key knowledge and remembered it sufficiently to make good decisions and take appropriate actions. We will then gain insights to help us make decisions about which elements of our learning designs should be kept and which need improvement.

LTEM is a significant improvement over the Kirkpatrick-Katzell Four-Level Model of evaluation because it has learning wisdom baked into it. The Kirkpatrick-Katzell Model nicely encouraged the learning field to look not just at learning, but also at behavior change and organizational results. Unfortunately, the Four-Level Model failed to discourage the measurement of attendance and completion. It failed to encourage the measurement of remembering. Most problematically, it failed to distinguish between less important learning outcomes from more work-realistic learning outcomes. Indeed, it put all learning outcomes into one bucket, which it called "Level 2 Learning." In that bucket were put the regurgitation of trivia, meaningless recall and recognition, meaningful recall and recognition, realistic decision-making, authentic task practices, and skills testing. Because all learning was blended into one big bucket of undifferentiated smoothie, learning teams inevitably lost their bearings. They measured learning at its most impoverished levels and never noticed that their evaluations told them nothing about their learners' competence in making work-realistic decisions or engaging in work-relevant tasks.

You're the CEO; what do you want your employee learners to be able to do? Memorize terms and definitions? Or make real work decisions and carry out authentic work tasks? The Kirkpatrick-Katzell Four-Level Model enticed your learning team to ask questions about terminology, definitions, and knowledge, when they should have been assessing whether employees could make better decisions and carry out work-relevant tasks.

LTEM has specific targets for decision-making competence and task competence. It encourages—and perhaps compels—your learning team to consider measuring learning beyond learner surveys and knowledge.

You can see for yourself what LTEM encourages and discourages in its eight tiers. The details below may be more than you need to know as CEO, but I'm including specifics so you can refer to this later when your learning team starts talking about the LTEM tiers.

- *Tier 1—Attendance/Completion.* LTEM makes it clear that measuring attendance or course completion rates is insufficient to validate learning results. Why insufficient? Because learners may attend or complete a course but still not learn; or they could learn the wrong things or become demotivated or cynical. This doesn't mean your learning team shouldn't measure attendance or completion rates, but it does mean that—when they share learning results with you—they shouldn't brag about the number of people they trained or about course completion rates!

- *Tier 2—Learner Activity.* Measuring learner activity during learning—for example, their attention, interest, and participation—should also not be used to validate learning results. Learners may engage in learning activities but still fail to learn what they need to learn. Don't be fooled when your learning team tells you that 95% of your learners engaged in online discussions during the leadership development course. That's great, but were the discussions illuminating or just proforma? Did they get beneficial insights from their fellow learners, or did they hear empty platitudes? Did they come to believe more strongly in your strategic direction, or did they become more cynical? Measuring learner activities in learning is not a sufficient way to validate learning.

- *Tier 3—Learner Perceptions.* Measuring learner perceptions through some sort of learner survey is the most common method of measuring learning outside of measuring attendance—but it is the method most fraught with dangers. I've written the definitive book on how to design learner surveys—and, even though I believe learner surveys can be well designed, I strongly advocate that they should *not* be our sole source of information. You'll notice I've put learner surveys at LTEM Tier-3, signifying that, though they can provide valuable information, they should be augmented with more objective measures. As CEO, you might ask your learning team whether they are using Performance-Focused Learner Surveys rather than traditional learner surveys, and you might ask whether they are augmenting their learner surveys with measurements at LTEM Tier-5, Tier-6, Tier-7, and Tier-8. Don't beat them up if they are just getting started and are only using Performance-Focused Learner Surveys. That's a good place for them to start improving their evaluation process. But don't let them end there!

- *Tier 4—Knowledge.* Measuring knowledge is another common learning-evaluation approach. Nothing wrong with measuring critical knowledge—especially if it foundational for making good decisions—but too often learning teams measure knowledge that's easy to measure rather than measuring how people might use that knowledge in realistic decision-making. Also, learning teams tend to measure knowledge right at the end of learning, when knowledge is top-of-mind—easy for learners to remember. This all-too-common practice blinds your learning team to potential failures in their learning designs. When reported out to you that learners passed the knowledge test, you might ask these questions: *Is the knowledge they are asked about critical to their work? Did they show they could remember the knowledge at least a few days later? Was the test of knowledge rigorous enough to really separate out those who fully comprehended from those who just knew enough to guess the correct answers? Can they use the knowledge in work-relevant decision-making?* The bottom line is that measuring knowledge is often insufficient to validate learning, but measuring learner knowledge can be valuable in helping your learning team diagnose learner comprehension and remembering of work-relevant concepts.

- *Tier 5—Decision-Making.* LTEM Tier-5 represents the first level that is adequate to certify the kind of competence required to lead to learning transfer. We want learners to use what they've learned to make realistic, relevant decisions. Here again, as in LTEM Tier-4, it is remembered competence that is the higher goal. If learners show decision-making competence only during the learning event, but can't show it three or more days afterward, we can't really certify full success. Ideally, we'd like them to remember for at least a week or two, but I specify three days because much of the research I've reviewed shows that differences in understanding and remembering begin to show up after three days. LTEM Tier-5 is a significant improvement compared to previous learning-evaluation models. It encourages your learning team to measure and determine whether your learners can use what they've learned when faced with work-realistic scenarios. I often tell my learning-evaluation workshop audiences that LTEM Tier-5 is the sweet spot in learning evaluation; for a modest investment in the development of well-crafted scenario questions, we as learning professionals gain critical insights about the strengths and limitations of our learning programs.

- *Tier 6—Task Performance.* LTEM Tier-6 is fulfilled when learners can perform relevant, realistic actions while making the decisions that enable those actions. Again: Remembered task competence is the goal. It is not enough to show competence right after something is learned, when everything is top-of-mind— but learners must be able to demonstrate competence after a delay of several days or more. This tier, like LTEM Tier-5 decision-making competence, is also a high-value-add opportunity, especially for some content areas. For example, if you want your employees to be able to use PowerPoint to make effective presentations, the most telling evaluation would focus on their ability to make a presentation. An LTEM Tier-6 evaluation of their task competence—of an actual presentation they deliver within the training—would be ideal. But a warning: Not all competencies are easy to measure at LTEM Tier-6. For some topics, it might be too expensive, too dangerous, or too unwieldy to measure task competencies. For example, in measuring oral communications skills, it is probably too expensive and awkward to hire actors to interact with all our learners. In such a case, measuring at LTEM Tier-5 focusing on people's decision-making skills within conversations would likely be more workable.

- *Tier 7—Transfer to Work Performance.* LTEM Tier-7 is the first tier that focuses on work performance rather than performance in learning. When we talk about "learning transfer," we're really talking about work behavior—or, more specifically, we're aiming to determine whether a learning program caused improvements in employees' work behavior. When we measure transfer, we are really measuring Key Behavior Indicators (KBIs) or metrics that align with our KBI targets. We are measuring whether salespeople trained on handling objections are using the techniques when customers raise objections, and whether they are using them appropriately. We are measuring whether mine supervisors are speaking with their operators when they see them failing to deal with a hazard in the pits. We are measuring whether people trained on the new IT system are using the system as intended. Measuring transfer is not easy. First, we must outline workable KBIs and determine how they can be measured. Then, we must determine whether the training actually made a difference or whether other factors were involved. Here we get into whether we need a comparison-group design, pre-assessments versus post-assessments, or some sort of time-series design. Measuring transfer is complicated, and usually costly—only sometimes worth the investment. Don't be fooled when your learning team tells you a simple survey of learners will be enough to measure transfer. It won't! Carefully designed surveys can give some indication of behavioral outcomes, but, by themselves, surveys can't determine whether the results were due to training or to some other non-training factors.

- *Tier 8—Effects of Transfer.* LTEM Tier-8 measures our ultimate outcomes, our Key Performance Indicators (KPIs). We hope managers who coach better don't just coach better. We hope that those they coach will produce better results, better KPIs. We hope the training helped them create higher quality outputs, raise revenues, reduce costs, improve safety, produce more innovative work products, and the like. LTEM specifically highlights the effects of transfer on a variety of stakeholders, including beneficiaries, learners, the organization, customers, sponsors, coworkers/family/friends, investors, community, society, and the environs. Your learning team shouldn't measure the impact on all these stakeholders—certainly not every time they measure (that would be too expensive). But they should consider the options. Measuring KPIs at LTEM Tier-8 requires some of the same methodologies as used for measuring Key Behavioral Indicators (KBIs) at LTEM Tier-7. Your learning team must determine the evaluation study design to use, how to collect the data, and whether it is easily available. Measuring at LTEM Tier-8 is generally costly and shouldn't be undertaken in a willy-nilly manner.

Final Words About LTEM

My description of LTEM has been brief, and I'm leaving out a ton of details about how to make it work. Indeed, the workshop I teach on learning evaluation—*The LTEM Boot Camp*—requires about 24 hours of learning activities because of all the subtleties involved. I share LTEM with you to give you a sense of the kind of things your learning team should be looking to measure—while also giving you a window into the complexities of measuring learning evaluation. If your learning team is doing great learning evaluation, they deserve a ton of credit because, as you can see, it's not as simple as it looks.

LTEM is not a panacea, but it is a significant improvement over previous learning evaluation models based on the Kirkpatrick-Katzell Four-Level framework. It adds several doses of learning wisdom. It nudges learning teams to see that measuring attendance, completion rates, and learner activity is inadequate. It shows that measuring knowledge is not enough—that knowledge doesn't equal competence or performance. LTEM highlights the importance of decision-making and task performance. It makes clear that learning interventions must support both comprehension and remembering, and, when we measure learning, we must account for the forgetting curve by measuring after a delay. LTEM reinforces the importance of measuring actual transfer to real work. It also reminds us that the ultimate goal of learning is not just behavior change but also achieving results for a variety of stakeholders.

LTEM is a learning-evaluation model, but it is having a profound impact on learning teams in other ways as well. As Elham Arabi documented in her doctoral dissertation, learning teams that use LTEM are likely to be more attuned to the importance of improved learning designs. It's too soon to expect that academic researchers have fully delineated the causal factors of how LTEM inspires learning teams, but it's easy to imagine a learning team looking at LTEM and thinking, "Well, if learning programs should be evaluated by measuring decision-making and task performance, we probably ought to give learners more practice in making decisions and more opportunities to practice the kind of tasks they'll be asked to do in their work." Getting a learning team to think like this is an extraordinary leap forward. We know from the scientific research that massive learning gains occur when learners get realistic practice making decisions and accomplishing tasks. That's how learning evaluation should work—inspiring better learning designs!

A few more caveats about LTEM. It was designed as a *learning* evaluation framework. It was designed specifically to help learning teams evaluate the effectiveness of a learning intervention to support and inspire learners to transfer what they've learned to their work. Learning wisdom was baked into the framework! LTEM was *not* intended to measure other types of interventions. It was not intended to measure nudges, habits, context triggering, job aids, or performance support tools. In short, LTEM is the beginning of better learning evaluations; it is not the culmination of the journey from learning to performance.

For you as CEO, here are my final words of wisdom about the LTEM framework. LTEM is a major improvement in learning evaluation, but it's not the only framework your learning team ought to utilize. They should also consider building evaluation practices based on the LEADS framework—starting with the decisions they need to make and then building evaluation and diagnostic methodologies to get data to make those decisions. They should also look to the literature on cognitive biases, survey design, data science, and the many related fields of study that can shed light on the vast complexities of learning evaluation. They should be reading Daniel Kahneman, Jerry Muller, and other experts who have studied cognitive functioning, data utilization, and fields related to assessment. Your learning team should also be reading experts in learning so they can align learning evaluation with how people learn. Learning evaluation isn't rocket science; it's much more complex!

You'll remember at the beginning of this book I called bad learning evaluation the root of all evil in the workplace learning field. It is so true! With good measurement, reality comes into focus. We can deal with reality—making plans to keep what works and improve what's not working. Good learning evaluation enables virtuous cycles of continuous improvement. Poor learning evaluation keeps us locked into feeble traditions and poor learning practices, blind to what we cannot see. Please give your learning team the permission and resources to help them do learning evaluation right. It truly impacts every aspect of your learning team's thinking and performance.

Organizations that do good learning evaluation create a competitive advantage. Those who do the difficult work to become excellent in learning evaluation create a hard-to-imitate sustainable competitive advantage.

Chapter 36

Performance-Focused Learner Surveys

Aside from measuring attendance and course completions, learner surveys are the most common method used in evaluating learning. In Chapter 8 on the crap-data problem, I described how traditional smile sheets are virtually uncorrelated with learning results. What this means in practice—if your learning team is still using traditional smile sheets—is that when they get high marks, they could have a very effective course but almost equally likely they could have a very ineffective course. When they get low marks, they could have a poorly designed learning experience or a well-designed one. With traditional smile sheets we just can't tell.

Surveys are useful because they are relatively easy to create and administer, but they too often suffer from poor designs that do not carve through the fog of subjective responses. Fortunately, by using performance-focused learner surveys, we can gather meaningful data.

Learner surveys are worth doing, but only if they are done right. Indeed, in my work with hundreds of organizations over the past decade—from Bloomberg to Oxfam to Genentech to the CDC—I've seen how performance-focused learner surveys produce leverageable data while also creating momentum for learning teams to measure how well the learning enabled improved decision-making, task competence, and behavior change. In this chapter, I briefly explain how performance-focused learner surveys work, why they're important, and how you as a senior leader can help.

Performance-focused learner surveys aim to accomplish three things: (1) measure learning effectiveness, (2) produce actionable data, and (3) enable the learning team to nudge advantageous thoughts and actions.

Traditional smile sheets tend to focus on learner satisfaction and course reputation. This focus is insufficient because learners may like a learning experience but not learn, or learn the wrong things, or quickly forget what they've learned. It's better to focus on learning effectiveness—as much as surveys enable.

Performance-focused learner surveys are designed to align with what we know about workplace learning. They focus on key learning factors like learner comprehension, ability to remember, motivation to apply what they've learned, the after-learning support they are likely to receive, and the learners' sense of self-efficacy.

Performance-focused learner surveys can focus on all variety of other constructs as well, depending on the goals a learning team has in evaluating. For example, I have created questions that focus on the following:

- How well the training exemplifies an organization's values.

- Whether the training provided spaced repetitions.

- Whether the online training kept learners' attention.

- How much realistic practice the learners felt they received.

- Whether the training prepared learners to deal with real-world obstacles they anticipate facing.

- Which elearning tools were utilized during the learning.

- The goals learners hope to achieve based on the learning.

- Whether conference speakers provided a practically useful session.

- How deeply a mentoring relationship has progressed.

- How effectively the training created a sense of belonging.

Recently I've been working with Ingeborg Kroese, an expert in diversity, equity, inclusion, and accessibility (DEIA). For almost three years we've been crafting questions to support organizations in measuring how well their training programs are supporting their DEIA values—not just in diversity training, but in all training. We are continuing to improve the questions and will soon share these with the field, making them available at no charge.

Performance-focused learner surveys can also use questions that nudge thinking and action. For example, a question about after-learning supports sends a message that what happens after learning is important. Depending on the answer options, it can also nudge managers to support training, nudge instructors to stay in contact with learners, and nudge learning architects to ensure job aids are likely to be utilized by learners.

As a senior leader, you can support your learning team by encouraging them to use performance-focused learner surveys—while also providing them with the resources and support they'll need as they transition away from traditional smile sheets. Such a transition is one of the best ways to get your learning team to begin upgrading its learning evaluation efforts. Building better learner surveys should only be a first step; it's good to also measure things like decision competence, ability to complete tasks, and job performance, but it's a great way to build momentum.

Section Eight
Advanced Topics

Section Eight—Theme

Section Eight covers a wide range of important topics under the heading "advanced topics." While the rest of the book focuses on fundamentals, this section explores highly beneficial practices that are often overlooked.

Chapter 37—Customer Education

In this chapter I make the case that customer education can be a powerful way for organizations to motivate customer loyalty, build partnership-like relationships with customers, limit customer frustrations, and attract new customers. One danger is to focus only on customer training. Customer education must go beyond what is required when you train your employees. One example is the distinction between pre-sales and after-sales customer education. I introduce "customer success management," a relatively new approach to customer engagement strategy. I warn against taking a one-size-fits-all training regimen and I encourage a problem-solving approach.

Chapter 38—Adding Learning to Leadership Development

I describe a hidden opportunity in leadership development to supercharge your managers into force multipliers. By helping your managers learn and utilize learning as one of their central competencies, they can do more in supporting their teams to learn more fully in the flow of work. By adding "learning" into leadership development programs, we can help managers engage more of their team members in actively strategizing about the work, in being creative and innovative, in learning more capably, and in supporting social learning.

Chapter 39—Integrating Values and Ideas Across Your Learning Efforts

In this chapter I provide examples that show how repetitions provided over multiple channels are critical to persuasion, branding, motivation, and organizational success. From this essential nugget, I argue that learning teams ought to integrate organizational values and key ideas over many learning programs, while also seeking to embed engaging repetitions in employees' work contexts as well.

Chapter 40—Training to Help Your Employees

I make a simple case in this chapter: that learning teams should do more to consider how their learning programs benefit their learners. I show how this produces benefits for organizations in terms of employee engagement, loyalty, and recruiting. I describe many ways that learning teams can focus their attention on learners, including building evaluation metrics that track benefits to learners.

Chapter 41—Compliance Training: Effectiveness and the Law

Compliance training is required, of course, but should it also be made effective? In this chapter I describe how most compliance training is poorly designed—and what your organization can do to make it effective.

Chapter 42—Learning in the Workflow

In this chapter I argue that learning in the flow of work can be leveraged more than it is today, going beyond brown-bag lunches and communities of practice, which are in the workplace but not in the flow of work. I identify 10 practices and argue that, as learning teams strive more and more to help employees leverage workflow learning, additional methodologies will be developed.

Section Eight—Notes for Learning Professionals

Each of the chapters in this section is critical for our success. When we do customer education, we must do good learning design, but we must also do more to provide real value for our organization's customers. When we design leadership training, we should add learning to our curriculum of topics—helping leaders leverage learning. We should stop thinking of our courses in silos, but instead align to mission-critical business goals by integrating repetitions of values and key ideas over many courses and initiatives. When we create compliance training, we should remember that aiming also for effectiveness may be in the best interest of our organization and fellow employees. We should also invest in helping teams and individual contributors leverage workflow learning to their advantage.

Chapter 37
Customer Education

As CEO, you certainly know there are two main audiences for training: your employees and your customers. In this chapter, I focus on customer education.

All organizations want happy customers—or beneficiaries in mission-driven organizations. Customer education is more important for some organizations than for others, but, as the world becomes more technology driven, effective customer education will be needed more than ever. Consumers need help using their phones, computers, and other devices. They need guidance in assembling new products, troubleshooting, and buying parts. They need help in making investment decisions, insurance decisions, and making retirement plans. In business-to-business activities, complex equipment like planes, front loaders, medical instruments, and software-as-a-service products require training to enable customers to use them quickly, successfully, safely, and with minimum frustration.

Customer education can be divided into pre-sale and post-sale efforts. Much of customer education today is post-sale: After customers make a purchase, we train their people on how to use our products and services—ideally, we help them to do their jobs better.

Pre-Sale Customer Education: In pre-sale customer education, we need to educate customers who influence buying decisions, providing them with foundational information so they can make informed decisions. Many businesses focus only on enticing customers to buy their products and services, but this is a faulty strategy. It's more productive to view pre-sale customer education as a way to provide meaningful information to the marketplace.

In today's complex world, helping customers make buying decisions is critical to their success—and to yours. If you nudge customers to buy a product or service that is not right for them, you're going to have unhappy customers—customers who will share their bad experience with colleagues, friends, and associates in your industry, or even on social media.

In the short term, you may sell more to your uninformed customers, but eventually another company will educate them properly and they'll grab your customer base, who will have lost trust in your brand. Just as importantly in today's world—where we business leaders proclaim our interest in a broader bottom line—by educating our customers, we can create a spiral-up toward better products and services. The better informed our customers are, the better products and services we will build. This benefits not only our customers, but our nations and our societies.

If we really want to help our customers, we must help them avoid the myths and misconceptions that float around the internet and in trade associations and communities of practice. We must first and foremost provide them with foundational information that supports them in making good decisions.

Post-Sale Customer Education: In post-sales customer education—where we put most of our efforts—our traditional goal has been to avoid customer frustrations. Customers who can't use their new products are customers who will return their products, share their grievances with the world, and avoid our company long into the future.

But customer education should not just be an investment in avoiding customer frustration. As CEO, you don't just want satisfied customers; ideally, you'd like to give rise to customer advocates—people who will actively sing the praises of your products, services, people, and brand. This is especially important in a world that is hyper-connected.

So, what does good post-sale customer education look like? First, it follows the research-aligned learning principles described earlier in the book. Learners must be inspired to pay attention to the learning materials in ways that support learning. They must be supported in comprehending key information and procedures. They must be motivated to use what they've learned. They must get realistic practice and be able to put what they've learned into practice immediately. They must have on-the-job supports to help them overcome obstacles as they put their learning into practice. These science-backed learning imperatives are critical, but they are just one part of a successful customer education practice.

There are important differences between training employees and training customers. In designing learning for customers, learning teams may have a harder time getting access to their learners' work contexts—making it more difficult to design learning that is fully relevant. Similarly, we too often train customers and never see them again. We lose touch and so we don't have the ability to learn what worked and what didn't. We don't know the obstacles our learners faced or the workarounds they developed. When we lose touch with our customer-learners, we also can't provide them with post-learning supports—of the kind that the learning-transfer research shows are critical.

Of course, not all customer education professionals have these problems. Some create trusted-advisor relationships with users. Some teach systems that routinely track usage, gaining data that makes visible the outcomes of their organization's training efforts.

Your customer-education team knows the importance of understanding their learners' work contexts. They likely lament the obstacles they face in not having more access. Still, too many accept these obstacles as immutable constraints rather than pushing for more access to their learners' work situations. They have learned that you and the rest of the organization often won't support their efforts in getting insight about your customers' work contexts. As usual, when training is seen solely as information sharing, people outside of learning think the learning team should just compile content and present it to customers.

You and your customer education team must do more! If you want your customer-education efforts to be the powerful force it can be, you must change the paradigm. As CEO, you can help by making sure customer education is intimately integrated as a partner in your operations rather than being an isolated add-on.

__Marketing Rationale:__ I'll get back to recommended practices, but, first, let's look at the marketing reasons for customer education. Those who study marketing—the researchers who do the hard work of sifting through the complexity of marketing programs and their business results—have found that organizations that focus on customer success, not just customer satisfaction, achieve better results. As *Harvard Business Review* authors Andris Zoltners, Prabhakant Sinha, and Sally Lorimer have written:

> *When a business buyer makes an initial purchase from a seller, it's only the start of the value exchange between the two. Most of the mutual value accrues over time as the customer benefits and both continues and expands purchasing.*

Customer success management (CSM) is a relatively new field, but it is rapidly growing, as evidenced in job boards filled with vacancies for customer success managers. To be clear, customer success management should be distinguished from value-based selling and customer relationship management—both of which are important components of an overall customer strategy. Customer success management is not just about selling and relationships. It goes much deeper and is focused directly on ensuring that customers feel their suppliers are actively helping them achieve their goals.

Research on customer success management demonstrates a range of complexities—with many factors contributing to success. Suppliers are perceived as providing value to the extent that they exhibit a customer orientation, that they demonstrate competence across their organization, and that key individuals—those who interact most closely with the customer— are seen as having high competence. CSM researchers Prohl-Schwenke and Kleinaltenkamp did an extensive analysis of what customers want and found many factors related to operational efficiency, effectiveness, and competitive advantage. Customers also valued personal factors like task simplicity, perceived control, pressure reduction, uncertainty reduction, social comfort, and personal reputation.

The Role for Customer Education: Take note! Many of the factors above can be supported by good customer education—but only if your customer-education team is empowered to connect closely with your customers and your customer-operations people (product support folks, technicians, trouble-shooters, customer-support representatives).

More specifically, your customer-education operation itself should aspire to be problem solvers, and product experts, not just information presenters. The best already do this! They should not just provide one-time trainings but should be focused on continual process improvement. They should be in constant contact with your product support folks—learning where customers are having problems so they can improve the training to focus on these key roadblocks. They should also have clear lines of communication with your product design team—letting them know the features that are hardest for your customers to learn so that more intuitive product designs can be created.

To avoid having your customers switch to your competitor's products and services, your *post-sale* customer education efforts should focus more on providing information and support on your own products and services rather than educating customers on the market in general. However, this is much less a worry if you are educating current customers who might incur substantial switching costs to move to a competitor.

A few final hints from the research on customer education. Customers tend to be motivated to learn your products, but some are more motivated than others. Many are motivated out of curiosity and a goal to continually improve their skills in using your products. Many are motivated because they want to be able to share what they've learned with their colleagues or their broader communities of practice.

To create the most effective customer education programs, your learning team must avoid a one-size-fits-all learning design. They should treat novices differently than more experienced customers. They should provide ongoing learning experiences for expert customers—engaging them in supporting each other in learning, seeking their insights, supporting them in sharing what they've learned, and generally focusing on building a partnership relationship with them.

Your role as CEO is to help your customer-education team become partners with other operation units, to set clear expectations that research-aligned learning designs should be used, and that customer education must go beyond information presentation to fulfill a role more aligned with the goals of customer success management. You can also help by placing your customer-education team outside your L&D unit, perhaps aligned with your customer success unit, or marketing, or product development. Whatever you do, don't outsource customer education to a third party—third parties will focus almost entirely on training, while ignoring or downplaying the critical role of relationships, expertise, and trust.

Chapter 38
Adding Learning to Leadership Development

Leadership training—usually aimed at people who supervise others—is likely one of your organization's most costly training efforts. Unfortunately, much of what passes for leadership training is weak and misguided. I know. I was a leadership trainer.

I'm a big believer that managers are the key to organizational success. If your leadership training is lacking, your organization will be lacking.

Leadership training suffers from several problems. First, it is often based on popular business books that claim to have leadership insights, but many of the recommendations made are not based on science or are based on pseudoscience, including surveys of managers, sketchy personality instruments, and, recently, false allusions to neuroscience. Second, much of leadership training is based on the "sheep dip" model of training: giving managers a brief content dump and assuming they will transform into great leaders. Leadership training should aim to change long-held habits of action, and that's impossible unless the "training" involves a long-term coached journey to new ways of thinking and new behaviors. Third, leadership training doesn't typically teach managers about learning and human performance—the powerful stuff from psychological science. That's what I'm going to focus on in this chapter—how your leadership training can add insights and practices around learning and performance.

Obviously, in this short chapter, I'm not able to detail every skill you should teach your managers. Instead, I will share some killer leadership skills.

Noticing. In one of my workplace audits, I job-shadowed managers in retail stores. Most treated their assistant managers and clerks as drones. Managers would "walk" the store and point out problems to fix—sometimes writing a task list, sometimes dictating a task list as they led their reports around the store. With this practice, there was only one set of eyes on the store! The few brilliant managers I saw did the opposite. They asked their assistant managers and clerks to run a section of the store (even a small section)—prompting them to notice what was good or bad in their section and asking them to fix problems as they arose. These managers had 20 pairs of eyes noticing things in their stores. Since organizational success is partly about marshaling employee attention, these managers created more successful stores. But they also created learners: people who look around for opportunities and problems to solve.

Coaching for Learning. Most people aren't very good at coaching others. They make some fundamental mistakes they wouldn't make if they knew learning a little bit better. And I'm not talking about long coaching relationships. I'm talking about employees helping each other—observing, getting questions, giving advice. Too often, we in the coaching role jump right in and give advice. Often, we just fix the problem for the other person. This happens a ton with digital technologies. Someone asks, "How do I do X?" And we say, "Let me see your screen; I'll fix it." We fix it and the person learns virtually nothing. If we approached coaching from a learning perspective, we might show them, then ask them to try it on their own. We might even go further and have them do the task half an hour later to give them spaced retrieval practice—supporting their ability to remember! There's more to say about coaching, but you can see how even some simple fixes can produce good results.

Creativity. Management, as typically practiced, is about getting stuff done. Managers help employees focus their attention toward outcomes. That's great and seems natural and right, but a getting-stuff-done focus is the opposite of creativity. Good managers sometimes slow their teams down—going slow to go fast. "Measure twice, cut once." But that's still a getting-stuff-done approach—not one designed to engender creativity and innovation. But what should we teach managers and informal leaders about creativity? First, we need to teach them when to push for creativity and when to push for directed action. Second, we need to get them to see innovation as a process that goes beyond creativity. Here are the components of such a process:

1. Having one or more unrequited goals.

2. Noticing stimuli from which to generate insights.

3. Generating one or more insights.

4. Accepting an insight (as worthy and worth the risk).

5. Remembering or being reminded of the insight.

6. Relating the insight to one or more unrequited goals.

7. Deciding to utilize the insight.

8. Creating something workable from the insight.

9. Persuading others to accept and utilize the insight.

10. Tweaking and finalizing implementation of the insight.

There's more I could say about the process but notice how creativity goes beyond generating ideas. It involves goal-directed thinking, the ability to be bold in the face of obstacles and resistance, persuasion of stakeholders, cycles of experimentation and improvement, and generally, a long-term process that goes from generating creative ideas to workable innovations.

Leaders can be taught and supported in creating a work-team culture where creativity thrives. They can be taught how to monitor the creativity of their work teams so they can make improvements if creative practices are weaker than desired. We can provide managers with prompting tools that encourage better creative practices, and ensure we give substantial practice and support in using these tools. We can train senior leadership—like you—how to set the tone for a creative workplace.

Social Learning. Every time we interact with others, we learn something. All too often, however, we learn that we are right in what we believe. Status-quo learning is fine. We need it so our world doesn't crumble into uncertainty. On the other hand, we also need learning that improves us—that transforms the way we see things into something new and better. Managers can influence the way people interact. They can't control other people's interactions and thinking, but they can influence it in subtle and powerful ways. As an example, imagine managers—after their teams complete a project—asking these simple questions, "What did we do well? What mistakes did we make? What should we do better for next time?" With these simple words managers send powerful messages: that we will hold ourselves accountable, that we will always strive to get better, that we speak hard truths, that we aim to learn from our successes and our failures. With these types of simple interactions, work cultures, performance, learning, loyalty, and love are built.

Noticing the Human Element. I mentioned noticing before—helping managers notice important work artifacts—but a topic worthy of a separate section is helping managers notice the human element that surrounds them every day. Many of us get promoted into management because we're good at doing tasks. We become experts in noticing the tangible things in our work context, but we are much less focused on the human beings in our midst. When I was a leadership trainer, my audiences were filled with people who had moved up the technical ranks—who had spent a much higher percentage of their cognitive investigations focusing on technical things and much less time focusing on people. They had, as a result, learned more about things than people! Leadership development, at its core, should help managers learn about people.

Learning About Themselves. As humans, we are a bundle of actions ready to be triggered by the stimuli and contexts we encounter. Ideally, these prepared actions—or preassembled ways of thinking—will be triggered in the right place at the right time. To improve these situation-action plans, we must develop some self-knowledge about our behavioral tendencies—both the good and the bad. One method, common in leadership-development programs, is to use multi-rater feedback to give those being trained insights into how others see them. This is a useful practice, but the instruments typically utilized are commercially developed to cover general sets of competencies—often missing the behavioral factors that can push personal improvement. Multi-rater surveys don't get specific enough; they don't get to the situation-action level. They might survey people with a question stem like, "Uses his/her time effectively." Note how a person answering that question has to make a global judgment and, worse, they have to make it using a scale with fuzzy distinctions, for example between "strongly agree" and "agree."

A person getting feedback is left without clear knowledge. They may sense a red-flag warning but not know what to focus on. Let's look at an example. On the time dimension, managers need to know whether they are allocating the right amount of time to planning, coaching, reviewing work, etc. They need to know whether they have set up their work environment optimally to minimize distractions and stay focused. They need to know whether they are scheduling their tasks at the right time of day to support productive thinking. They need to know whether they are selecting tasks to support their psychological frame of mind in the moment. The managers we guide in leadership development are not going to get any of this nuance with generally-worded questions like, "Uses his/her time effectively" or, "Can be counted on to follow through with promises."

Conclusions About Learning in Leadership Development. To create a competitive advantage with leadership development, you need to start with good content that, if understood and utilized, would improve manager performance. Generally, it will be safer to choose topics based on science, not popular leadership gurus and anecdotes. Leadership development should be seen as a long, never-ending journey that requires managers to self-motivate and manage—at the same time the organization provides support and resources for the journey. Finally, leadership development can be supercharged by focusing on learning-and-performance factors as mentioned above—helping managers and informal leaders notice what they couldn't notice before, coach in ways that spur learning in others, engender creativity and innovation, enable social and workflow learning, and parlay their own personal learning, among other things.

Chapter 39
Integrating Values and Ideas Across Your Learning Efforts

The best learning teams don't think in silos. They don't treat each training course as a separated and isolated island. Instead, they inculcate values and key ideas across training, and they enlist managers to reinforce those values and ideas as they manage their teams.

You, as CEO, have certainly been preached to about the power of an empowering vision for your company. Come on! Admit it! All the shock-jock leadership gurus of the past 30 years! Please! It's almost cliché by now! But whether you buy into this hype or not, let's dissect it. What is an empowering vision supposed to do? It's supposed to infuse energy, purpose, and guidance into your organization and all its people. And how does it do that? Through repetition from credible, powerful sources (you and other leaders within your organization). Having a vision works only to the extent that it is repeated and resonates with those who hear it!

What about the power of your company's brand—the image your products and services have in the marketplace? How are these brand perspectives created? Through repetition over time! Through conceptual consistency! And, most importantly for us here, through the intentional effort to create a constellation of product, marketing, communication, and organized teamwork.

What have we learned about learning that relates to visioning and branding? We've learned that repetitions spaced over time—reinforced in a variety of ways—lead to learning, remembering, and action!

Relegating a learning event into a silo is the antithesis of what works in practice! We've already seen how learning programs are more powerful if they are spread over time, with repetitions intentionally arranged for maximum impact. But why should we stop there? Aren't some concepts and ideas so valuable that they bear repeating and reinforcing wherever possible?

Suppose you want your managers to engender more creativity from their teams. Specifically, you want them to enlist their teams in ideation, experimentation, and breadth learning (i.e., learning from a wide range of topics). You could provide your managers with one course on creativity management. Indeed, that's not a bad way to get them started. But what would you do if you really, deeply felt that creativity was the key to your organization's success? You would integrate creativity management into other training courses they take, including in such courses as change management, diversity and inclusion, sexual-harassment prevention, conflict resolution, SharePoint, and more!

But you wouldn't end there. You would add the topic of creativity not only to your managers' trainings; you'd add it to their managers' trainings and their direct reports' trainings. You might also add it to your managers' KPIs, their overarching goals, or their performance reviews. You might integrate creativity into your 360-degree multi-rater diagnostic tools, into your organization's meeting template or practices, into your teams' OKR planning, and into your messaging as a senior leader.

Obviously, you don't want to go max inculcation for every topic. That would create a nightmare scenario of information overload. But aren't some topics and ideas in your organization so critical that they deserve special reinforcement? How about your company's values, core principles, and new strategic initiatives? Don't these deserve repetition?

And what about fortifying your company to take advantage of generative AI? Your learning team can help you develop a competitive advantage by embedding GenAI project work into many courses across your organization—that is, many non-GenAI courses!

I give you one warning: You better damn well prioritize these strategic topics into a small handful. But let me give you another critical warning as well: Your learning team shouldn't just repeat a list or repeat key points when they set out to reinforce these strategically important topics! Ugh! That would be boring, eye-rollingly obvious, and feel more oppressive than empowering!

The best way to integrate topics across learning events is to surprise learners with exercises, questions, and activities that are related to the main topic, but that also simultaneously reinforce a targeted strategic topic.

Your learning team can also use learner-survey questions that target these strategic topics, ascertaining whether they've been covered in other courses. Your learning team can also build nudges into prompting tools that remind employees of the importance of the strategic topics. Your learning team can also support your organization's managers by creating meeting templates, recommending performance goals, or providing activity interventions that reinforce and push the use of the strategic topics.

By integrating strategic values and ideas, you create a competitive advantage. It is well past time that learning teams align learning to organizational imperatives by utilizing messaging campaigns over multiple learning and workplace events.

Chapter 40
Training to Help Your Employees

Too often training is delivered with too little thought given to the employees who are trained. This seems crazy, but sometimes we think too narrowly—treating learners like assets rather than as creatures imbued with inherent worth who deserve to be treated with dignity, as people with agency, as people whose well-being is at stake. Members of your learning team are caring and compassionate professionals, but L&D traditions and organizational power structures are often blind to these issues. I'll discuss this in a moment. First, a common story.

My neighbor, a computer programmer, worked in a unit of a large organization. In her department the focus was on using high-powered telescopes to investigate heavenly bodies. I met her on the sidewalk a year ago and she talked about her hunger to get early retirement. When I asked why, one of the things she mentioned was the ridiculous training regimen she's been under. She's a long-time employee but has had to take the same trainings as newbies—wasting her time and distracting her from her work. She is given some of the exact same trainings every year—again wasting her time. And here is my favorite: Her whole department had to take a course on laboratory safety and harmful materials, but not one person in her department worked in a lab or ever encountered lab materials.

This story has two morals:
- This kind of training silliness can become a major irritant to employees, who may then seek to leave or disengage—especially when they experience other irritants. Certainly, this is a waste of time and resources.
- As employees are forced to take inappropriate or poorly designed training, they tend to enter other learning events—even important ones—with malaise and a lack of attention.

The members of your learning team may be personally compassionate, but, unfortunately, the learning-industry credo and commandments tend to consecrate organizational performance above all else. This is evidenced in our traditional insistence on measuring learning impact on "business results," in dictating for learners the training objectives they ought to have, and in outlining a strict regimen of courses that are required, regardless of previous experience or training.

This kind of parochial focus has its dangers. First, employees treated as only a means to an end often become disloyal or leave their organizations—or end up not giving a rat's ass in the work that they do. Second, unmotivated learners are not good learners.

A major root cause of these problems is that our L&D metrics don't even register any flux or friction on these issues. Learners are rarely if ever asked if the learning helped them beyond the narrow benefits for their current positions. We have no sense of whether learners were inspired, energized to engage in further learning, jolted to creative outputs, or motivated to share what they've learned.

Our learning evaluations ask questions limited in their focus on whether the employees can use the skills taught. We measure their knowledge. We measure whether they were able to use their new skills in their work. We almost never ask them whether the learning might help them in their careers, whether they gained transformational insights, whether they were awe-inspired, or whether they were boosted to actions that might change their lives.

Here's a question for you and your learning team: Do you provide training only to improve employee performance, or do you also provide training as a perk of employment?

A recent client of mine in the life-science industry is revamping their training to compete with a competitor who has been grabbing the best people in the industry—largely because of their renowned academy! Training is not just for learning; more and more, it's about the reputation of your organization as a great place to work. Do your employees see training as a benefit of working for your organization?

Not all your employees will see training—and learning opportunities more broadly—as important to them, but two forces in today's economy are making learning and development central to your company's reputation as an employer. First, with accelerating innovations and technological advances, employees are hungry to develop themselves. Second, in today's tight job market, employees are more willing to switch organizations and demand better working conditions and perks.

If learning is a benefit, then we might design training differently. We might also train managers differently and encourage them to prioritize employee learning to a greater extent—providing more and better coaching, task variation, team feedback, challenge, and opportunities for independent decision making.

As asserted in the recent U.S. Surgeon General report, *Workplace Mental Health & Well-Being*, employee growth opportunities are one of the essential elements in a healthy workplace environment. Learning *"provides opportunities for individual intellectual, social, professional, and emotional growth. Learning helps workers meet deadlines and reach goals at work, while promoting healthy social interactions. Without learning or working towards shared goals, workers can start to feel stagnant, frustrated, and ineffective."*

Chapter 41

Compliance Training: Effectiveness and the Law

You do compliance training for a lot of reasons, such as for prevention of sexual harassment, lockout tagout, ergonomics, lab safety, health information, hazardous materials, financial and securities regulations, and data security. Compliance training helps you meet regulations, protects your company from lawsuits, maintains your company's reputation when things go wrong, keeps your employees loyal, and protects your employees' health, wellbeing, and safety.

And very often (though not always) you do it just to cover your ass.

Often, employees are required to engage in compliance training once a year or at some set interval. Organizations like yours are very careful to collect data showing that your employees have paid attention while engaging in training, have taken a quiz and passed it (or have been successful in some other form of assessment), have attended and completed training, or have signed off and/or acknowledged that they understand key concepts and rules.

Organizations like yours might have two meta-goals in creating compliance training. You could aim to create training that IS EFFECTIVE in improving or maintaining employee behaviors. Alternatively, you could ensure that your training PROTECTS your organization. Yes! You can do both, but mostly you don't!

I'm not a lawyer, but I'm going to tell you what the law is NOT doing now for the most part, as far as I can tell (being that I'm not a lawyer, you should not take this as legal advice, lest I get sued). I'm also going to share with you an important secret. I'm going to tell you what the law *should* be doing. And I'll issue this warning: What the law should be doing, the law *can* do; and what the law can do, it can do tomorrow!

First, let's begin with learning. When thinking about training and development, we must always think about how learning works—before we think about anything else. When people learn something in January, they may forget it by April. They may remember it in March, but not care much about it, having gone on to focus on other things. People may learn something in January, but by February their boss or coworkers might convince or cajole them into alternative attitudes, beliefs, or behaviors.

The four deadly sins here are forgetting, forgoing, forestalling, and forbidding. Let me explain. Employees will *forget* what they've learned unless the original learning designs specifically support remembering, learners are reminded of what they learned, or they have done additional learning in the interim. Employees will *forgo* putting into practice what they've learned unless they believe in the practice itself, unless they are incentivized, and/or unless they are nudged into action. Employees will be *forestalled* in following through when they don't have the time and resources to act on what they've learned (including the inability to practice what they've learned). Employees will feel they are *forbidden* to put into practice what they've learned when they face resistance against the rules or practices recommended in the training. Resistance happens all the time with compliance training. Some of your employees just don't believe that women, or people of color, or LGBTQ workers deserve equal treatment. Some don't believe that insider trading, cannabis use, or slacking are wrong.

If you want to create compliance training that works to improve the actions and health of your employees; if you want to have compliance training that does more than protect your organization from legal liability and that effectively improves your organization's operations, it is NOT acceptable to do perfunctory yearly training! It is also not acceptable to think training is the whole solution!

To create compliance education that works, try this:

- Design compliance training to support long-term remembering, utilizing spaced repetitions and realistic practice.

- Provide reminders at least every three months. Ensure that people's managers are reinforcing the desired actions regularly—and effectively. Maybe even forgo training and focus on this!

- Ensure that learners get time and encouragement to put into practice what they've learned soon after the training ends. Where targeted situations are infrequent, provide simulated practice.

- Ensure that key worksite stakeholders are also on board with the recommendations, and that incentives and people's sense of identity are aligned with the recommendations.

- Ensure that cues in the worksite nudge appropriate behaviors.

- Evaluate compliance training by tracking compliance incidents.

Chapter 42
Learning in the Workflow

We employees are learning all the time—not just when we sit in a training class, read a book, or peruse an instruction manual. We learn when we struggle to figure out how to fix a piece of equipment. We learn when we watch others perform a task or behave in a meeting. We learn when a more experienced person pulls us aside and gives us advice. We learn when we see a younger colleague use an app to reduce their workload.

When we learn as we do our work, we are learning! This workflow learning happens all the time. It happens naturally. But here's the thing: Workflow learning is not always leveraged for maximum results. Not all employees take advantage. Some work contexts stifle this type of learning. Sometimes people learn the wrong lessons. Sometimes they become more entrenched in bad practices and bad thinking.

Your learning team should focus not just on formal training. It should also help your employees leverage workflow learning to their advantage. It should help your managers engender workflow learning within their teams. It should figure out ways to keep key concepts fresh in people's minds. This includes organization-wide values, principles, and cultural touchstones, as well as department-level critical ideas like safety practices on the manufacturing floor, agile practices among your developers, and customer-service attitudes with your customer-facing employees.

Your learning team has certainly heard about workflow learning—although maybe not by that name—and they have likely even tried to leverage it in your organization. Unfortunately, too often these efforts have devolved into crude attempts to give people formal learning in disguise. Brown-bag lunches, webinars, special interest groups, communities of practice, and repositories of information like wikis and SharePoint pages. These efforts are not necessarily bad; they can be useful. But they are not even touching the surface of what is possible.

Indeed, most of these efforts are really outside the flow of work. Yes, they are in the workplace, but they occur when employees step away from their actual work. To create transformational workflow learning, your learning team should be helping your employees leverage the work context. They should be helping employees develop habits of mind that nudge good thinking tuned to key work situations. They should encourage practices that nudge desirable behaviors. They should help inculcate attitudes and ways of being that promote useful behaviors and discourage useless or harmful behaviors.

One irony is that your learning team will need to use formal training to support all this work. They can integrate the teaching of good practices across multiple courses. They can teach your managers good practices so they can spread the practices throughout your organization. They should use other approaches too, but formal training is where they have considerable leverage.

Let me share some concrete examples. One thing that helps teams do better work is when everybody feels empowered to contribute. This has several benefits. Morale is improved, teammates bring more energy to their work, good ideas and more ideas are surfaced, teams are better able to communicate and collaborate, trust is strengthened. This can all break down when one or just a few people dominate. A simple workflow-learning hack—which I mentioned in the chapter on leadership—is to end projects and meetings with three simple questions. "What did we do well?" "What did we not do well?" "What can we do better for next time?"

These simple questions supercharge teamwork. They send important messages like the following: We're likely doing good work. We're likely to have made some mistakes. We're better off focusing on the future rather than dwelling on the past. We hold ourselves accountable for making improvements in our work. We need every single person to think strategically about our work—about what's going well and what's not going well.

Think of the learning that this simple hack enables! Instead of one person dominating the thinking of the team, multiple brains are working in parallel. Instead of just muddling through, people are actively looking for ways to improve as they think critically about the work. Isn't this a profound way to learn in the flow of work?

There must be hundreds of learning-in-workflow hacks that your learning team could help spread throughout your organization. They could include these hacks in training programs or in leadership development efforts. They could role-model and facilitate groups in using these hacks. They could seed hacks in partnership with some of your early-adopter managers— thereby gathering lessons learned and champions who could communicate their successes and spread tested beneficial practices. They could create campaigns to share these hacks with your managers and employees who might use them.

They could also integrate these hacks as practical nuggets throughout your organization's training programs. So, for example, as your employees take a course on how to maximize innovation, they could be provided with learning-in-the-workflow hacks to help them generate more creative ideas. As your employees attend training on how to utilize a new technical tool, they could be provided with learning-in-the-workflow hacks that help them remember, help them create a prompting tool, or help them reflect.

Although I can't be exhaustive—because there are infinite possibilities—let me share several learning-in-the-workflow hacks to illustrate the power and potential of these tools.

1. **Challenging Work Projects**

   When employees are challenged with work projects, they are pushed to learn. To enable such learning, they can't be stressed too far, and they will need support and coaching to ensure they learn the right values, principles, and skills—but carefully curated challenges are a great way to promote learning.

2. **Pre-mortems**

   A pre-mortem asks individuals or teams to imagine that a future project or process will have gone terribly wrong—and to brainstorm all the ways that might have happened. Teams can be seeded with categories of failures, for example, Amy Edmonson's six sources of failure (i.e., sabotage, inattention, inability, task challenge, uncertainty, experimentation). By engaging in a thoughtful pre-mortem, individuals and teams surface blind spots and learn more completely about the work in which they will engage.

3. **Experimentation**

   When teams are willing to try something new, they will learn about cause and effect in their work context. A-B testing is an example, discussed earlier in Chapter 32. When we don't experiment, we only know what we've seen before; we don't know what might be possible. By experimenting, we learn new possibilities and enable new futures. Also, by allowing experimentation, we nudge ourselves to think beyond what we see now—we push ourselves to be open to new learning and new ideas.

4. **Conversational Wrangling and Dissent**

   Scientists now think that humans evolved to learn from each other in collegial adversarial conversations. Many brains have more knowledge than fewer brains, and since all our brains harbor ideas and remembrances that are faulty, we as a group will be more successful if we surface our ideas and wrangle with them together. To make this work, we must be open to dissent and embrace those who voice uncomfortable ideas.

5. **Preparatory Cognition**

   As humans we have millions of concepts in our heads. At any one time, some of these concepts are more likely to be utilized than other concepts. They are more accessible from long-term memory. As we carry out a task this afternoon, the thinking we did this morning can impact what we learn from our afternoon task. If we think about safety issues in the morning, we'll be more likely to think about safety issues as we work through tasks in the afternoon—thus learning about how safety relates to those tasks. Team leaders can seed their teams with information to prepare them to learn from their work.

6. *Enhanced Guided Cognition*

Like preparatory cognition, enhanced guided cognition prepares employees' minds to think differently about issues they are contemplating. But whereas general preparatory cognition simply brings a broad range of concepts to mind, enhanced guided cognition helps employees focus on specifically vetted ideas— with the goal of improving their contemplations and enabling them to make better decisions. Consultants should do this, but too often don't, especially now that design thinking has become ubiquitous and misused. They play this game of asking client groups what they think about an issue and then merely collect and organize those results. They should first guide those groups to think more fruitfully about the issues they are being asked about.

7. *Triggered Cognition*

Prospective memory is the capacity to nudge oneself or others to remember to do something in the future. When we leave an envelope by the door so that we remember to mail it, we are setting up our environment to trigger our prospective memory. We can use this same mechanism to spur us and our teams to learn. When a meeting agenda includes a review of project goals before the work of the meeting begins, those goals are more likely to be considered as part of the team learning and decision-making process.

8. *Subconscious Learning and Problem Solving*

Problem solving requires learning. When we're stuck on a problem, we navigate through different options—learning what works and what doesn't. Getting ourselves unstuck isn't always easy. Obviously, we'll need to think deeply and productively about what to do. Once we've done this, often it's best to stop working on the problem for a while and let our subconscious mind work on solutions as we think about other things.

These are just a few examples of the many ways that workflow learning can be augmented by your learning team. As CEO, you can certainly use these and other workflow-learning hacks on your own, but you can also help create a permission structure for your learning team to be creative in how they help your employees with these workflow initiatives.

Section Nine

Managing Your Learning Team

Section Nine—Theme

Section Nine focuses on how to manage your learning team. In this section we'll look at your learning leader, often known as your Chief Learning Officer. We'll look at the strategic elements your learning team must focus on to gain a competitive advantage. We'll examine a learning-request process that enables your learning team to align with organizational stakeholders and set the stage for effective learning and performance-improvement interventions. We'll talk about the dangers of giving too much weight to industry awards, which are often flawed. Finally, in a chapter that summarizes the main points in the book, I provide you with a guide to help you think about your learning team's budget. I specifically provide recommendations on what to invest more in and what to invest less in.

Chapter 43—Your Learning Leader

Here I talk about how you should select your Chief Learning Officer. I argue that learning leaders ought to be drawn from people experienced in L&D, not just any business leader. I recommend having your CLO report directly to you or another senior leader—but *not* to HR, because most HR leaders are risk averse and your learning team must be able to innovate. I also provide a list of the traits required for your CLO.

Chapter 44—How to Tell If Your Learning Leader Is Doing Good

In this chapter I offer over 20 specific sets of questions you can use to evaluate the performance of your learner leader and the learning operations they inspire.

Chapter 45—Your Learning Team Should Have a Strategy

Here I provide a list of 28 strategic imperatives for your learning team—focus areas to consider as they plan their L&D work.

Chapter 46—Full-Factor Learning Request Process

One of the biggest issues in L&D is that most learning teams, when they get a request for a new course, just focus on how to create the course. As they partner with the managers who requested the new course, they often fail to surface the possibility that training might not be the right solution, that other factors beyond training may need to be leveraged, and that the learning experience might need to be augmented to ensure it has the desired impact. To overcome this "order-taker" issue, I share an extensive learning-request process your organization can adapt to raise important considerations.

Chapter 47—Outsourcing Your Learning Team

In this chapter I review the benefits and dangers of outsourcing your learning team. Mostly I warn against the dangers, recommending outsourcing only when you need to reengineer your organization's learning and performance-improvement practices—and even then, only outsourcing your learning leadership and only doing it on a temporary basis to accelerate the improvements required.

Chapter 48—What If Your Learning Team Wins Awards?

Here I warn that most industry awards are based on poor criteria and are a waste of time and resources for your learning team. Not all, but most.

Chapter 49—Learning Vendor Awards Are Just as Problematic

Here I warn you not to judge learning vendors based on awards.

Chapter 50—Investing in Learning for a Competitive Advantage

In this final chapter, we get to the bottom line. Here I share budgeting advice, describing what to invest more in and what to spend less on.

Section Nine—Notes for Learning Professionals

In this last section, I share with CEOs how they can manage those who lead their organization's learning efforts. For us as learning professionals, the insights in this section can guide our thinking about our strategic direction and help us move beyond our traditional order-taker role. We must augment training to full effectiveness while looking beyond training to performance improvement. Finally, before our senior leaders twist our arms, we should reorganize our budgets for the new roles we will play in building learning and performance practices that create a competitive advantage.

Chapter 43
Your Learning Leader

Who's in charge of learning and development in your organization? Do they have the title Chief Learning Officer, Head of Training, VP of Talent? Or is it Chief Executive Officer? Hmmm. Ah! Sorry! That's too tangential, but you are a role model for learning.

Certainly, you have one person assigned to lead your learning efforts—it doesn't really matter what you call them. Unfortunately, many CEOs are botching this, putting the wrong person in charge. Here's what a great organizational learning leader should be:

- Tasked with creating learning that leads to benefits for the organization aligned with "business" needs.

- Tasked with creating learning that benefits employees and other key stakeholders, including the beneficiaries of those learning programs, employees' coworkers, customers, investors, families, communities, society, and the environs.

- Tasked with enabling improved work performance beyond learning interventions, using performance-activation and learning-in-the-workflow approaches.

- Wholly responsible for hiring staff—not subjected to the request, "Can you find a place for Joe in training?"

- A member of your senior team—and specifically NOT housed under your Human Resources unit. I'll explain why in a moment.

- A person who has spent a serious amount of time working in learning and development—NOT someone passing through.

- A person with a deep understanding of learning and learning-to-performance practices.

- A person with knowledge and affection for the learning and performance sciences, and a person who knows how to balance practical priorities with evidence-based wisdom.

- A person responsible for voicing and enabling the ethical and social dimensions of employee learning.

- A person responsible for supporting managers and informal learning leaders throughout your organization.

- A person with knowledge of the functional and cultural milieu in which your organization operates—whether in small or large businesses, in the nonprofit world, or in government, military, education, etc.

One of the biggest mistakes you CEOs make is putting your learning unit under the aegis of Human Resources. This is a monumental mistake, but it's understandable. "HR is all about people; learning is about people; therefore, learning should be under HR." Here's the problem. Your HR people have been trained and drilled and have become experts in the practice of risk avoidance. They focus on laws and regulations! Virtually in every instance, they will kill your learning unit—making the focus about vetting content, not effective learning design; pushing everything to stay the same, rather than encouraging the creativity and experimentation required for significant improvement; discouraging attempts by your learning people to reach into the organization to support after-training efforts and managers. You will not get a competitive advantage by having a risk-averse learning team.

Another big mistake you CEOs make is putting a know-nothing in charge of your learning team. I'm exaggerating for effect, but here's what I mean: On the surface, it may seem sensible to take a person from another part of your organization and put them in charge of learning. Maybe you want to help your learning team align with business concerns. Maybe you want to instill some business discipline or help your learning team become more data-driven or shake your learning team out of some malaise.

I'm being facetious when I say that these business-focused leaders know nothing. They know a ton. Many of them are wicked-smart and know they need to let their learning-and-development experts drive the direction. I've heard many stories of these leaders trying to be useful. It just doesn't matter! Would you put a salesperson in charge of your legal team? How about putting a finance person in charge of HR, or a developer in charge of biotech science? Sure, in rare cases, maybe! But as your go-to strategy? Hell no!

There's even research to show that, when teams are managed by people with no background in the issues at hand, the teams are much less creative—and innovation is exactly what you need from your learning teams in general, and especially right now when they have been handcuffed for so long!

One warning for you. Don't just hire a Chief Learning Officer who's been in learning and development for a long time. There are too many senior members of the field who still don't know learning at a deep level, who are too susceptible to traditions and fads and fancy new technologies. You probably can't tell the good ones from those with silvery tongues who talk a good game. Get help when you hire your senior learning people! Use the list above to craft job requirements. Hire an outside consultant to help you cut through the bullshit! I'm not talking about recruiters—they don't know anything about learning. I'm talking about research-to-practice experts in the workplace learning field.

Hiring a new Chief Learning Officer is one of the most important decisions you'll make. Don't let your organization sleepwalk through the same old process. Prioritize this; get help and hire an enlightened learning leader.

Support for Your Chief Learning Officer:

Your CLO needs support. Don't leave them on an island. There are three things that are critical in lending support.

First, enable your CLO to have a small leadership team, maybe 3-6 people who have some of the same characteristics required of a good learning leader. They should have deep knowledge of learning and experience in the practice of workplace learning and performance improvement. They should be learners themselves, the kind of folks who revel in continuous learning and self-improvement. They should have people skills—able to lead and learn from others, able to coordinate action, and able to get stuff done.

One advantage of a leadership group for your learning team is that it multiplies the vision and energy to get things accomplished. It also serves to nurture and develop future learning leaders—which will help you maintain a competitive advantage as people move in and out of your organization. Finally, having people work together provides a necessary but hidden advantage. Having a leadership team prevents CLO burnout by maintaining practical and emotional support, a critical but little-recognized requirement for sustaining the productivity of change agents.

The second channel of support critical for CLOs comes from the other members of your leadership team (your organization's leadership team). CLOs need close relationships with other senior leaders. Your organization benefits when your CLO learns the language and norms and practices used throughout the organization—and when your CLO develops relationships across the enterprise. Your organization also benefits when members of your leadership team gain insights into the thinking and functioning of your learning team. Benefits are also created when learning initiatives can be smoothly coordinated from the top levels across your organization.

The third pillar of support required for your CLO is outside expertise. To do their best, CLOs must be working from a knowledge base of evidence-based best practices. None of us know everything and all of us have blind spots. Our leaders must be learners, but they must also supplement their knowledge from time to time. You'll help your CLO immeasurably by enabling and resourcing them (and their leadership team) to periodically hire experts in the learning and performance sciences, in learning technology, in evaluation, in GenAI, and in other areas of need.

Obviously, such support should be beneficial, *not* performative. Your CLO should be careful not to bring in celebrity thought leaders just to make a splash or gain a photo opp. Experts should be hired for purpose. Invitations should only be offered to carefully vetted consultants under the rigors of cost-benefit thinking.

Chapter 44

How to Tell If Your Learning Leader Is Doing a Good Job

As CEO, one of the toughest parts of your job is managing managers who oversee areas you know little about—and especially areas that produce results that are hard to measure. Basic research is hard to measure over the short run. Suppose your biotech company rules out multiple avenues for finding a cure for cancer—are you making progress or just mucking around? It's hard to know what's really going on, and so it's hard to manage. It's even harder to manage the manager!

Managing schools is extremely difficult—as Bill Gates and other business leaders have found when their many education solutions have flopped. Humility is earned. Education and learning are extremely difficult to manage because the outcomes are so diffuse, so long term, so variable from person to person. Managing learning efforts is hard. Managing those who manage learning is even harder! Especially if you only have a passing knowledge of the work that gets done.

How do you know how well your learning leader is doing? We've already discussed how your learner surveys are likely meaningless, how attendance and elearning completions are meaningless, and how opinions from learners and their managers can give you false confidence. Employee engagement surveys don't give you good data on the state of your learning initiatives. Fancy dashboards and beautiful data visualizations are hiding data weaknesses. Industry awards are often misleading. Experience and advanced university degrees and other pedigrees are unreliable indicators. The happiness and morale of your learning team are not enough either.

Oh, my goodness, it's easy to be completely in the dark! So many false signals sent your way—the fog of managing learning-and-development leaders. I am so sorry!

But there's some good news. I can help! I can't give you perfect knowledge here in this book, but I can shine a light on things to look for. And remember: The first thing you're going to want to do is encourage your learning leader to start using better metrics, which will help you get better insights over time. For now—even before you get better data—here's what to look for to judge your learning leader.

- Does the learning team have a process in place for the continuous improvement of their learning designs? It should!

- Does the learning team regularly experiment with new learning designs? Do they regularly engage in A-B testing? Do they routinely improve their designs based on evidence?

- Does the learning team provide more than just training and elearning? It should also provide prompting tools, promote improved learning in the workflow, help managers better guide learning, and support teams and individuals learning on their own—among other things.

- Does the learning team have a full-factor learning request process that seeks to (1) determine whether some factor other than training might produce results, (2) gather ideas for other performance supports, (3) ask requestors what they and their units can do to support the learning proposed, and (4) compile a list of how learners' managers can support learning and application. See the next chapter for my recommended process.

- Does the learning team rely on learner surveys that utilize standard Likert-like questions focused on learner satisfaction and the reputation of the learning event? It should NOT! First, it should not rely on learner surveys alone. Second, it should use learner surveys that focus on learning effectiveness: performance-focused learner surveys using the distinctive questioning approach!

- Does your learning team utilize rigorous learning-evaluation methods that (1) help them determine whether they are creating beneficial outcomes, (2) support learners in learning, and (3) enable them to improve their learning designs?

- Does the learning team reject or redirect requests for training on a regular basis? It should! Especially when training is unlikely to fix the issue, or the content proposed is some fad-of-the-year idea not backed by research, or the timeframe for the training is too far away from actual work performance, or the learning design requested is ineffective.

- Does the learning team design learning for results? They should! Specifically, they should specify the results they expect to create for the organization, for the targeted beneficiaries of the learning program, for learners, for coworkers, for family/friends, for customers, for investors, for the community, society, and environs. They can say, "no benefits expected" or, "possibly negative effects expected" for these stakeholders, but they shouldn't ignore any of these in doing their learning evaluations.

- Does the learning team align their work to your organization's "business" goals and initiatives? They should! Are they integrating messaging about strategic initiatives into many or all of your learning programs? Are they building accountability for these initiatives by measuring themselves against related metrics?

- Does the learning team regularly upskill themselves? They should! They should regularly engage in training or education or self-directed learning or community learning—to gain new ideas on how to use learning technologies, science-of-learning best practices, and other social-science findings related to learning and performance improvement.

- Do leaders on the learning team regularly network with key "business" stakeholders? Do they take time to learn the business, and operations, and products/services, and the organization's customers and benefactors? Do they communicate to their teams to educate them on organizational functioning and priorities?

- Does the learning team regularly bring in specific outside expertise to get diagnostic feedback on their current practices? They should! In a complex field like workplace learning and performance, we all have blind spots, and it's worth getting a few days of an independent consultant's time to kick the tires. After all, we get our bodies and cars inspected once a year!

- Does the learning team invest time in applying for awards in the learning field? They should NOT! Most awards programs gather far too little information and evaluate it unreliably. It would be better for your learning team to seek outside review from credible, research-informed experts.

- Does the learning team put a high priority on having a large catalog of courses that employees can access? They should NOT! Learning repositories can be useful, but they should NOT be a priority. See Chapter 20 for a full analysis.

- Does your learning team outsource a large portion of its work to an embedded third party? Usually, it should NOT! Embedded outsourcing partners too often create busy-work that is not aligned with priorities—and they are damned expensive!

- Does your learning team have a recruiting and hiring process that prioritizes a strong background in research-informed learning design and performance design? It should! It should also have a strong onboarding program that teaches these skills to ensure that key learning principles are a high priority for all.

- Does your learning team have a proactive process to determine the true learning needs of your employees—a process that goes beyond simple surveying, but instead looks to uncover real needs, not just perceived needs.

- Does your learning team have a set of clear ethical principles that they utilize in making decisions and designing their programs? Do they evaluate or review their success in this area?

- Does your learning team consider individual differences relevant to effectiveness and belonging? Are they sensitive to diversity, equity, inclusion, and accessibility? Do they evaluate their success in these areas?

- Does your learning team take pains to validate the content being taught—using job-task analysis, gathering expert knowledge, compiling common mistakes, and engaging in reviews of scientific research where available and providing a reasonable cost/benefit return? They should!

- Does your learning team routinely provide or encourage after-training support, including reminders, coaching, practice, and management support? They should! Not always, and only in relation to the benefits to be gained, but after-training support should be a regular consideration because it is so important for learning transfer.

- Does the learning team routinely demonstrate that they have been successful in creating organizational results? No! Don't fall for this trick! Your learning team should NOT make this a priority. Proving organizational results is a highly costly endeavor, so it should never be routine! Second, by pushing to demonstrate success, your learning team will likely produce biased findings that "show" their value.

- Do members of your learning team stay focused on building learning products, avoiding extra efforts like spending time learning about employee performance contexts, or following up on learners to see how they engage the learning and apply it to their work? Egads! If your learning team is just cranking out programs, they are not doing their job. To create good learning, they must understand employees' performance contexts, they must see how employees are engaging with their learning interventions, and they must see what happens after learning—when employees have opportunities to apply the learning in their work situations.

And of course, there are many things you should expect from your learning team that you expect from all units in your organization. The items below are important too, but you'll get more of a competitive advantage by focusing on the recommendations above.

- Is your learning team clear about their aims?
- Do they set clear and measurable objectives?
- Do they get things done on time?
- Do they advocate forcefully and persuasively for their budgets?
- Do they stay within those budgets?
- Do they work well with other units?
- Do they work well within their own teams?

- Is performance rewarded and promoted?
- Does everybody have an equal chance to thrive?
- Do they tell the truth and focus on what's important?
- Do they document their best practices and lessons learned so that organizational wisdom is not lost?
- Do they work toward cutting unneeded costs?
- Do they represent your company well in public?
- Do they work effectively to minimize negative environmental effects of their operations?

Chapter 45
Your Learning Team
Should Have a Strategy

Duh! Of course, your learning team should have a strategy, but here's the question: What should it strategize about? When I taught business strategy in my leadership development workshops, I taught that strategy is about how to differentiate yourself—to make your products, services, and brand "differently better" in ways relevant to your customers (or "beneficiaries," if you're in a government, nonprofit, or social-purpose business). Strategy is also about choosing *how to get to* "differently" better—by determining what to do and what *not* to do. The secret to strategy is guiding organizational attention, team attention, and individual attention!

Ideally, your learning team should play an integral part in supporting your organization's strategy. To give you a competitive advantage, your learning team must be differently better than other organizations' learning teams.

To help you guide your learning team, I'm providing you with a list of learning team deliverables. It is designed specifically to help your learning team go beyond insufficient old-school training-and-development approaches. It is inspired by recent advances in the learning and performance sciences, by a focus beyond learning toward performance improvement, by a business and organizational focus, and by an employee focus.

I am specifically not providing a list of the capabilities required of your learning team. Such a list is beyond the scope of this book—and I'm specifically not including one because (1) such lists quickly become unwieldy and impractical, (2) capability requirements change quickly with time and advances in technology, (3) capability and lists of competencies can push teams to focus on their activities rather than their goals, and (4) it's better not to micromanage teams but to enable them to determine how to reach the goals suggested in the list of deliverables.

Note, however, that—while I'm not dictating capabilities here—your learning team should consider and plan for the capabilities they need to be able to build and deploy the deliverables below. They don't have to do everything, but they should consider their full set of options.

I am also not suggesting any specific strategic planning process. Instead, I'm providing a list of focal areas for your learning team to consider as they do their strategic planning. Specifically, by providing focal points, I'm preventing your learning team from generating strategic plans that ignore critical leverage points. Too many strategic planning initiatives fortify the top-of-mind preconceptions of the participants. The outcomes feel good because the participants' thinking is reflected in the outcomes; however, because only top-of-mind considerations were surfaced, many critical constructs were not even considered. By having a focal list of critical considerations, your learning team will be much more likely to hit on innovative and unique ideas—the kind that lead to competitive advantages.

Learning Team Deliverables:

Included are items your learning team should consider providing to your employees and organization—not everything all at once, but to be used as a list of high-opportunity delivery targets! To make the list easier to read, I've divided it into categories—but the items are more important than the category names. Indeed, some of the items can fit under more than one category. What you want to avoid is having your learning team simplify their efforts down to the category names, because, by doing that, they'll likely ignore important opportunities to provide value.

Information and Knowledge

1. ***Training and eLearning***
   Helping employees learn important concepts and skills.

2. ***Knowledge Access***
   Giving employees quick, reliable look-up access to info they know they need, and automated context-based info when they don't know they need it.

3. ***Social Learning***
   Augmenting opportunities for employees to learn from one another (in ways that are productive), through individual sharing and group learning.

4. ***Organizational Literacy***
   Keeping employees aware of the external forces relevant to their jobs and the internal mechanics that sustain operations, outputs, and success.

Learning Support

5. ***Job Experience***
   Putting employees in new roles to give them experience in a wide variety of work contexts.

6. ***Learning Acceleration***
   Enabling employees to be more effective in their own learning and be more effective in helping others learn.

7. ***Decision-Making***
   Educating and supporting employees in making effective decisions—enabling wisdom around data gathering and analysis, avoiding cognitive biases, etc.

Practice and Reinforcement

8. ***Practice and Feedback***
   Enabling employees to practice and improve their skills.

9. ***Remembering Support***
   Providing systems and practices to support employees in remembering information that is critical to them and their work.

10. ***Reminding***
    Using periodic reminders to enable additional reflection and to keep ideas, concepts, skills, and tendencies accessible from memory.

Enabling Change

11. ***Creativity and Innovation***
    Enabling employees to generate creative ideas and take those ideas through the long and arduous process to innovation.

12. ***Change Championing***
    Educating and supporting employees in leading complex organizational change initiatives.

Organizational Development

13. ***Management Development***
    Supporting managers in helping their teams be more productive.

14. ***Work Culture***

    Supporting managers and others in creating routine practices and ways of thinking that benefit employees and organizational productivity.

15. ***Talent Strategy***

    Considering and planning for long-term talent needs—aiming to satisfy needs for the organization, for units and teams, and for individual employees. Yes! Our talent strategies must view employees as equal partners.

Work-Context Supports

16. ***Prompting Tools***

    Providing tools, checklists, job aids, performance support, and signage that directly prompt action.

17. ***Nudging***

    Enabling the setting of context triggers to increase the likelihood that desirable thoughts and behaviors are nudged into action.

18. ***Memory Accessibility***

    Creating strategies for keeping important goals, values, and behaviors consciously top-of-mind and subconsciously active and influential.

19. ***Context Enablers***

    Examining and modifying work contexts to ensure that performers have appropriate tools, rules, practices, norms, expectations, and time.

20. ***Context Obstacles***

    Examining and modifying work contexts to ensure that performers have sufficient freedom from obstacles, distractions, complexity, and noise.

Self-Direction Supports

21. ***Self-Direction***

    Supporting and enabling employees in their efforts to be proactive in their own learning, context triggering, development, and work performance. Also, encouraging and enabling more employees to be more self-directed.

22. ***Habit Formation***

    Supporting employees in developing good habits and weaning themselves off bad habits.

23. ***Coaching, Mentoring***

Provide coaches and/or mentors to employees to provide guidance and support for individual development.

Content and Practice Improvement

24. ***Content Vetting***

Providing research and analysis services to vet content to ensure its validity, relevance, and cost effectiveness.

25. ***Outside Expert Reviews***

Providing teams with access to experts to provide unbiased diagnostic reviews and recommendations for improvement.

Employee Health and Well-Being

26. ***Well-Being***

Examining employees' physiological, psychological, and financial states—then lessening stressors and optimizing feelings of safety, belonging, and well-being.

27. ***Employee Empowerment***

Enabling employees to have their individual and collective voices influence important employment-related decisions and practices.

28. ***Employee Dignity and Respect***

Enabling employees to be valued and respected—to be assumed worthy, to be granted grace, to be able to be their authentic selves.

All right, that's 28 focus areas! Your learning team should have points of view and strategies for delivering each of these. They should also prioritize—emphasizing some all the time, and some only occasionally or periodically. And note that a "learning strategy" should really be thought of as a "learning and performance-improvement" strategy!

Responsibility for accomplishing goals within these areas can be shared with other units in the organization, but your learning team should offer expertise and/or support in how to carry out these functions. For example, your managers are in the prime spot to promote creativity, but your learning team should be ready to facilitate idea-generation meetings and provide training on how to facilitate the creative process.

The bottom line on learning strategy is simple. By focusing on providing the most powerful—and most leverageable—learning-and-performance factors, your learning team will create a competitive advantage for your organization!

Chapter 46
A Full-Factor Learning Request Process

Your learning team is often asked to develop or purchase training programs. Too often, huge opportunities are lost in this process and too much money is spent on training that won't work at all or won't work as well as it could. The following process can be used as a template to help your organization maximize learning benefits—while also minimizing unwarranted costs. Using it, even if you modify it to your organization's specific needs, will help educate key players in your organization to the most critical leverage points of learning and performance.

Here it is:

1. If you have a preference, what type of learning or performance-improvement intervention are you requesting? Because learning-and-performance interventions can blend methods, feel free to select more than one:

   - Training delivered in a classroom, seminar room, etc.

   - Training delivered online through computers, tablets, or phones.

   - Educational experiences through local or online universities.

   - Knowledge-repository development and support.

   - Community of practice development and support.

   - Mentorship and/or coaching for executives, managers, employees.

   - Prompting tools development (e.g., job aids, checklists, performance-support tools, signage, etc.).

   - Diagnosis of worksite and employee performance factors.

   - Research on worksite and employee performance factors.

   - Training or support specifically focused on learning—to help you and your team better utilize learning as a performance enhancer.

   - I'm not sure—but want to partner with you on the learning team to determine what might be effective.

2. [Optional—We can talk about this later.] Now, in your own words, describe the learning intervention you are envisioning. Don't overthink this; we just need your initial thoughts at this stage.

3. Why is this intervention needed now? Select the ONE or TWO most important drivers of this need.

    - There has been a long-term performance problem.

    - There is a new performance problem.

    - We'd like to take advantage of a new opportunity, but we can't until people have new skills.

    - There is a new system, tool, product, software package, or piece of equipment that needs to be learned.

    - We are taking a new strategic or tactical direction, and we need to get everyone on the same page.

    - Somebody important suggested that this training is needed.

    - We need to ensure that people are up to date with the latest thinking in their field.

    - We need to ensure that people are aware of specific new knowledge, techniques, or procedures.

    - We must do training to meet regulatory rules or legal compliance.

    - We want to offer learning opportunities that provide employees with career skills they can use now and in their future work.

    - We want people to think more creatively and be more innovative.

    - We have tried everything else we can think of, but nothing has worked, so we want to try something different now.

4. [Optional—We can talk about this later.] Now, in your own words, why is this intervention needed now?

5. What other factors might be limiting the performance of the employees who are targeted by the learning intervention? Please list anything that might be relevant. This step is crucial because we don't want to utilize resources on training or learning if some other factors are really at play.

6. We don't want to focus only on learning if other factors need to be tweaked as

well. Select as many of the following factors you think MAY be at play in the performance problem/opportunity you are targeting for improvement. Note that, if these issues are too sensitive, we can talk them through later.

- Lack of clear goals.
- Lack of time to accomplish tasks.
- Too few people to get the work done.
- Too little budget to obtain needed resources.
- Inadequate tools, equipment, and systems.
- Inadequate management or leadership.
- Poor teamwork.
- Unclear standards of performance.
- Poor employee morale.
- Inadequate or inappropriate incentives for performance.
- Lack of an engaging or inspiring purpose for the work.
- High levels of stress.
- Unethical, illegal, or inappropriate behavior.
- Too many unproductive procedures, rules, or paperwork.
- Unhelpful personalities or work-style conflicts.
- Unhealthy or unsafe work situation.
- Discrimination, bias, and/or unfair treatment of some workers.
- I'd rather talk about these off the record.
- Other?

7. In your own words, what workplace factors will have to be modified to obtain the desired results?

8. What are you willing to do to ensure the success of the learning or performance-improvement intervention that is created? Select all the following that you are willing to be involved in:

- I will provide help in the design of any learning program.

- I will provide help in the design of any performance-improvement intervention.

- I will participate in the full program as a learner myself—whether the actual program or a pilot version.

- I will participate in an executive overview as a learner myself.

- I will participate as a trainer or facilitator when the program is ready to be deployed.

- I will tell my direct reports (and teammates, if I'm not in a formal management role) that they are expected to learn and implement what they learn.

- I will ask each of my direct reports or teammates to implement 1-3 specific action plans after the training.

- I will follow up with each of my direct reports or teammates to ensure they have followed through on their action plans.

- I will provide the learning team with feedback about the learning or performance-improvement intervention a month after the program ends, whether I am asked or not.

- I will create my own mini-courses (on relevant concepts and skills) and deploy these after my direct reports or teammates have completed their training or learning programs—to ensure they are reminded of key concepts, and they know how important this is.

- I will NOT be directly involved, but I will guide, support, and monitor the performance of those who will be (for example, I will be attentive to the support given by learners' managers).

- I will do whatever it takes. Please count me in as a full partner.

- I will do the following (please provide detail):

9. If you are NOT the learners' manager yourself, or there are other learners' managers involved, what will you expect those managers to do?

- Help in the design of any learning program.

- Provide help in the design of any performance-improvement intervention.

- Participate in the full program as learners themselves—whether the actual program or a pilot version.

- Participate in an executive overview of the learning program as learners themselves.

- Deliver or facilitate some or all of the learning or performance-improvement program.

- Tell their direct reports that they are expected to learn and implement what they learn.

- Require each of their direct reports to implement 1-3 specific action plans after the training.

- Follow up with each of their direct reports to ensure they have followed through on their action plans.

- Provide the learning team with feedback about the learning or performance-improvement intervention a month after the program ends, whether asked or not.

- Create their own mini-courses (on relevant concepts and skills) and deploy these after their direct reports have completed their training or learning programs—to ensure they are reminded of key concepts and they know how important this is.

10. Finally—and most importantly—what do you want to accomplish in making this request?

    - What do you expect people to be able to do differently?

    - What organizational results do you expect as a result of this initiative?

    - What benefits to employees do you expect?

    - What benefits, if any, to employee families and friends, to the community, society, environs?

11. The learning-and-performance department will contact you within one week to (1) review your request with you, (2) determine what level of additional analysis may be needed, and (3) decide on whether to consider your request for implementation.

The suggested process above is critical for two reasons. First, it educates your managers that (1) training is not the only solution, (2) training may not be the best solution, (3) even if training is required, other factors also need to be utilized, (4) learners' managers play a key role, (5) after-training follow-through is critical, (6) learning can be designed to benefit employees and other stakeholders, and, among other things, (7) the learning team can help diagnose issues and provide a number of solutions—not just training.

You might ask, well, why do we need such a process? Why can't we just train managers that these things are important? Come on, now! If you've read this far into the book, you should remember that people forget, they get distracted, they need to have their attention guided sometimes to be fully effective. It's great to train them on the seven concepts above, but that won't be enough. By having a research-inspired set of questions your learning team can use every time a training request is made, it focuses the attention of your managers and your learning team toward learning-design considerations they should be thinking about—that they would certainly not remember fully without such a tool.

The process above is also critical because it wildly increases the likelihood that effective interventions will be created, and that money, time, and resources won't be wasted.

I would recommend that your learning team incorporate the questions above into a survey tool for simple and effective responding—and that they track responses over time to look for trends and make adjustments in their outreach and operations.

Your learning team will also need to develop a follow-up process to (1) interview the people and teams who submit requests and (2) develop criteria for deciding the fate of the requested interventions. An impersonal set of questions like those suggested is not enough—it's just a start! It's critical that your learning team follow up with an empathetic conversation with the person or people who requested the training.

Your learning team also needs to be authorized to reject requests when training is unlikely to create benefits, when learning supports are unlikely to be delivered, or when stakeholders are unwilling to take responsibility for learning support and follow-through. In other words, your learning team should be entrusted with the same responsibility as other key units within your organization.

This level of tough-love responsibility will not be easy for your learning team. They're likely to feel uneasy when your Executive Vice-President of Sales—or R&D, Marketing, Operations, etc.—makes a training request that has dubious merit. You're going to have to lend support and sanctify the learning team's new learning-request process.

You might consider role-modeling it, too! The next time you yourself are involved in thinking about training for your senior managers, for high potentials, for some strategic initiative, go through the process yourself. Answer the questions, go through the interview, reflect on your experience, and then share your enthusiasms with your team and managers throughout the organization.

Chapter 47
Outsourcing Your Learning Team?

Within the past three decades, one of the biggest movements in business has been outsourcing. Instead of having a group of employees carry out some function, organizations outsource that function to a third party. Reasons cited for outsourcing include (1) enabling the organization to focus on what it does best, (2) reducing labor and operations costs, (3) freeing up internal resources to focus on high-priority needs, (4) avoiding difficult-to-manage operations, (5) gaining access to hard-to-find capabilities, and (6) mitigating risk by outsourcing dangerous, unethical, and polluting operations.

Outsourcing has its dangers, of course, including a risk to your organization's reputation, difficulty in quality control, risk to your organization's intellectual property, stagnation in technology and practices, lack of responsiveness, difficulty in managing outsourced operations, losing control, becoming dependent, and lack of oversight.

Some functions may be no-brainers to outsource because they are not central to your organization's success, and they entail few risks. Hiring a landscaping service, a food-service company, or a cleaning company are relatively safe options for outsourcing.

What about outsourcing your learning function? What benefits might be gained? The greatest benefit may be finding world-class expertise, particularly if you can find an outsource partner that has a strong bench of research-informed learning practitioners.

Outsourcing might be useful if your learning function needs a complete reset—if it is stuck on ineffective practices, if it is resistant to improvement, if it is filled with too many legacy employees, if it is chronically understaffed.

You might also want to outsource only portions of your learning function. Your learning-technology infrastructure is a good candidate. Too many organizations like yours stifle their learning efforts by creating roadblocks through their IT organization. Your learning team wants to pilot innovations, but your IT department throws up roadblocks or slow-rolls the implementation. If you could find an outsourcing partner that maintains and continually improves its learning-technology platforms, this may create benefits. Other partial-outsourcing targets include learning evaluation and course creation.

What about the dangers of outsourcing your learning function? Over the years, I've heard many horror stories where outsourcing companies made a mess of things, but I also speak from firsthand experience as a subcontractor to a renowned training outsourcing company. What I saw back then was appalling. They cared more about their own revenues than they did about the success of the client. They had an account manager embedded in the client site I worked in—they weren't stupid to the point of admitting that person's sales role, but the person's overarching goal was to look for new work within the client, whether the work was useful or not.

Here are some things to worry about in outsourcing your learning function. Outsource partners have little incentive to utilize rigorous learning-evaluation approaches. They want to show you data that makes them look good. They don't want to show you data that makes them look like they are working toward improvements—even though this is a good practice. If you do hire an outsourcing partner, find one who uses rigorous metrics and demonstrates a history of measuring and improving their learning interventions.

I'm also worried that outsourcing partners will push you toward a training-first ethos and be unable to nudge your organization toward a performance-focused view of learning. Training is easy. When you outsource training, your outsourcing partner can easily show you that they delivered the training and that your employees liked it. But how will they implement in-depth discussions with your managers about non-training supports? As outsiders, they are unlikely to have a high level of trust. How will they push back when your managers ask for training that is unlikely to overcome the real performance issue? How will they take risks to innovate when bad news may lose them next year's contract?

And what about the idea of creating an organizational culture, a shared vision and set of values? How can an outsourced trainer be persuasive in conveying and getting your employees to identify with these precious concepts? Also, how is an outsourcing partner going to support workflow learning—when they are distant from the actual work you do? How will they be trusted to observe critical operations, sit in sensitive meetings, etc.?

Outsourcing may hold promise, but the learning-and-development function is strategically important, so the risks of outsourcing may just be too high. Two alternatives are available to you. First, you might use a temporary outsourcing approach, bringing in a strong learning-leadership team for a few years to build a team and inculcate rigorous practices. You might also use the recommendations in this book to charge your current learning team with reinventing itself, but you must be fair to them—providing resources, permissions, and technology and enabling them to hire expertise on an as-needed basis.

Finally, if you do outsource, find a partner who honestly cares about your employees and your company's success—one that makes your folks stronger, not dependent.

Chapter 48
What If Your Learning Team Wins Awards?

How do you know whether your learning team is any good? This is a critical question. Your learning team drives productivity, innovation, motivation, and employee loyalty. If your learning team is excellent, you as CEO want them to continue doing what they're doing. You also want to pay them well to keep them from being lost to other organizations. If your learning team is mediocre, you're going to want to drive an L&D change—for the health of the organization and the viability of your own job!

One of the ways your learning team sends false signals to you is when they apply for awards in the learning-and-development field. It's not their fault, really—they are not responsible that the award criteria are too often bogus.

Trade associations benefit from sponsoring these contests in two ways. They attract eyeballs to their magazines and websites. We humans can't resist knowing who's best. I'll bet even you have peeked at a top-10 list. Trade associations also love these contests because they keep people as loyal paying members. Everybody wants to feel part of an organization that includes the top such-and-such learning departments in the world!

Here's the problem. The criteria used for most of these learning-industry awards are not meaningful. Indeed, many of them encourage the wrong kinds of practices. I'm not going to name names here—because past winners will feel bad and trade association lawyers might try to sue me—but here are some of the criteria that are used:

- Number of hours of training delivered organization-wide.

- Number of trainers.

- Average class size.

- Average training hours per person.

- Learner-survey ratings.

In fairness, the contest applications ask meaningful questions as well, like whether the organization has a succession plan for key performers, whether there is job shadowing, whether tuition is reimbursed. They also ask applicants to write essays to confirm that they are adding to innovation, being part of the organizational strategy process, and so forth.

You might be amused to know that, on one application, an applicant organization can receive up to one-half point if senior leadership is *"involved in the design, development, or marketing of a training program."* Your contribution as CEO was worth half a percent!

The sad truth is that these award contests are often complete bullshit! Applicants are awarded points for all kinds of crazy things. They get credit for certain levels of company turnover, even though there is no accounting for different types of organizations, different market circumstances, etc. Applicants are awarded points if they were listed as a winner the year before, or if they report they have a "training infrastructure," or if they say they have job rotations—regardless of whether the rotations are thoughtfully implemented.

These contests can hurt organizations applying for awards as well as organizations that simply use the criteria to develop their learning-and-development strategies. The criteria may encourage an organization to willy-nilly do evaluations at each Kirkpatrick level regardless of what makes sense, cut or add trainers just to have a "good" ratio, invest in unwarranted technologies, start an innovation initiative just to have one, etc.

Here's my recommendation to you: Do not allow your learning team to apply for these awards—to spend time on these extensive application processes—except in the rare cases where the criteria are valid, rigorous, and informed by research.

If your team previously won an award, don't assume they deserved it—and don't assume they didn't. The criteria are so tangential—and the review process is so sketchy—that any award they won is almost certainly unpredictive of their competence.

In lieu of this external whitewashing, have your team build its own set of criteria for success, vetted by research-to-practice experts—then ensure the outcomes are monitored and reported quarter to quarter and year to year.

To evaluate the performance of your team, seek outside research-to-practice experts to conduct periodic audits and set up evaluation systems so progress can be monitored on a regular basis.

In 2006 I became so despondent that our learning-industry awards were encouraging mediocre practices that I created an award to acknowledge people who were utilizing and/or advocating for research-aligned practices. The Neon Elephant Award—given annually to the person, people, or organizations who have best supported research-aligned learning methods—has been awarded 18 times. It is a small contribution, and it doesn't capture the full extent of practitioners doing great work, but it has guided learning teams like yours toward ideas and thought-leaders likely to inspire effective learning designs.

Chapter 49
Learning Vendor Awards
Are Just as Problematic

Your learning team members are not the only ones who can win bogus awards. So can vendors in the learning field, who will regale your learning team and senior managers with all their awards and accolades. These awards are sometimes and somewhat indicative of quality. Winners are probably not terrible; they're probably in the top 50%, but the best vendors may not be represented in the awards. Anybody who looks solely at awards to choose a vendor is a damn fool. And, oh my, you won't believe how these awards get issued. Before I go into the details, I need to emphasize that many vendors are meticulous in avoiding unscrupulous award programs and the organizations that sponsor them. Do NOT write off a vendor just because they have won awards!

You're a businessperson, so let me describe the business model at work here. There are a number of these award-distribution companies in the learning field. Let me call them ADCOs (for Award Distribution Companies). They attract eyeballs to their websites and publications, and they charge vendors for advertising. The vendors, when they advertise, are basically paying for the eyeballs. There is nothing inherently wrong with that—this is a common business model in today's interconnected world. Indeed, this content-based advertising model goes back to newspapers, magazines, etc.

There are two ways in which these awards have problems. First, some of the awards are associated with money spent. Application fees skew the applicant base to larger, more established firms, and to vendors willing to play the awards game. Some awards restrict applications, only allowing vendors to take part if one of their customers applies. So, vendors offer to pay the application fees and write the application if organizations like yours agree to submit the application. Your people are being asked to allow your organization's reputation to be used to benefit a vendor who may or may not deserve accolades. Of course, your learning team has an incentive to look good in winning an award, so the offer of free application fees and free labor seems good—and we tend not to think about the ethics or legal exposure of these questionable exchanges.

Sometimes, vendors pay to play more indirectly, doing extensive advertising with an ADCO and hoping their application is examined with appreciative judgments to translate into platinum, gold, or silver awards.

Let me give you a real example (the name and identifying information of ADCO withheld to avoid a lawsuit). In this ADCO's category for the top learning evaluation companies, they don't list any of the organizations widely seen as leaders in learning evaluation. They did NOT list Jack and Patti Phillips's ROI Institute, The Kirkpatrick Partners, Rob Brinkerhoff's Brinkerhoff Institute, or my consulting practice—even though I'm a known leader in learning evaluation. None of us paid to play, so none of us were listed.

The second problem for these vendor awards arises when the award-assessment process is weak—especially because reviews of products and services are conducted in a manner that is inadequate to the task. So, for example, say that you—yes, YOU—had to select the best-in-category learning product (maybe your category was "workshops on coaching," or "short elearning programs," or "training-on-smartphone authoring tools," etc. Suppose your reputation, job, or life depended on creating a fair and valid assessment and ranking within the category you were reviewing. Would you accept a 20-minute video developed by the marketing department of each company as the only thing you saw for your review? What about looking at just a written application with answers to questions about hours of training delivered, number of trainers, or sales of your training products? Or answers to essay questions? Would you accept these third-person affidavits or would you prefer to observe the learning product in action and track its results? Obviously, to create a valid assessment process, you'd want experts to evaluate real products and real results, not marketing videos or answers on applications.

The official judges in these contests are largely volunteers. After talking with a bunch of them, I'm convinced they generally work in good faith despite the poor questions asked, the inappropriate criteria, etc. Still, some judges tell tales of feeling they don't have enough information to make good selections. One judge told me how he thought none of the applicants in his category were worthy of an award, but that the ADCO had pushed back and told him he should be appreciative of the work people put in on the application.

The incentive for these ADCOs is to give as many awards as possible. You won't be astonished to hear that ONE of these ADCOs recently gave out more than 500 awards in *one* year, including about 200 gold medal awards. And that's just one of about a dozen of these awarding organizations. If one company can give 500 awards, they must not really be worth much in the first place!

The bottom line: Keep your people away from these awards and don't let awards sway your organization's purchasing decisions!

Chapter 50

Investing in Learning for a Competitive Advantage

We're coming to the end of this book. You're still the CEO and I am, I hope, still your trusted guide. You're now going to turn to me and ask, "Okay, Thalheimer, you've convinced me of a bunch of things, but now let's get down to numbers. What's this going to cost me?"

It's my book, so I get to be a wise-ass here. I will turn to you and ask, "What's it going to cost you... if you don't do anything, if you keep the status quo, if you only namby-pamby nibble around the edges?" Pausing for effect, I will add, "What'll it cost you if your employees are less motivated, less skilled, less productive, less effective, less healthy, less innovative, less loyal, less, less, less, less, less—less than they could be?"

I can't tell you exactly how to allocate your learning team's budget, but I can tell you what you should budget less for and what you should budget more for.

Budget Less For:

- Off-the-shelf course repositories (because these tend to focus mostly on content and have very limited practice or application).

- Training courses that don't provide substantial realistic practice.

- Vendors who deliver courses, unless those courses have validated, unique content, sufficient practice, and application support.

- Travel or time for learning-team industry awards efforts.

- Traditional smile sheets and surveys of learners that purport to measure behavior change and business results.

- Tuition reimbursement for your learning team (because currently too many graduate programs teach poor learning practices—even though they seem to be getting better).

- Efforts that utilize learning myths and misconceptions.

- ROI and other learning evaluation methods primarily designed to prove the value of learning. ROI has its place, but there is too much emphasis on it.

- Fancy dashboards and other data visualizations, unless the data underlying the visuals is valid and meaningful.

- Leadership training based on popular books, unless these books are based on good-faith compilations of rigorous scientific evidence (and there are too few of those!).

- Classroom training that requires substantial travel (because it costs more, utilizes more employee time, pollutes more, and is not generally more effective than online learning).

- Tests of knowledge—unless the knowledge is queried using well-designed work-realistic scenario questions.

- Training programs delivered to learners more than a month before the learning can be applied to real work (because learners forget).

- Training that is not needed—that is, where the performance problem or opportunity is not likely to improve with training, and where improving knowledge, skill, or belief won't make a difference.

- Unproven technologies, unless you're running small experiments to further explore innovations.

- Training, where prompting tools are likely to be more effective and/or cost efficient.

- Adding business leaders to your learning team who have no background in learning and performance (because they will be relatively expensive, they'll have an impossible learning curve to climb, and they're more likely to get in the way than to be helpful).

- Legacy employees assigned to your learning team (some employees who have a true passion for learning are gems, but, in general, don't saddle your learning team with relatively expensive dead weight).

Look above at all the ways you can save money! As Leidy Klotz's research shows, while our tendency as humans is to add to our efforts, it can be even more beneficial to subtract. Then, after you subtract, you can do more of the good stuff. See the list below.

Budget More For:

- Learning needs analysis and work-context analysis (to determine if and which learning is needed, which learning supports are needed, and which performance activators may be helpful).

- Improved learning evaluation, including performance-focused learner surveys (upgrading from traditional smile sheets) and measuring decision-making and task competence.

- A-B testing (to enable your learning teams to make decisions based on data, not opinion).

- Independent reviews of your learning designs, by unbiased experts in research-inspired learning design.

- Professional development for your learning professionals—focused on research-informed practices, the performance sciences, advanced technologies, and avoiding myths and misconceptions.

- Building, testing, and improving a full-factor learning request process—for example, like the one I outlined in Chapter 46.

- Additional supports for remembering and application, including realistic practice activities, spaced repetitions, contingency preparation, and feedback—added to every (or almost every) training program.

- Innovation, experimentation, pilot testing of new learning and performance methods.

- An agile process of learning design and development, building rapid prototypes, testing, and improving—rather than designing and then building everything as originally planned.

- An in-house system of team learning, reviewing every project openly, fairly, critically; and asking four questions: what did we do well, what did we do poorly, what factors were at play, what should we do better for next time?

- Well-designed, strategically valuable customer education. Not only can such efforts support your brand in a content-marketing way; they can also enable your organization to be a good citizen by sharing expertise.

Final Words of Wisdom

I'm ending the book here. It seems a good place to end—after talking about money, resources, and priorities. Yes, there are subtleties and intricacies I've left unexplored in the book. Still, I've given you everything you need to create a world-class, kick-ass job of managing and supporting your learning team. You now have all the tools and knowledge you need to make learning a competitive advantage for your organization.

Unleash your learning team! They are good people. They believe deeply in the work they are doing. Support them, help them continue to develop their skills, help them do good work, help them help your employees and your organization.

Sharing the Wealth

If you've found value in this book, please share it with your leaders and with other leaders outside your organization (maybe not your competitors). I know it's probably not something you normally do, but consider getting in touch with me to share a few sentences of praise or write a blurb on Amazon.

Being in Touch

If you think I can help your organization, feel free to get in touch. Through my Work-Learning Research consulting practice, I help empower learning-and-performance professionals and help organizations like yours get the most out of learning. You can write me at my work email address (will.thalheimer@worklearning.com) or go to the Work-Learning Research contact page and set up a short online meeting with me. https://www.worklearning.com/contact/.

Thank You!

Finally, let me thank you for reading what I've written. This is my life's work: helping people learn. To me—outside my family, friends, country, and world—it is everything!

About the Author...
Will Thalheimer, PhD, MBA

Will Thalheimer is a consultant, learning expert, researcher, learning architect, speaker, and writer. He holds an MBA from Drexel University and a PhD in Educational Psychology: Human Learning and Cognition from Columbia University. He has worked in the learning-and-performance field since 1985—playing a diverse set of roles, including leadership trainer, instructional designer, simulation architect, project manager, business product line manager, researcher, speaker, author, and consultant.

Beginning in 1998, Dr. Thalheimer dedicated his career to bridging the gap between research and practice in the workplace learning field—founding Work-Learning Research as his research and consulting practice. His clients have included giant multinationals, elearning companies, government agencies, trade associations, and universities.

Since the early 2000s, Dr. Thalheimer has been publishing seminal articles and reports of relevance to the work-learning field. In 2007, Dr. Thalheimer published a research-to-practice report titled *Measuring Learning Results: Creating Fair and Valid Assessments by Considering Findings from Fundamental Learning Research*. Since then, he has been the learning-and-development field's most innovative expert in learning evaluation—publishing the book *Performance-Focused Smile Sheets: A Radical Rethinking of a Dangerous Art Form* in 2016 and the second edition in 2022, *Performance-Focused Learner Surveys: Using Distinctive Questioning to Get Actionable Data and Guide Learning Effectiveness*, revolutionizing learner surveys. Will also created LTEM (the Learning-Transfer Evaluation Model) in 2018, a replacement for the Kirkpatrick-Katzell Four-Level Model. He also devised a brand-new approach to learning evaluation: LEADS (Learning Evaluation As Decision Support), introduced formally in this book.

Will has also published a series of ground-breaking research-to-practice reports and articles related to learning design: *Instructional Objectives: A Work-Learning Research Instructional Research Report* in 2002; *Aligning the Learning and Performance Contexts: Spontaneous Remembering* in 2002; *Simulation-Like Questions: How and Why to Write Them* in 2002; *How to Calculate Effect Sizes from Published Research: A Simplified Methodology* with Samantha Cook in 2002; *The Learning Benefit of Questions* in 2003; *Research that Supports Simulations and Simulation-Like Questions* in 2003; *Bells, Whistles, Neon, and Purple Prose:*

When Interesting Words, Sounds, and Visuals Hurt Learning and Performance—a Review of the Seductive-Augmentation Research in 2004; *Spacing Learning Events Over Time: What the Research Says* in 2006; *Repetition: A Work-Learning Research Instructional Research Report* in 2006; *Questioning Strategies for Audience Response Systems: How to Use Questions to Maximize Learning, Engagement, and Satisfaction* in 2007; *Providing Learners with Feedback—Part 1: Research-Based Recommendations—Part 2: Peer-Reviewed Research* in 2008; *Using Linguistically, Culturally, and Situationally Appropriate Scenarios to Support Real-World Remembering* in 2009; *How Much Do People Forget?* in 2010; *The Decisive Dozen* in 2013; *Why the World Needs Research Translators* in 2015; *Kirkpatrick Model Good or Bad? The Epic Mega Battle!* with Clark Quinn in 2015; *Mythical Retention Data & The Corrupted Cone* in 2015; *Research Besmirched—When Practitioners Just Don't Believe! Why Research is the Best Source of Information, Even When It has Limitations and Flaws!* in 2016; *Brain Based Learning and Neuroscience—What the Research Says!* in 2016; *Does eLearning Work? What the Scientific Research Says!* in 2017; *Donald Kirkpatrick was NOT the Originator of the Four-Level Model of Learning Evaluation* in 2018; *Learner Survey Results are NOT Correlated with Learning Results* in 2019; *Factors That Support Training Transfer: A Brief Synopsis of the Transfer Research* in 2020; *The Work Performance Field: Innovative Ideas from Our History to Our Future* in 2021; *Maximize Your Training Results with One Powerful Question* in 2022; *LTEM After Five Years* in 2023; and *Training Works! Says the Science!* in 2023.

Dr. Thalheimer is regularly asked to lead learning-audit workshops, write articles, do research, and give keynotes on the topic of learning measurement, presentation science, and research-based learning design. Will co-created with Matt Richter the innovative L&D Conference. Will also co-founded with Matt Richter the professional membership organization LDA (The Learning Development Accelerator)—where research-aligned practices are encouraged. He also created the Serious eLearning Manifesto with Michael Allen, Julie Dirksen, and Clark Quinn. He also founded the Debunker's Club, a group devoted to debunking learning myths and promoting research-based practices in learning. Will also curates one of the most prestigious awards in the workplace learning field: the Neon Elephant Award, given annually to the person, people, or organizations who have best supported research-aligned learning methods.

In 2021 Will Thalheimer joined TiER1 Performance as Principal. After 2.5 years as an employee, Will restarted Work-Learning Research in 2023, where he has rededicated himself to empower learning professionals to get the most from learning while helping organizations build strategic learning and performance practices. Will can be reached through LinkedIn or through his contact page: https://www.worklearning.com/contact/.

Chapter Notes
Research, Evidence, Reflections

Some of the content shared in this book deserves commentary or research support. Not every chapter requires this, so I'll just share when it's important to do so.

Chapter 1—Introduction

I don't know. I wonder whether I went over the line in calling out senior leaders. Did you appreciate it, or did you bristle? Maybe both?

Chapter 2—First Do No Harm

I share the following only because it's interesting. None of us needs to know this.

The phrase, "First Do No Harm," is commonly attributed to the Hippocratic Oath, but, while those sentiments were loosely in the original and early versions of the oath, the exact wording was not—even more true because the words used were in an earlier form of Greek. By the way, most scholars don't believe Hippocrates wrote the oath. Interestingly, the oath encouraged physicians to hold their medical teachers equal to their own parents and to make them a partner in their livelihoods, even to the extent of sharing their own money with their teachers if their teachers were in financial need. And please, dear reader, I am your humble servant. If I am your teacher, you should feel no obligation to my financial needs. But thanks for buying the book! Importantly, I learned all this from Wikipedia! Please consider supporting the community of "teachers" represented there!

Chapter 3—Training and Development Related to Organizational Success

In the chapter I share research that shows training and development tends to work to support organizational success. Here in the chapter notes, I provide more details about that research.

This is the recent meta-analysis that found strong evidence for the relationship between training and organizational performance. To be clear, they found that investments in training were positively correlated with business performance. They also found that training's impact has been increasing over time:

- Garavan, T., McCarthy, A., Lai, Y., Murphy, K., Sheehan, M., & Carbery, R. (2021). Training and organisational performance: A meta-analysis of temporal, institutional and organisational context moderators. *Human Resource Management Journal*, *31*(1), 93–119. https://doi.org/10.1111/1748-8583.12284

Many of the same authors also highlighted weaknesses of measuring the organizational impact of training. Specifically, researchers made recommendations to themselves that more research and improved methodologies were needed to ensure that training's causal impact can be more clearly supported in the research.

- Garavan, T., McCarthy, A., Sheehan, M., Lai, Y., Saunders, M. N. K., Clarke, N., Carbery, R., & Shanahan, V. (2019). Measuring the organizational impact of training: The need for greater methodological rigor. *Human Resource Development Quarterly, 30*(3), 291–309.

Here is another recent meta-analysis that demonstrates the positive impact of training. These researchers focused on the benefits of training on attitudes and motivations.

- Uslu, D., Marcus, J., & Kisbu-Sakarya, Y. (2022). Toward optimized effectiveness of employee training programs: A meta-analysis. *Journal of Personnel Psychology, 21*(2), 49–65.

Here is a classic research review of the training field:

- Salas, E., Tannenbaum, S. I., Kraiger, K., & Smith-Jentsch, K. A. (2012). The science of training and development in organizations: What matters in practice. *Psychological Science in the Public Interest, 13*(2), 74–101.

In addition to training's impact on organizational performance, researchers who take care in investigating specific types of training have found that training typically creates robust benefits.

In a recent meta-analysis that covered 335 studies, leadership development training led to strong benefits as rated by participants and demonstrated in learning results, behavior change, and organizational results.

- Lacerenza, C. N., Reyes, D. L., Marlow, S. L., Joseph, D. L., & Salas, E. (2017). Leadership training design, delivery, and implementation: A meta-analysis. *Journal of Applied Psychology, 102*(12), 1686–1718.

Team training—that is, training teams to work together more effectively—has been found to produce robust, positive outcomes.

- Hughes, A. M., Gregory, M. E., Joseph, D. L., Sonesh, S. C., Marlow, S. L., Lacerenza, C. N., Benishek, L. E., King, H. B., & Salas, E. (2016). Saving lives: A meta-analysis of team training in healthcare. *Journal of Applied Psychology, 101*(9), 1266–1304.

In addition to these results, researchers continue to examine factors that promote training improvements. For example, a recent meta-analysis showed that the work context impacts training results, with key factors being the learners' motivation to transfer, and peer and supervisor support for training application.

- Hughes, A. M., Zajac, S., Woods, A. L., & Salas, E. (2020). The role of work environment in training sustainment: A meta-analysis. *Human Factors, 62*(1), 166–183.

Researchers have also examined learner motivation to tease out the factors that are most important in creating the benefits elicited by such motivation.

- Chung, S., Zhan, Y., Noe, R. A., & Jiang, K. (2022). Is it time to update and expand training motivation theory? A meta-analytic review of training motivation research in the 21st century. *Journal of Applied Psychology, 107*(7), 1150–1179.

Researchers have looked at pre-training interventions and found which approaches create more benefits.

- Mesmer-Magnus, J., & Viswesvaran, C. (2010). The role of pre-training interventions in learning: A meta-analysis and integrative review. *Human Resource Management Review, 20*(4), 261–282.

Researchers have looked at after-action reviews (AARs) to find out which components are most important in creating AARs' benefits.

- Keiser, N. L., & Arthur, W. (2022). A meta-analysis of task and training characteristics that contribute to or attenuate the effectiveness of the after-action review (or debrief). *Journal of Business and Psychology.* Advance online publication.

Researchers have looked at online training to determine what works to keep learners engaged.

- Lee, J., Sanders, T., Antczak, D., Parker, R., Noetel, M., Parker, P., & Lonsdale, C. (2021). Influences on user engagement in online professional learning: A narrative synthesis and meta-analysis. *Review of Educational Research, 91*(4), 518–576.

The conclusion from these many examples—and these represent only a few of the vast numbers of studies conducted on training and workplace learning—is that (1) there is strong evidence that training works and (2) some specific learning methods work better than others.

Chapter 4—Weakness at the Heart of the Learning Field

The United States Bureau of Labor Statistics says that people wanting to become training-and-development professionals need *"a bachelor's degree, work experience, and strong communication skills."*

Let's compare this to other professions. Architects need to *"complete a bachelor's degree in architecture, gain relevant experience through a paid internship, and pass the Architect Registration Examination."* Mechanical engineers *"typically need a bachelor's degree in mechanical engineering or mechanical engineering technology. Every state requires mechanical engineers who sell services to the public to be licensed."* Computer programmers *"typically need a bachelor's degree to enter the occupation. Most programmers specialize in several programming languages."* Accountants typically need a bachelor's degree in accounting or a related field, and completing certificate programs, *"such as becoming a licensed Certified Public Accountant (CPA), may improve job prospects."* Market Research Analysts *"typically need a bachelor's degree. Some employers require or prefer that job candidates have a master's degree."* Physical therapists *"need a Doctor of Physical Therapy Degree (DPT). All states require physical therapists to be licensed."*

Many professions require licensing or certification beyond a bachelor's degree, but not in the learning-and-development field. Certainly, licensing or certification is not required in all professions, but it does tend to be true for professions where people's work performance is critical and for professions that have the highest degrees of credibility.

In the learning-and-development field, we don't begin to expect higher requirements until we get to the management level. As the Bureau of Labor Statistics reported, to become a training-and-development manager, people typically need *"a bachelor's degree or master's degree and related work experience."*

Personally, I don't give a damn whether a person has an advanced degree or not. I have seen fools with PhDs and brilliant research translators who had only bachelor's degrees. But it is telling that, on average, the educational requirements for learning professionals are relatively low compared to vocations that have the same high level of impact.

One of the dirty little secrets in the L&D field relates to conference attendees. What percentage of a conference's attendees are attending that conference for the first time? What would you guess? Maybe 20% or 30%, with most people having attended the conference in the past? It's difficult to know for sure, but I once attended a large trade association's business meeting where they reported that well over 50% of their conference-goers were new to their international conference and exhibition each year. This is another indication that the learning-and-development field is always in flux.

Chapter 5—Remembering and Forgetting

Hermann Ebbinghaus is famous for his learning and forgetting curves—and his name is thrown around with explosive abandon in the learning field. He did brilliant work and was a seminal figure in moving learning-and-memory research forward starting in the late 1800s. Unfortunately, those who cite his work as a blinding badge of honor don't usually report on the limitations of his research. In his memory research, he didn't study many people; he studied only himself. He didn't use normal learning materials; he used nonsense syllables. It was great work—transformative—but we cannot use his numbers and expect our learning and forgetting results to be the same.

Wikipedia's review: https://en.wikipedia.org/wiki/Hermann_Ebbinghaus.

In 2010, I examined an *ad hoc* set of important research studies that measured how much people forgot over time. I looked at over 50 research comparisons and found a range of forgetting from 0-94%. I also found that, in some experiments, people didn't forget; they were able to recognize or recall more over time. Just to be clear, here is a representative sample of the range of findings, representing the amount of forgetting: -53%, -16%, 2%, 12%, 19%, 26%, 39%, 54%, 63%, 82%, 89%. The findings are all over the place! So don't let people tell you that people forget a certain amount in a certain amount of time. First, they are wrong. Second, they are nudging us to believe we can't influence the amount of forgetting. We can! By using good learning-design methods, we can minimize forgetting and support remembering!

Here's a link to learn more: https://www.worklearning.com/2010/12/14/how-much-do-people-forget/.

Chapter 6—Author's Introduction

In this chapter, I shared a little about myself to give you—as a reader—a sense of whether you could trust me. I did *not* embellish, but I didn't highlight all the many mistakes I've made in my career—particularly as I've worked on my own as an independent consultant for over 23 years. That probably sounds impressive to some, but there were many years when things weren't working well enough to meet my goals and my family's aspirations. On the other hand, I learned a ton trying different approaches to make a go of it. Passionate struggle is a great educator. I also didn't tell you how terrible I once was as a trainer and presenter, or the boneheaded ways I managed projects as a young professional. And my delusions of competence right after I got my MBA, they were historic, and now hysterical. I never told anyone—not anyone—until now, but right after I got my MBA degree, I actually applied for a job as a CEO. What a blind, over-confident puppy was I. Hmm. Maybe I still am! But I do know enough now that I would never again apply for a job as a CEO. Your job is safe from me!

Chapter 7—How to Use This Book

Wisely! With open eyes and an open heart, passionate about making improvements.

Chapter 8—Learning Data Is Often Crap Data

In 2022 and 2023, when I was a Principal at TiER1 Performance, we surveyed learning professionals from around the world in our annual Learning Trends Survey. When asked which learning evaluation metrics were used most frequently in their organizations, the highest percentages were for attendance and/or completion rates at about 68% and learner perceptions via surveys at about 63%. The next highest percentages were much lower. Knowledge of key concepts was measured by only about 41% of organizations. Learners' competence on the tasks they were taught was measured by only 35%. Ability to make decisions was measured by 22%. Work performance was measured by 26% of organizations. How well training supported organizational results was also measured by only about 25% of organizations surveyed.

Most organizations measure attendance and completion rates because it's easy to do from their LMS (their learning management system). Most measure learner perceptions through surveys because it's a tradition and fairly easy to do.

But here's the thing. Organizations don't rely on attendance or completion rates to tell them how effective the learning is; they rely mostly on learner surveys. So what does the science say about learner surveys?

As mentioned in the chapter, the following two meta-analyses, together examining over 150 scientific studies, found correlations between traditional smile-sheet ratings and learning at an r = 0.09.

- Alliger, G. M., Tannenbaum, S. I., Bennett, W., Jr., Traver, H., & Shotland, A. (1997). A meta-analysis of the relations among training criteria. Personnel Psychology, 50, 341–358.

- Sitzmann, T., Brown, K. G., Casper, W. J., Ely, K., & Zimmerman, R. D. (2008). A review and meta-analysis of the nomological network of trainee reactions. *Journal of Applied Psychology, 93*(2), 280–295.

Similar levels of low correlation were found in university teaching, with an r = 0.20 in the meta-analysis below.

- Uttl, B., White, C. A., Gonzalez (2017). Meta-analysis of faculty's teaching effectiveness: Student evaluation of teaching ratings and student learning are not related. *Studies in Educational Evaluation, 54*, 22-42.

Similar low correlations were found in healthcare training, with an r = 0.03 in the meta-analysis below.

- Hughes, A. M., Gregory, M. E., Joseph, D. L., Sonesh, S. C., Marlow, S. L., Lacerenza, C. N., Benishek, L. E., King, H. B., Salas, E. (2016). Saving lives: A meta-analysis of team training in healthcare. *Journal of Applied Psychology, 101*(9), 1266-1304.

It was looking at these values that motivated me to find a better method for improving learner surveys, resulting in the award-winning book, *Performance-Focused Learner Surveys: Using Distinctive Questioning to Get Actionable Data and Guide Learning Effectiveness (Second Edition)*. Later in this book, I'll talk more about learner surveys.

Chapter 9—Other Learning Evaluation Failures

Who said the following, and in what publication did they say it?

The Kirkpatrick Model *"is antithetical to nearly 40 years of research on human learning, leads to a checklist approach to evaluation...and, by ignoring the actual purpose for evaluation, risks providing no information of value to stakeholders..."*

Here's the citation:

- Salas, E., Tannenbaum, S. I., Kraiger, K., & Smith-Jentsch, K. A. (2012). The science of training and development in organizations: What matters in practice. *Psychological Science in the Public Interest, 13*(2), 74–101.

The journal is a top-tier scientific journal, and the researchers are among the most renowned in training research.

Who said this, and where was it from?

"Kirkpatrick's framework is not grounded in theory and the assumptions of the model have been repeatedly disproven over the past 25 years."

Here's the citation:

- Sitzmann, T., & Weinhardt, J. M. (2019). Approaching evaluation from a multilevel perspective: A comprehensive analysis of the indicators of training effectiveness. *Human Resource Management Review, 29*(2), 253–269.

Again, the researchers above are among the most respected, and the journal is in the top quartile in terms of influence.

Here's my article that outlines Raymond Katzell's role in the development of the Kirkpatrick-Katzell Four-Level Model of Evaluation. Every time I run into Jack Phillips—the legendary expert on ROI in learning evaluation—he tells me how important a contribution I made in daring to write this article.

- Thalheimer, W. (2018). *Donald Kirkpatrick was NOT the Originator of the Four-Level Model of Learning Evaluation*. Available at: https://www.worklearning.com/2018/01/30/donald-kirkpatrick-was-not-the-originator-of-the-four-level-model-of-learning-evaluation/.

Here is LTEM (The Learning-Transfer Evaluation Model):

- Thalheimer, W. (2018). *The Learning-Transfer Evaluation Model: Sending Messages to Enable Learning Effectiveness*. Available at: https://www.worklearning.com/ltem/.

Chapter 10—Training Is NOT Always the Answer

In this chapter I emphasized the problem that, too often, people in organizations assume training is the solution. Even without much or any analysis, they just contact their learning team and order some training. Your learning-and-development folks hate this, but they usually feel forced to go along with these requests for training. How do I know my fellow learning professionals don't like being order-takers? They talk about it *all* the time. Here are 10 titles from actual conference sessions, magazine articles, and social media posts:

- From Order Taker to Performance Partner.

- What If They Just Want Order Takers?

- Order Taker or Impact Maker?

- From "Order Taker" to Stakeholder: How L&D Can Earn a Seat at the Table.

- The L&D Conundrum: Relevance or "Order-Taking?"

- Moving from Order Taker to Business Partner.

- From Order Taker to Learning Facilitator.

- Transforming Learning & Development from Order Takers to Value Creators.

- Don't Just Be an Order Taker: Effective Training Needs Assessments.

- Pitch Two Options to Move from Order Taker to Trusted Partner.

As the words above attest, your learning team knows it can provide more value to your organization if it can push beyond the expectation that they should just be order-takers. One of my goals in writing this book is to help organizational managers and learning teams have more productive conversations around how to improve performance. The first step is for everyone to take a step back and not assume that training is the answer.

Chapter 11—Training Does NOT Work Alone

Richard Clark, renowned learning researcher, told me that the following was the best review of the learning-transfer research ever written.

- Thalheimer, W. (2018). *Factors that support training transfer: A brief synopsis of the transfer research*. Available at: https://worklearning.com/catalog/.

Maybe he was being nice to me.

Since that review was published, more reviews of training transfer have been written, showing that non-training factors play a critical role in training success.

- Jackson, C. B., Brabson, L. A., Quetsch, L. B., & Herschell, A. D. (2019). Training transfer: A systematic review of the impact of inner setting factors. *Advances in Health Sciences Education, 24*(1), 167–183.

- Casey, T., Turner, N., Hu, X., & Bancroft, K. (2021). Making safety training stickier: A richer model of safety training engagement and transfer. *Journal of Safety Research, 78*, 303–313.

Here also is a classic research article—a meta-analytic review of many research studies. It also finds evidence that learning transfer is influenced by factors beyond training.

- Blume, B. D., Ford, J. K., Baldwin, T. T., & Huang, J. L. (2010). Transfer of training: A meta-analytic review. *Journal of Management, 36*(4), 1065-1105.

To be fair, many learning-transfer researchers have lamented the state of the transfer research, and my review offered a rather scathing indictment of the extent to which the past research had relied on subjective assessments of transfer. The weight of evidence clearly shows that non-learning factors have a profound impact on learning transfer—but future research will more decisively uncover the factors at play.

Chapter 12—Your Learners Don't Always Know Learning

In this chapter, I led with a story of how CEOs in 2005 said they trusted their employees to give them good feedback about learning success. I will first describe that research and then I'll share some other research that paints a different picture. I will also describe the strengths and weaknesses, in general, of this CEO research. Finally, I will provide example after example of research studies showing that learners often have misconceptions about learning.

The CEO Research

In 2005, ASTD (the American Society for Training and Development, now the Association for Talent Development) partnered with IBM and interviewed 26 C-suite executives (CEOs, etc.) and 26 CLOs (Chief Learning Officers). It is rare to get time with C-suite executives, so this is a rare and thus important study. Led by Tony O'Driscoll, Brenda Sugrue, and Mary Kay Vona, the study was an important early contribution in gauging CEO perceptions of learning and learning evaluation. One of the most striking findings from the study was that C-suite executives *"emphasized the challenge of linking learning to business results and appear comfortable with correlations and stakeholder perceptions over direct evidence of learning's strategic value."* The Chief Learning Officers were getting the same messages from their C-suite leaders. One said, *"Our efforts in tracking ROI for learning are greater than the demands of our senior executives."* A second CLO was quoted as saying, *"We're striving to come up with better ROI metrics that truly connect to business value. But senior executives are not demanding this from us. They are comfortable with anecdotal observation."*

The IBM and ASTD research cited above was reported in:

- O'Driscoll, T., Sugrue, B., Vona, M. K. (2005). *The C-Level and the Value of Learning.* In TD, October 2005.

In 2008 and 2009, Jack and Patti Phillips surveyed CEOs about their views on learning evaluation and found substantially different findings than those reported above. They published their results in book form in 2010. Jack and Patti run the ROI Institute and are globally recognized for their seminal work in learning evaluation. They are also good people and are known for their generosity in the learning-and-development field. I engaged with them in a friendly debate at the Learning Development Conference in 2020. Jack and I have had many discussions over the years about issues in learning evaluation, and he has written testimonials for my book on Performance-Focused Learner Surveys. In short, I trust Jack and Patti to do good work.

They surveyed 96 CEOs and gave them a list of eight types of learning measurements that might be utilized. The CEOs rank-ordered their preferences. The top preference was *"Impact: 'Our programs are driving our top five business measures in the organization.'"* The second highest preference was *"ROI: 'Five ROI studies were conducted on major programs yielding an average of 68% ROI.'"* In contrast, learner reactions to the learning experience were rated last, application of the learning to employee jobs was rated fourth, and industry awards were rated third.

Some caution is urged in interpreting these results. Most importantly, the survey may have inadvertently primed the respondents to focus on financial considerations above other considerations. The first question on the survey asks for the CEOs to report the annual budget for learning and development. The third question asks the CEOs to describe their approach to investing in learning and development. The critical question is the fifth question—the one that asks CEOs to rank their preferences. It is likely that the two earlier questions elevated their reported preference for impact and ROI and deflated the other categories of evaluations.

It should be noted that the dangers of priming effects on surveys were not widely known until recently. Indeed, the O'Driscoll, Sugrue, and Vona study (2005) also primed constructs in the questions it asked—mostly focused on the alignment of learning with strategic business goals.

What are we to conclude from two studies of CEOs that have produced different results, both of which may have had some methodological limitations? Probably, we should view both results with skepticism. Incidentally, there are zero studies in refereed scientific journals about CEO perceptions of learning and learning evaluation.

What's especially notable is that, despite the weakness of the evidence, a majority of the industry's evaluation thought leaders have been telling the industry that, if we learning professionals don't provide proof of training's impact, we will be removed or have our resources and autonomy taken away. This seems to be a highly contrived suggestion.

What's more likely is that CEOs generally focus very little of their time on the learning-and-development function—and their perspectives on learning are somewhat loose and subject to contextual influences. In the Phillips study, they found that, on average, CEOs were three levels above their Chief Learning Officers! Think about that! When the top learning leader is three levels removed, the CEO is spending very little time thinking about learning and development. Indeed, this is a prime motivation for this book: to help CEOs develop clearer insights about how L&D works.

Here is the citation for the Phillips research:

- Phillips, J. J., & Phillips, P. P. (2010). Measuring Success: What CEOs Really Think About Learning Investments. ASTD Press.

Let's go back to the surveying we've done so far with CEOs. It's important to paint a full picture so we understand what the research shows and so we see clearly what was and wasn't measured.

Even more troubling than the general weaknesses pointed out above is that the surveys and interviews done with CEOs completely failed to ask questions about specific learning factors. They did ask about learning outcomes in general, but they did not clarify how learning teams might use learning data to improve the effectiveness of learning. They didn't ask specifically about the value of measuring employees' competence in making decisions or taking actions. In short, they focused on a limited subset of what we might measure—and omitted some factors that are central to learning success.

This blind spot has been one of the central weaknesses in the learning-and-development field for decades. We've been pushed to measure all the wrong things—business results and learner perceptions provide faulty guidance for the practice of learning. Training certainly influences business results, but the causal factors involved are difficult to discern—and are very costly to measure. Learners consistently make faulty attributions about what works in learning, so relying on learner surveys—especially traditional smile sheets—provides learning teams with unreliable guidance for learning design.

The Research Showing That Learners Don't Always Know Learning

How do we know learners are unreliable sources of learning guidance? There is a ton of research over many years on learners' faulty decision making. Let me provide examples.

Zechmeister and Shaughnessy found that learners are overly optimistic about their ability to remember what they've learned, so they tend to fail to give themselves enough repetitions. The title of their research article highlights learners' faulty thinking.

- Zechmeister, E. B., & Shaughnessy, J. J. (1980). When you know that you know and when you think that you know but you don't. *Bulletin of the Psychonomic Society, 15*(1), 41–44.

Karpicke, Butler, and Roediger—researchers from Roediger's famous lab at Washington University—found that learners fail to utilize retrieval practice to support long-term remembering, even though retrieval practice is one of the most powerful learning methods.

- Karpicke, J. D., Butler, A. C., & Roediger, H. L. III. (2009). Metacognitive strategies in student learning: Do students practise retrieval when they study on their own? *Memory, 17*(4), 471–479.

Kendeou and van den Broek found that learners don't always overcome their incorrect prior knowledge when reading. Indeed, those with misconceptions end up with more faulty knowledge than those without prior misconceptions even after reading the correct information.

- Kendeou, P., & van den Broek, P. (2005). The Effects of Readers' Misconceptions on Comprehension of Scientific Text. *Journal of Educational Psychology, 97*(2), 235–245.

Prinz, Golke, and Wittwer followed up on this line of research and found that not only did those with prior misconceptions learn more poorly as they read, but they also made *"more overconfident predictions of their conceptual and procedural text comprehension than students who had fewer misconceptions."*

- Prinz, A., Golke, S., & Wittwer, J. (2018). The double curse of misconceptions: Misconceptions impair not only text comprehension but also metacomprehension in the domain of statistics. *Instructional Science, 46*(5), 723–765.

Renkl showed that learners often fail to use examples in ways that would foster deeper learning. Where some learners support their own learning by thinking about examples in terms of underlying principles and the meaning underlying each example, other learners learned less because they didn't process the examples productively. In this research, more than half of learners used poor explanation strategies.

- Renkl, A. (1997). Learning from worked-out examples: A study on individual differences. *Cognitive Science, 21*(1), 1–29.

Benjamin, Bjork, and Schwartz found that learners can get fooled by the ease with which they could recall information from memory. While retrieval fluency is often a good predictor of knowledge, it can be an unreliable predictor when response concepts are highly accessible from memory.

- Benjamin, A. S., Bjork, R. A., & Schwartz, B. L. (1998). The mismeasure of memory: When retrieval fluency is misleading as a metamnemonic index. *Journal of Experimental Psychology: General, 127*(1), 55–68.

Finn and Tauber found that learner confidence is not always a good prediction of learning.

- Finn, B., & Tauber, S. K. (2015). When confidence is not a signal of knowing: How students' experiences and beliefs about processing fluency can lead to miscalibrated confidence. *Educational Psychology Review, 27*(4), 567–586.

Hofseth, Toering, Jordet, and Ivarsson studied elite youth soccer players—highly successful yet still learning their craft. Those players who had overrated their abilities, compared to ratings given by their coaches, went on to lower career success than their peers who had rated their abilities lower.

- Hofseth, E., Toering, T., Jordet, G., & Ivarsson, A. (2017). Self-evaluation of skills and performance level in youth elite soccer: Are positive self-evaluations always positive? *Sport, Exercise, and Performance Psychology, 6*(4), 370–383.

Dunlosky and Nelson found that learners' predictions of their ability to remember the second word in a word pair when given the first word—for example, remembering "tree" when presented with the word "ocean" in the "ocean-tree" word pair—were worse when they were asked to estimate right after learning the word pair than if they were asked to estimate after a slight delay (i.e., after more than half a minute). This and other similar experiments showed that learners' judgments of learning were improved if they were compelled to "test" their ability to remember after a delay—something learners rarely do on their own. Indeed, in an earlier experiment, Nelson and Dunlosky found that *all* their learners produced better accuracy when asked to estimate their judgments after a delay compared to estimating immediately.

Fortunately, learners can be trained or nudged, through various means, to improve their judgments of learning, as demonstrated in later studies—for example, by Koriat and Bjork in 2005 and Bui, Pyc, and Bailey in 2018. And to be clear, learners who are learning from more complex learning materials have also benefitted significantly after being trained to overcome their ineffective learning practices. Roelle, Schmidt, Buchau, and Berthold warned learners about the dangers of being overconfident and found large improvements in learning for adult learners—27% better than those who had not been trained. Again, these kinds of results show the value that learning teams can bring to learning design when they use research-inspired practices.

- Dunlosky, J., & Nelson, T. O. (1994). Does the sensitivity of judgments of learning (JOLs) to the effects of various study activities depend on when the JOLs occur? *Journal of Memory and Language, 33*(4), 545–565.

- Nelson, T. O., & Dunlosky, J. (1991). When people's judgments of learning (JOLs) are extremely accurate at predicting subsequent recall: The "delayed-JOL effect." *Psychological Science, 2*(4), 267–270.

- Koriat, A., & Bjork, R. A. (2005). Illusions of Competence in Monitoring One's Knowledge During Study. *Journal of Experimental Psychology: Learning, Memory, and Cognition, 31*(2), 187–194.

- Bui, Y., Pyc, M. A., & Bailey, H. (2018). When people's judgments of learning (JOLs) are extremely accurate at predicting subsequent recall: The "Displaced-JOL effect". *Memory, 26*(6), 771–783.

- Roelle, J., Schmidt, E. M., Buchau, A., & Berthold, K. (2017). Effects of informing learners about the dangers of making overconfident judgments of learning. Journal of Educational Psychology, 109(1), 99–117.

When it comes to training, it's our hope that those communicating—trainers and/or learning designers—are being effective. Further, we assume that those giving a presentation have accurate information about whether they are successfully communicating. Unfortunately, this assumption is wrong. Keysar and Henly found that speakers are overly optimistic about their success in communicating.

Others have found similar results. Fay, Page, and Serfaty, over two studies, found similar speaker misperceptions, but argued that they can be adaptive when speakers are nervous and might otherwise be perceived as less credible. Kleinlogel, Renier, Schmid Mast, and Toma found that speakers performed better when they were confident that they were performing well. One caveat on these studies is that the "speakers" were not professional speakers. It seems likely that experienced trainers experience much less cognitive interference from performance anxiety. Trainers are still likely to be overconfident in their performance—we humans are inherently overconfident—but they are less likely to benefit from overconfidence than the participants in these research studies.

Recently, Lau, Geipel, Wu, and Keysar found that both speakers and listeners overestimated how effective their communications had been—and this was true even when speakers spoke to listeners in a language the listeners did not understand! Though both speakers and listeners were aware that the listeners couldn't understand the speaker's words, both overestimated how successful they had been in communicating. Relating this finding to training, we might imagine a trainer who is overconfident that she is being successful communicating concepts and also imagine learners who are similarly overconfident that they are understanding what the trainer is trying to communicate.

Here's one more study showing that communications are often assumed to be effective when they are not. Chang, Arora, Lev-Ari, D'Arcy, and Keysar examined communications in a hospital setting. Specifically, they were interested in how successful physician interns were in communicating to others when they were handing off patient information. What they found was, *"the most important piece of information about a patient was not successfully communicated 60% of the time"* even though the communicator believed they had communicated that information!

- Keysar, B., & Henly, A. S. (2002). Speakers' overestimation of their effectiveness. *Psychological Science, 13*(3), 207–212.

- Fay, N., Page, A. C., Serfaty, C., Tai, V., & Winkler, C. (2008). Speaker overestimation of communication effectiveness and fear of negative evaluation: Being realistic is unrealistic. *Psychonomic Bulletin & Review, 15*(6), 1160–1165.

- Fay, N., Page, A. C., & Serfaty, C. (2010). Listeners influence speakers' perceived communication effectiveness. *Journal of Experimental Social Psychology, 46*(4), 689–692.

- Wang, J. J., Miletich, D. D., Ramsey, R., & Samson, D. (2014). Adults see vision to be more informative than it is. *The Quarterly Journal of Experimental Psychology, 67*(12), 2279–2292.

- Chang, V. Y., Arora, V. M., Lev-Ari, S., D'Arcy, M., & Keysar, B. (2010). Interns overestimate the effectiveness of their hand-off communication. *Pediatrics, 125*(3), 491–496.

- Lau, B. K. Y., Geipel, J., Wu, Y., & Keysar, B. (2022). The extreme illusion of understanding. *Journal of Experimental Psychology: General, 151*(11), 2957–2962.

- Kleinlogel, E. P., Renier, L., Schmid Mast, M., & Toma, C. (2020). "I think that I made a good impression!": Meta-perception improves performance in public speaking. *Social Psychology, 51*(6), 370–380.

DiMenichi and Tricomi in two separate experiments found that learners preferred competitive conditions where they got feedback about their relative comparison to the performance of others. But they learned more in non-competitive conditions where they got feedback only on their own performance.

- DiMenichi, B. C., & Tricomi, E. (2015). The power of competition: Effects of social motivation on attention, sustained physical effort, and learning. *Frontiers in Psychology, 6*, Article 1282.

- DiMenichi, B. C., & Tricomi, E. (2017). Increases in brain activity during social competition predict decreases in working memory performance and later recall. *Human Brain Mapping, 38*(1), 457–471.

Von Hoyer, Kimmerle, and Holtz found that learners who were given an extra opportunity to search for information on the internet—after having taken a test on the information—increased their confidence on the information tested for both correct and incorrect answers. The fact that confidence increased even on incorrect information shows another flaw in learners' ability to learn. Fortunately, in some circumstances, learners can be nudged to have better metacognitive accuracy by reflecting on the success of their retrieval efforts—as demonstrated by Robey, Dougherty, and Buttaccio.

- von Hoyer, J. F., Kimmerle, J., & Holtz, P. (2022). Acquisition of false certainty: Learners increase their confidence in the correctness of incorrect answers after online information search. Journal of Computer Assisted Learning, 38(3), 833–844.

- Robey, A. M., Dougherty, M. R., & Buttaccio, D. R. (2017). Making retrospective confidence judgments improves learners' ability to decide what not to study. *Psychological Science, 28*(11), 1683–1693.

As the many studies reported above show, we humans—both as we learn and as we communicate to support others in learning—are filled with delusions and misperceptions about the effectiveness of learning practices. If these studies aren't enough, there have been three recent reviews of the scientific research showing that learners often have incorrect intuitions about learning. Each reviews dozens of studies showing that learners often make metacognitive mistakes in thinking about learning.

- Brown, P. C., Roediger, H. L., III, & McDaniel, M. A. (2014). *Make It Stick: The Science of Successful Learning*. Cambridge, MA: Belknap Press of Harvard University Press.

- Kirschner, P. A., & van Merriënboer, J. J. G. (2013). Do learners really know best? Urban legends in education. *Educational Psychologist, 48*(3), 169–183.

- Rhodes, M. G. (2016). Judgments of Learning: Methods, Data, Theory. In J. Dunlosky & S. K. Tauber (Eds.) The Oxford Handbook of Metamemory. Oxford University Press.

Chapter 13—Why Your Experts Aren't Always Great at Teaching

There is a general tendency for we human beings to overestimate how successful we have been in communicating.

- Lau, B. K. Y., Geipel, J., Wu, Y., & Keysar, B. (2022). The extreme illusion of understanding. *Journal of Experimental Psychology: General, 151*(11), 2957–2962.

- Tullis, J. G., & Feder, B. (2023). The "curse of knowledge" when predicting others' knowledge. *Memory & Cognition, 51*(5), 1214–1234.

- Nickerson, R. S. (1999). How we know—and sometimes misjudge—what others know: Imputing one's own knowledge to others. *Psychological Bulletin, 125*(6), 737–759.

Experts have an especially difficult time in communicating to those who are non-experts.

- Hinds, P. J. (1999). The curse of expertise: The effects of expertise and debiasing methods on prediction of novice performance. Journal of Experimental Psychology: Applied, 5(2), 205–221.

- Zhang, T., Harrington, K. B., & Sherf, E. N. (2022). The errors of experts: When expertise hinders effective provision and seeking of advice and feedback. *Current Opinion in Psychology, 43,* 91–95.

Speakers, in particular, often overestimate their ability to communicate clearly.

- Keysar, B., & Henly, A. S. (2002). Speakers' overestimation of their effectiveness. *Psychological Science, 13*(3), 207–212.

- Chang, V. Y., Arora, V. M., Lev-Ari, S., D'Arcy, M., & Keysar, B. (2010). Interns overestimate the effectiveness of their hand-off communication. *Pediatrics, 125*(3), 491–496.

Being overconfident in how we are being perceived as speaker can be useful—particularly to bolster our performance as we speak—to help us avoid the anxiety we have of being judged negatively. But overconfidence in how we are being perceived is not the same thing as being overconfident about our success in communicating.

- Kleinlogel, E. P., Renier, L., Schmid Mast, M., & Toma, C. (2020). "I think that I made a good impression!": Meta-perception improves performance in public speaking. *Social Psychology, 51*(6), 370–380.

- Fay, N., Page, A. C., Serfaty, C., Tai, V., & Winkler, C. (2008). Speaker overestimation of communication effectiveness and fear of negative evaluation: Being realistic is unrealistic. *Psychonomic Bulletin & Review, 15*(6), 1160–1165.

The common practice of searching the internet to help us create presentations or write reports may exacerbate our overconfidence.

- Pieschl, S. (2021). Will using the Internet to answer knowledge questions increase users' overestimation of their own ability or performance? *Media Psychology, 24*(1), 109–135.

- von Hoyer, J. F., Kimmerle, J., & Holtz, P. (2022). Acquisition of false certainty: Learners increase their confidence in the correctness of incorrect answers after online information search. *Journal of Computer Assisted Learning, 38*(3), 833–844.

- von Hoyer, J. F., Kimmerle, J., Cress, U., & Holtz, P. (2024). False certainty as an unwanted side effect of knowledge acquisition in computer-based online search and content learning. *Computers & Education, 208,* 1–10.

- Flanagin, A. J., & Lew, Z. (2022). Individual inferences in web-based information environments: How cognitive processing fluency, information access, active search behaviors, and task competency affect metacognitive and task judgments. *Media Psychology.* Advance online publication.

But both automated and human help can make us overconfident as well.

- Fisher, M., & Oppenheimer, D. M. (2021). Who knows what? Knowledge misattribution in the division of cognitive labor. *Journal of Experimental Psychology: Applied, 27*(2), 292–306.

Research shows that people are sensitive to communication problems when they are in two-way conversations—and do improve their messaging over time by using the feedback they get from these conversations.

- Micklos, A., Walker, B., & Fay, N. (2020). Are people sensitive to problems in communication? *Cognitive Science, 44*(2), Article e12816.

- Castillo, L., Smith, K., & Branigan, H. P. (2019). Interaction promotes the adaptation of referential conventions to the communicative context. *Cognitive Science, 43*(8), Article e12780.

Interestingly, when we make presentations, we don't often get the benefit of two-way communications. More generally, as we have conversations with people, if we don't encourage them to share their understanding of the concepts discussed, we are likely to overestimate how successful we've been in communicating.

Failing to get conversational feedback is especially problematic for people in authority, because subordinates are less comfortable sharing back. For example, managers tend to fail in giving constructive feedback to their direct reports.

- Schaerer, M., Kern, M., Berger, G., Medvec, V., & Swaab, R. I. (2018). The illusion of transparency in performance appraisals: When and why accuracy motivation explains unintentional feedback inflation. *Organizational Behavior and Human Decision Processes, 144,* 171–186.

One problem experts have in communicating is that they use abstract language when concrete language tends to be more effective.

- Hinds, P. J., Patterson, M., & Pfeffer, J. (2001). Bothered by abstraction: The effect of expertise on knowledge transfer and subsequent novice performance. *Journal of Applied Psychology, 86*(6), 1232–1243.

Experts may get nudged to use abstract language because doing so often signals that they are in a position of power.

- Wakslak, C. J., Smith, P. K., & Han, A. (2014). Using abstract language signals power. *Journal of Personality and Social Psychology, 107*(1), 41–55.

Fortunately, experts can be trained or nudged to be more effective in communicating, generally by understanding how their communications may fail and by seeking information about their success in communicating.

- Nückles, M., Wittwer, J., & Renkl, A. (2005). Information About a Layperson's Knowledge Supports Experts in Giving Effective and Efficient Online Advice to Laypersons. *Journal of Experimental Psychology: Applied, 11*(4), 219–236.

- Trinh, M. P. (2019). Overcoming the shadow of expertise: How humility and learning goal orientation help knowledge leaders become more flexible. *Frontiers in Psychology, 10,* Article 2505.

Still, experts often aren't in the best position to give advice or feedback. For example, expert tutors used less interactivity than less-experienced tutors—even though interactivity is beneficial in communicating.

- Herppich, S., Wittwer, J., Nückles, M., & Renkl, A. (2016). Expertise amiss: Interactivity fosters learning but expert tutors are less interactive than novice tutors. *Instructional Science, 44*(3), 205–219.

Research finds that experts can be worse at giving learners feedback than the learners' peers—those who are also engaged in learning.

- Double, K. S., McGrane, J. A., & Hopfenbeck, T. N. (2020). The impact of peer assessment on academic performance: A meta-analysis of control group studies. *Educational Psychology Review, 32*(2), 481–509.

While there is a substantial variability in the findings, generally peer feedback provides benefits—and may be especially beneficial for the peer who provides the feedback.

- Yu, Q., & Schunn, C. D. (2023). Understanding the what and when of peer feedback benefits for performance and transfer. *Computers in Human Behavior, 147*, 1–17.

Sometimes, experts are equal to peers in providing feedback. It is not always true that peers are better than experts in providing feedback.

- Huisman, B., Saab, N., van den Broek, P., & van Driel, J. (2019). The impact of formative peer feedback on higher education students' academic writing: A meta-analysis. *Assessment & Evaluation in Higher Education, 44*(6), 863–880.

Finally, we can't assume that the best performers give the best advice.

- Levari, D. E., Gilbert, D. T., & Wilson, T. D. (2022). Tips from the top: Do the best performers really give the best advice? Psychological Science, 33(5), 685–698.

Chapter 14—Avoiding Myths and Misconceptions

Learning Styles

There are very strong reviews showing that the learning styles notion is a myth worth avoiding. The Association for Psychological Science published a definitive review in 2008 from four of the top learning researchers.

- Pashler, H., McDaniel, M., Rohrer, D., & Bjork, R. (2008). Learning styles: Concepts and evidence. *Psychological Science in the Public Interest, 9*(3), 105–119. Available at: https://www.apa.org/pubs/journals/releases/edu-edu0000366.pdf

Famed educational researcher Daniel Willingham and colleagues conducted their own review and found learning styles a poor way to design learning.

- Willingham, D. T., Hughes, E. M., & Dobolyi, D. G. (2015). The scientific status of learning styles theories. *Teaching of Psychology, 42*(3), 266–271.

Here are two reviews, each examining aspects of one learning-styles approach—and both found them wanting.

- Klitmøller, J. (2015). Review of the methods and findings in the Dunn and Dunn learning styles model research on perceptual preferences. *Nordic Psychology, 67*(1), 2–26.

- Calderón Carvajal, C., Ximénez Gómez, C., Lay-Lisboa, S., & Briceño, M. (2021). Reviewing the structure of Kolb's Learning Style inventory from factor analysis and Thurstonian Item Response Theory (IRT) model approaches. *Journal of Psychoeducational Assessment, 39*(5), 593–609.

One researcher who once advocated for designing elearning differently based on people's cognitive learning styles did further research and now disavows learning styles.

- Cook, D. A. (2012). Revisiting cognitive and learning styles in computer-assisted instruction: Not so useful after all. *Academic Medicine, 87*(6), 778–784.

Researchers have begun to come to grips with the widespread dispersion of the learning styles myth—tracking its history, lamenting its current reach, and strategizing ways to limit the damage.

- Dekker, H. D., & Kim, J. A. (2022). The widespread belief in learning styles. In D. H. Robinson, V. X. Yan, & J. A. Kim (Eds.), *Learning styles, classroom instruction, and student achievement* (pp. 11–20). Springer Nature Switzerland AG.

- Olsen, A. A., Romig, J. E., Green, A. L., Joswick, C., & Nandakumar, V. (2022). Myth busted or zombie concept? A systematic review of articles referencing "learning styles" from 2009 to 2019. In D. H. Robinson, V. X. Yan, & J. A. Kim (Eds.), *Learning styles, classroom instruction, and student achievement* (pp. 39–57). Springer Nature Switzerland AG.

- Nancekivell, S. E., Shah, P., & Gelman, S. A. (2020). Maybe they're born with it, or maybe it's experience: Toward a deeper understanding of the learning style myth. *Journal of Educational Psychology, 112*(2), 221–235.

There are even research-based discussions that show how harmful the learning-styles myth can be for those designing learning.

- Nancekivell, S. E., Sun, X., Gelman, S. A., & Shah, P. (2021). A slippery myth: How learning style beliefs shape reasoning about multimodal instruction and related scientific evidence. *Cognitive Science, 45*(10), Article e13047.

- Yan, V. X., & Fralick, C. M. (2022). Consequences of endorsing the individual learning styles myth: Helpful, harmful, or harmless? In D. H. Robinson, V. X. Yan,

& J. A. Kim (Eds.), *Learning styles, classroom instruction, and student achievement* (pp. 59–74). Springer Nature Switzerland AG.

Lots of people deserve credit for debunking this damaging myth, but I don't want you to overlook an important new contribution from Daniel Robinson, Veronica Yan, and Joseph Kim, editors of a research-focused book on learning styles: *Learning Styles, Classroom Instruction, and Student Achievement.*

Finally, it's worth noting that individual differences between learners do not seem to matter for at least one of the major learning factors. Researchers have found that retrieval practice—the first learning research factor described in this book (in Chapter 22)—created benefits for all learners despite their varying traits as measured by three widely disparate instruments, including working memory capacity, grit, and need for cognition. Our belief that we should focus first on each learner and focus less on proven research-aligned learning strategies seems more dubious than ever.

- Bertilsson, F., Stenlund, T., Wiklund-Hörnqvist, C., & Jonsson, B. (2021). Retrieval practice: Beneficial for all students or moderated by individual differences? *Psychology Learning & Teaching, 20*(1), 21–39. https://doi.org/10.1177/1475725720973494

Indeed, in a recent study by Buchin and Mulligan, even differences in learners' prior knowledge did not impact the power of retrieval practice.

- Buchin, Z. L., & Mulligan, N. W. (2023). Retrieval-based learning and prior knowledge. *Journal of Educational Psychology, 115*(1), 22–35.

Microlearning and Attention-Span Workarounds

Researchers have found differences in attention across age groups but have not yet done sufficient longitudinal studies to see if human attention spans have been changing over time. Notable in this research is that the ability to sustain attention peaks when people are in their 40s and attentional strategies mature with age. The researchers point out that attention is highly trainable.

- Fortenbaugh, F. C., DeGutis, J., Germine, L., Wilmer, J. B., Grosso, M., Russo, K., & Esterman, M. (2015). Sustained attention across the life span in a sample of 10,000: Dissociating ability and strategy. Psychological Science, 26(9), 1497–1510.

If attention is trainable, doesn't that suggest that our worries about attention spans are misplaced? Indeed, recent research shows that attention is improved simply by having people go out into nature.

- Mason, L., Ronconi, A., Scrimin, S., & Pazzaglia, F. (2022). Short-term exposure to nature and benefits for students' cognitive performance: A review. Educational Psychology Review, 34(2), 609–647.

Interestingly, researchers have found a number of "effortless" ways to improve attention, again suggesting that attention-span worries are silly.

- Tang, Y.-Y., Tang, R., Posner, M. I., & Gross, J. J. (2022). Effortless training of attention and self-control: Mechanisms and applications. *Trends in Cognitive Sciences, 26*(7), 567–577.

Sustained attention peaks between 9 and 11 in the morning and then declines throughout the day.

- Riley, E., Esterman, M., Fortenbaugh, F. C., & DeGutis, J. (2017). Time-of-day variation in sustained attentional control. *Chronobiology International, 34*(7), 993–1001.

Attention is a complex phenomenon. As the brilliant researcher Michael Posner has reported, there are at least three attentional systems in the brain.

- Posner, M. I. (2016). Orienting of attention: Then and now. *The Quarterly Journal of Experimental Psychology, 69*(10), 1864–1875.

There are different ways to think about attention. One way is to look at how well people can avoid mind-wandering. Interestingly, where the research I cited above (Fortenbaugh and colleagues) found people peak in their 40s in terms of some attention measures, research shows that older adults are better at reducing mind-wandering than younger adults.

- Arnicane, A., Oberauer, K., & Souza, A. S. (2021). Validity of attention self-reports in younger and older adults. *Cognition, 206,* Article 104482.

Older adults tend to be more accurate at attention tasks, even if slower.

- Vallesi, A., Tronelli, V., Lomi, F., & Pezzetta, R. (2021). Age differences in sustained attention tasks: A meta-analysis. *Psychonomic Bulletin & Review, 28*(6), 1755–1775.

All this research—taken in total—suggests that our worries about attention spans are completely misplaced. They also give hints that we can improve attention quite easily. Certainly, learners don't require microlearning chunks to overcome attention issues.

eLearning Is Less Effective Than Classroom Training
The research on this will be fully covered in the notes from Chapter 18.

Training Is NOT Effective
The research on this was fully covered in the notes from Chapter 3.

Training Is Already Effective Enough
This is clearly not true, as evidenced by the many lines of research I describe in Section 4—The Powerful Practicality of the Learning Sciences. Chapters 23, 24, 25, and 26 show that large improvements in learning can result from more retrieval practice, context alignment, spacing, and feedback—practices that are too often neglected in the learning field.

Also, training researchers have long lamented the state of practice.

- Salas, E., Tannenbaum, S. I., Kraiger, K., & Smith-Jentsch, K. A. (2012). The science of training and development in organizations: What matters in practice. *Psychological Science in the Public Interest, 13*(2), 74–101.

The Learning Pyramid

Earlier, I detailed the work of researchers who have debunked the learning pyramid.

- Thalheimer, W. (2015). *Mythical Retention Data & The Corrupted Cone.* Available at: https://www.worklearning.com/2015/01/05/mythical-retention-data-the-corrupted-cone/.

Brain Science and Neuroscience

Earlier I compiled the research writings of neuroscientists who were largely skeptical that neuroscience—on its own—would quickly improve learning practice.

- Thalheimer, W. (2016, 2018). Brain Based Learning and Neuroscience—What the Research Says! Available at: https://www.worklearning.com/2016/01/05/brain-based-learning-and-neuroscience-what-the-research-says/.

Bloom's Taxonomy

Scientific researchers have long been concerned about Bloom's Taxonomy.

- Furst, E. J. (1981). Bloom's taxonomy of educational objectives for the cognitive domain: Philosophical and educational issues. *Review of Educational Research, 51*(4), 441–453.

- Seddon, G. M. (1978). The properties of Bloom's *Taxonomy of Educational Objectives* for the cognitive domain. *Review of Educational Research, 48*(2), 303–323.

Concerns about the original 1956 Bloom's Taxonomy were significant enough that researchers attempted a major rewriting of the taxonomy.

- Anderson, L. W., Krathwohl, D. R., Airasian, P. W., Cruikshank, K. A., Mayer, R. E., Pintrich, P. R., Raths, J., Wittrock, M. C. (2001), *A Taxonomy for Learning, Teaching, and Assessing: A Revision of Bloom's Taxonomy of Educational Objectives,* Longman, New York, NY.

Still, the concerns and limitations of Bloom's Taxonomy persist—regardless of the form it takes. For example, researcher Pooja Agarwal has found that the prediction from Bloom's Taxonomy that fact learning supports higher-order thinking is false.

- Agarwal, P. K. (2019). Retrieval practice & Bloom's taxonomy: Do students need fact knowledge before higher order learning? Journal of Educational Psychology, 111(2), 189–209.

70-20-10

The only research study done on 70-20-10 has found it wanting. Moreover, the inconsistencies and sloppy scholarship are well documented.

- Johnson, S. J., Blackman, D. A., & Buick, F. (2018). The 70:20:10 framework and the transfer of learning. *Human Resource Development Quarterly, 29*(4), 383–402.

- Clardy, A. (2018). 70-20-10 and the dominance of informal learning: A fact in search of evidence. *Human Resource Development Review, 17*(2), 153–178.

Different Generations Must Be Taught Differently

Researchers have not found much evidence that different generations must be taught differently.

- Lai, K.-W., & Hong, K.-S. (2015). Technology use and learning characteristics of students in higher education: Do generational differences exist? *British Journal of Educational Technology, 46*(4), 725–738.

Also, the similar idea that people raised during the age of widespread computer usage—so-called "digital natives"—learn differently, has also been debunked.

- Calvo-Ferrer, J. R. (2020). Exploring digital nativeness as a predictor of digital game-based L2 vocabulary acquisition. *Interactive Learning Environments, 28*(7), 902–914.

People Don't Need Training; They Can Look It Up

People can improve their knowledge by looking up information.

- Donovan, A. M., & Rapp, D. N. (2020). Look it up: Online search reduces the problematic effects of exposures to inaccuracies. *Memory & Cognition, 48*(7), 1128–1145.

Of course, that is not central to real-world performance. The research above shows that we *can* improve our accuracy: (1) when we have time, and (2) when we are nudged to look up information. Much of the time, this is not how real-world cognition works.

We know that we all encounter both accurate and inaccurate information; however, without some sort of intervention, we are not likely to be as skeptical and discerning as we should be. People are generally unaware of their susceptibility to inaccurate information.

- Salovich, N. A., & Rapp, D. N. (2021). Misinformed and unaware? Metacognition and the influence of inaccurate information. *Journal of Experimental Psychology: Learning, Memory, and Cognition, 47*(4), 608–624.

- Salovich, N. A., & Rapp, D. N. (2022). How susceptible are you? Using feedback and monitoring to reduce the influence of false information. *Journal of Applied Research in Memory and Cognition.* Advance online publication. https://doi.org/10.1037/mac0000074

Finally, people with less knowledge or no knowledge in a domain can't learn as effectively as those with knowledge. So even when people are able to look up information, they won't be as successful as those who were earlier trained in that area of expertise.

- Witherby, A. E., & Carpenter, S. K. (2022). The rich-get-richer effect: Prior knowledge predicts new learning of domain-relevant information. *Journal of Experimental Psychology: Learning, Memory, and Cognition, 48*(4), 483–498.

Learning Events Should Be Easy and Comfortable

World-famous learning researchers Robert and Elizabeth Bjork pointed out three decades ago that adding "desirable difficulties" to learning usually improves learning results. This finding has been replicated many times.

- Bjork, R. A., & Bjork, E. L. (1992). A new theory of disuse and an old theory of stimulus fluctuation. In A. F. Healy, S. M. Kosslyn, & R. M. Shiffrin (Eds.), *Essays in honor of William K. Estes, Vol. 1. From learning theory to connectionist theory; Vol. 2. From learning processes to cognitive processes* (pp. 35–67). Lawrence Erlbaum Associates, Inc.

- Bjork, R. A., & Bjork, E. L. (2020). Desirable difficulties in theory and practice. *Journal of Applied Research in Memory and Cognition, 9*(4), 475–479.

Fears that difficult learning might lead to more forgetting are unfounded, as the opposite is usually true.

- Bjork, R. A. (2015). Forgetting as a friend of learning. In D. S. Lindsay (Ed.) & C. M. Kelley (Trans.) & A. P. Yonelinas, H. L. Roediger II (Eds.), *Remembering: Attributions, processes, and control in human memory: Essays in honor of Larry Jacoby* (pp. 15–28). Psychology Press.

Chapter 15—Managers and Learning

In the chapter, I referred to ECRA (Engagement, Comprehension, Remembering, and Action) in regard to giving presentations. The idea, first put forth in my workshop called *Presentation Science*, is that all audience members are learners, and if we support them in learning we will have more effective presentations. In particular, we must support our audience members in being engaged, comprehending clearly, remembering, and being able to take action. Note that, in an earlier version of *Presentation Science*, I used "ELRA" as the acronym—where "Comprehension" had been "Learning." I recently decided to make the change because (1) the word "learning" has too many meanings, and (2) aiming for ECRA is all about learning.

In this chapter I also made the case that managers in organizations make a difference. This might seem obvious, but there is a wealth of research evidence for the beneficial impact of good managers. Let me share a few research sources here.

Giessner, Dawson, Horton, and West showed that, when mid-level managers increased their supportive leadership practices, they helped mitigate the stress-related outcomes exhibited by employees—like declines in job satisfaction and higher levels of absenteeism. Supportive leadership includes behaviors such as showing consideration, being accepting, providing guidance, and demonstrating a concern for others.

- Giessner, S. R., Dawson, J. F., Horton, K. E., & West, M. (2022). The impact of supportive leadership on employee outcomes during organizational mergers: An organizational-level field study. *Journal of Applied Psychology*. Advance online publication. https://doi.org/10.1037/apl0001042

Cao, Li, van der Wal, and Taris conducted a meta-analysis on the impact of leadership on workplace aggression, including incivility, employee interpersonal mistreatment, and bullying. They found that *"change-oriented, relational-oriented, and values-based and moral leadership (but not task-oriented leadership) were associated with reduced workplace aggression."*

- Cao, W., Li, P., C. van der Wal, R., & W. Taris, T. (2022). Leadership and workplace aggression: A meta-analysis. *Journal of Business Ethics*. Advance online publication. https://doi.org/10.1007/s10551-022-05184-0

Mazzetti and Schaufeli conducted a longitudinal study of how "engaging leaders" were better able to enable employee engagement and team effectiveness. *"Engaging leaders inspire, strengthen, and connect their followers, thereby satisfying their basic psychological needs of autonomy, competence, and relatedness, respectively."* The engaging-leader construct is based on the highly-respected self-determination theory of Deci and Ryan. Mazzetti and Schaufeli note that engaging leaders create impacts at both the individual and team levels.

- Mazzetti, G., & Schaufeli, W. B. (2022). The impact of engaging leadership on employee engagement and team effectiveness: A longitudinal, multi-level study on the mediating role of personal- and team resources. *PLoS ONE, 17*(6), Article e0269433. https://doi.org/10.1371/journal.pone.0269433

Bedi conducted a meta-analysis on leader outcomes and found (1) that leaders demonstrating morality and benevolence produced positive outcomes, and (2) leaders who exhibited authoritarian behaviors induced negative outcomes.

- Bedi, A. (2020). A meta-analytic review of paternalistic leadership. *Applied Psychology: An International Review, 69*(3), 960–1008.

Kim, Beehr, and Prewett did a meta-analysis on empowering leadership and found that leaders who were *"encouraging subordinates to take initiative, emphasizing subordinates' focus on goals, showing confidence in subordinates in order to increase their sense of self-efficacy and motivation, and providing developmental support in order to enhance subordinates' skills,"* produced the best outcomes.

- Kim, M., Beehr, T. A., & Prewett, M. S. (2018). Employee responses to empowering leadership: A meta-analysis. *Journal of Leadership & Organizational Studies, 25*(3), 257–276.

Again, I've chosen these examples largely at random from recent research—and they comprise only a very tiny subset of the research on the importance of good management.

Chapter 16—Managers' Performance Checklist

In this chapter, I shared a seven-item checklist your managers can use to think about the behavior and well-being of their direct reports—and themselves. A long and definite list of research citations could be compiled for each of the seven, but let me share just a few so you can have some trust that these truly represent powerful leverage points.

Employees who don't trust their bosses, coworkers, or organization are not going to be great employees. Here are just a few of many research studies that examine trust.

- Rodriguez, W. A., & Zhou, Z. E. (2023). How supervisor incivility begets employee silence: The role of trust in supervisor and perceived organizational support. *Occupational Health Science.* Advance online publication.

- Kähkönen, T., Blomqvist, K., Gillespie, N., & Vanhala, M. (2021). Employee trust repair: A systematic review of 20 years of empirical research and future research directions. *Journal of Business Research, 130,* 98–109.

- Kim, T.-Y., Wang, J., & Chen, J. (2018). Mutual trust between leader and subordinate and employee outcomes. *Journal of Business Ethics, 149*(4), 945–958.

Employees obviously need resources, tools, equipment, and time to carry out their jobs. Here are a few studies that looked at the importance of time and how it is managed.

- Bedi, A., & Sass, M. D. (2023). But I have no time to read this article! A meta-analytic review of the consequences of employee time management behaviors. *The Journal of Social Psychology, 163*(5), 676–697.

- Yang, M., Chen, H., & Li, S. (2021). The influence of working time characteristics on employee perceptions of physical and mental health: The moderating role of value orientations. *Current Psychology: A Journal for Diverse Perspectives on Diverse Psychological Issues, 40*(12), 6029–6044.

- Wang, X., Li, A., Liu, P., & Rao, M. (2018). The relationship between psychological detachment and employee well-being: The mediating effect of self-discrepant time allocation at work. *Frontiers in Psychology, 9,* Article 2426.

Unhealthy employees have more work-related issues, including absenteeism and productive losses.

- Wu, H., Sears, L. E., Coberley, C. R., & Pope, J. E. (2016). Overall well-being and supervisor ratings of employee performance, accountability, customer service, innovation, prosocial behavior, and self-development. *Journal of Occupational and Environmental Medicine, 58*(1), 35–40.

- Corbière, M., Zaniboni, S., Dewa, C. S., Villotti, P., Lecomte, T., Sultan-Taïeb, H., Hupé, J., & Fraccaroli, F. (2019). Work productivity of people with a psychiatric disability working in social firms. Work: Journal of Prevention, Assessment & Rehabilitation, 62(1), 151–160.

- Grossmeier, J., Mangen, D. J., Terry, P. E., & Haglund-Howieson, L. (2015). Health risk change as a predictor of productivity change. *Journal of Occupational and Environmental Medicine, 57*(4), 347–354.

Obstacles can derail performance, but improvements can be initiated, and employees can make changes to enable themselves to achieve goals.

- Buczel, M., Szyszka, P. D., Siwiak, A., Szpitalak, M., & Polczyk, R. (2022). Vaccination against misinformation: The inoculation technique reduces the continued influence effect. *PLoS ONE, 17*(4), Article e0267463.

- Alter, A. (2023). *Anatomy of a Breakthrough: How to Get Unstuck When It Matters Most.* Simon & Schuster. Adam Alter reviews research on how people and organizations get stuck and suggests a periodic "friction audit" to help get unstuck.

- Datu, J. A. D. (2021). Beyond passion and perseverance: Review and future research initiatives on the science of grit. *Frontiers in Psychology, 11,* Article 545526.

Incentives can impact employee performance significantly, but incentives are tricky because, while they sometimes support desired outcomes, at other times they push people to behave in counterproductive ways. Research has demonstrated that incentives can be effective if well designed.

- Thibault Landry, A., Gagné, M., Forest, J., Guerrero, S., Séguin, M., & Papachristopoulos, K. (2017). The relation between financial incentives, motivation, and performance: An integrative SDT-based investigation. *Journal of Personnel Psychology, 16*(2), 61–76.

A recent book by Uri Gneezy nicely compiles the research on incentives. It's also an enjoyable and useful read.

- Gneezy, U. (2023). Mixed Signals: How Incentives Really Work. Yale University Press.

Employee knowledge, skills, and attitudes are the lifeblood of organizational functioning. Research confirms the obvious: that employee knowledge matters.

- Campbell, J. P., & Wiernik, B. M. (2015). The modeling and assessment of work performance. *Annual Review of Organizational Psychology and Organizational Behavior, 2,* 47–74.

- Moehring, A., Schroeders, U., & Wilhelm, O. (2018). Knowledge is power for medical assistants: Crystallized and fluid intelligence as predictors of vocational knowledge. *Frontiers in Psychology, 9,* Article 28.

- Cokely, E. T., Feltz, A., Ghazal, S., Allan, J. N., Petrova, D., & Garcia-Retamero, R. (2018). Skilled decision theory: From intelligence to numeracy and expertise. In K. A. Ericsson, R. R. Hoffman, A. Kozbelt, & A. M. Williams (Eds.), *The Cambridge handbook of expertise and expert performance* (pp. 476–505). Cambridge University Press.

It's not just individual knowledge that matters, but how well organizations manage their human-resource practices to enable access to knowledge.

- Kehoe, R. R., & Collins, C. J. (2017). Human resource management and unit performance in knowledge-intensive work. *Journal of Applied Psychology, 102*(8), 1222–1236.

There is a ton of research on how people's thoughts and actions can be prompted with environmental stimuli. The books *Nudge* and *Influence* provide a variety of examples, but there are many other prompting methods—for example, through implementation intentions.

- Richard Thaler, Cass Sunstein. *Nudge: The Final Edition*. Learn more at: https://amzn.to/42WBiE8.

- Robert Cialdini, *Influence, New and Expanded: The Psychology of Persuasion*. Learn more at: https://amzn.to/3CRga7z.

- Wieber, F., Thürmer, J. L., & Gollwitzer, P. M. (2015). Promoting the translation of intentions into action by implementation intentions: Behavioral effects and physiological correlates. *Frontiers in Human Neuroscience, 9,* Article 395.

- Hoch, E., Scheiter, K., & Stalbovs, K. (2023). How to support learning with multimedia instruction: Implementation intentions help even when load is high. *British Journal of Psychology, 114*(2), 315–334.

Chapter 17—Stop Your Managers from Demanding Stupid Stuff

In the first example of managers asking for stupid stuff, I mentioned the MBTI, the Myers-Briggs Type Indicator. The MBTI is very popular for leadership training and other soft-skills training. Unfortunately, it is neither valid nor reliable. The same likely goes for DiSC, Strength Finders, and other popular personality diagnostics—for which there is very little scientific research.

The scary part is that the problems with the MBTI have been known for decades. In 2005, Pittenger reviewed the research on the MBTI and concluded with a scathing critique. Here is one example from his article: *"It is not evident that the instrument can compartmentalize accurately, consistently, and unambiguously individuals' personality into the 16 type categories created by the instrument. Consequently, using the MBTI as a consulting tool in corporate settings may be, in some instances, the equivalent of making promises that one cannot keep."*

- Pittenger, D. J. (2005). Cautionary Comments Regarding the Myers-Briggs Type Indicator. *Consulting Psychology Journal: Practice and Research, 57,* 210-221.

Brown and Reilly found that the MBTI was not related to one of the most trusted constructs in leadership research, transformational leadership.

- Brown, F. W., & Reilly, M. D. (2009). The Myers-Briggs Type Indicator and transformational leadership. *Journal of Management Development, 28*(10), 916–932.

Lake, Carlson, Rose, and Chlevin-Thiele found that human-resource practitioners put much more trust in the MBTI than researchers who study organizations. Effect size differences in ratings were huge, d = 1.97 and d = 1.88.

- Lake, C. J., Carlson, J., Rose, A., & Chlevin-Thiele, C. (2019). Trust in name brand assessments: The case of the Myers-Briggs Type Indicator. *The Psychologist-Manager Journal, 22*(2), 91–107.

Recent popular press articles do a good job of reviewing the critiques of the MBTI.

- Degado, C. (2021). *The Problem With the Myers-Briggs Personality Test.* Available at: https://www.discovermagazine.com/mind/the-problem-with-the-myers-briggs-personality-test.

- Grant, A. (2013). *Goodbye to MBTI, the Fad That Won't Die.* Available at: https://www.psychologytoday.com/us/blog/give-and-take/201309/goodbye-mbti-the-fad-won-t-die.

- Al-Shawaf, L. (2021). *Should You Trust the Myers-Briggs Personality Test?* Available at: https://areomagazine.com/2021/03/09/should-you-trust-the-myers-briggs-personality-test/.

Other similar personality diagnostics like the DiSC profile and Strength Finders also have virtually no scientific research published to support them. On the other hand, the Big Five and HEXACO diagnostic instruments are well researched—but are rarely used in organizations, even though they are available for free. While there may be other free versions available, here are two as examples:

- HEXACO: https://hexaco.org/hexaco-online.

- Big Five: https://bigfive-test.com/.

Chapter 18—Technology and Learning

In 1983, Richard Clark did a seminal research review on technology in learning. He reviewed meta-analyses and other findings and concluded that it wasn't the learning media that mattered; it was the learning methods that made all the difference. He got a strong reaction from researchers and practitioners who argued that some learning media might enable additional learning affordances, but the basic point has been repeatedly confirmed in the highest quality research. It's the learning methods that matter. Here are research and research reviews supporting the idea:

- Clark, R. E. (1983). Reconsidering research on learning from media. *Review of Educational Research, 53*(4), 445–459.

- Clark, R. E. (1994). Media will never influence learning. *Educational Technology Research and Development, 42*(2), 21–29.

- Robinson, D. H., & Bligh, R. A. (2016). An Interview with Richard E. Clark. *Educational Psychology Review, 28*(4), 875–891.

Here is the original—and now famous—critique of the media-doesn't-matter idea from Robert Kozma.

- Kozma, R. B. (1991). Learning with media. Review of Educational Research, 61(2), 179–211.

Here is a research review I wrote that examines the comparative benefits of elearning—for example, to classroom training. I reviewed several meta-analyses and other sources and found very strong evidence that, when learning methods are held constant, the learning media doesn't matter. That is, it doesn't matter whether a learning method was presented via elearning or classroom; it's the effectiveness of the learning method that matters. However, I also found that elearning tended to outperform classroom training because elearning developers tended to use more effective learning methods.

- Thalheimer, W. (2017). Does elearning work? What the scientific research says! Available at https://worklearning.com/catalog/.

Here's the secret to this debate. Both can be true. It can be true that learning methods, not media, are what create learning benefits. It can also be true that some learning media enable or nudge the use of better learning methods. I saw this in my research review on elearning. eLearning tended to outperform classroom training unless the learning methods were the same in both—in which case no learning differences emerged.

Here's a nice piece of research showing that the learning media didn't matter for learning effectiveness but did matter in the perception of the learners—which could impact their willingness to engage in future learning.

- Sung, E., & Mayer, R. E. (2013). Online multimedia learning with mobile devices and desktop computers: An experimental test of Clark's methods-not-media hypothesis. Computers in Human Behavior, 29(3), 639–647.

Finally, let me add that Richard Clark published an edited collection of essays on the great methods-vs.-media debate, which highlighted a variety of perspectives but didn't contradict the main conclusions expressed here.

- Clark, Richard E. (Ed). (2012). Learning from media: Arguments, analysis, and evidence, 2nd ed., (pp. 237-248). Charlotte, NC, US: IAP Information Age Publishing, xviii, 256 pp.

In this chapter I also made the claim that neuroscience does not have much to add regarding learning design. I had previously reviewed what neuroscientists themselves have said about neuroscience and learning. In essence, the conclusion is that neuroscience has promise but it is not yet providing practical insights on learning design. As the neuroscientists themselves have argued, without behavioral research neuroscience research cannot provide behavioral recommendations.

- Thalheimer, W. (2016, 2018). Brain Based Learning and Neuroscience: What the Research Says! Available at: https://www.worklearning.com/2016/01/05/brain-based-learning-and-neuroscience-what-the-research-says/.

Chapter 19—Classroom Training vs. eLearning

A few years ago, I reviewed the research on elearning and classroom training and wrote a well-received research-to-practice report on it.

- Thalheimer, W. (2017). Does elearning work? What the scientific research says! Available at: https://www.worklearning.com/catalog/.

I won't repeat here all that I wrote in that 30-page report, but I will say that research on elearning continues to find positive benefits.

Xu, Zhao, Zhang, Liew, and Kogut conducted a recent meta-analysis focused on self-regulated learning for online and blended learning (online and classroom). They looked at young learners, university learners, and workplace learners. They found positive benefits that were consistent with previous meta-analyses on self-directed learning largely focused on classroom learning.

- Xu, Z., Zhao, Y., Zhang, B., Liew, J., & Kogut, A. (2022). A meta-analysis of the efficacy of self-regulated learning interventions on academic achievement in online and blended environments in k-12 and higher education. *Behaviour & Information Technology*. Advance online publication.

Researchers continue to look for ways to improve elearning. Ekuni, Macacare, and Pompeia found that adding retrieval practice helped lessen the problem of learners engaged in multitasking while learning.

- Ekuni, R., Macacare, O. T., & Pompeia, S. (2022). Reducing the negative effects of multitasking on online or distance learning by using retrieval practice. *Scholarship of Teaching and Learning in Psychology, 8*(4), 269–278.

Witherby and Carpenter looked at the verbal and visual quality of recorded lectures delivered online and found that, while an instructor's verbal fluency impacted learner ratings, it did not impact learning. The visual quality of the slides had no impact.

- Witherby, A. E., & Carpenter, S. K. (2022). The impact of lecture fluency and technology fluency on students' online learning and evaluations of instructors. *Journal of Applied Research in Memory and Cognition, 11*(4), 500–509.

Carvalho, McLaughlin, and Koedinger found that giving learners varied spaced practice provides maximum learning benefits in an online learning environment.

- Carvalho, P. F., McLaughlin, E. A., & Koedinger, K. R. (2022). Varied practice testing is associated with better learning outcomes in self-regulated online learning. *Journal of Educational Psychology, 114*(8), 1723–1742.

These examples, picked largely at random, show that elearning is effective and is likely to continue improving in effectiveness if learning-science recommendations are followed.

There are many active and beneficial discussions and research efforts on the strengths and benefits of elearning. Here's one example from Dick Clark, one of the top researchers in learning.

- Clark, R. E., Feldon, D. F. and Jeong, S. (2022), Fifteen Common but Questionable Principles of Multimedia Learning, In R. E. Mayer (Ed.) *The Cambridge Handbook of Multimedia Learning* (Chapter 3). New York: Cambridge University Press.

Chapter 20—Large Course Repositories: Be Very Careful

An additional problem in courses taken voluntarily is that learners who have the most misconceptions— those who need the learning the most—may be more likely to exit a course before completing it.

- Chen, C., Sonnert, G., Sadler, P. M., Sasselov, D., & Fredericks, C. (2020). The impact of student misconceptions on student persistence in a MOOC. *Journal of Research in Science Teaching, 57*(6), 879–910.

Chapter 21—Generative AI: How Learning Can Help

In this chapter, I talked about the impact of AI on organizations and described how organizations' learning teams can help.

As I argued in the chapter, the history of technology demonstrates that general-purpose technologies are rarely stopped—they almost always become integrated into our daily lives. Mustafa Suleyman—AI pioneer and co-founder of two important AI companies, DeepMind and Inflection AI—argues persuasively in his stunning new book, *The Coming Wave,* that both AI and synthetic biology are poised to be widely leveraged, creating both benefits and disruptions. He advocates that we get our butts in gear and be prepared to enable the upside and contain the downside of these technologies.

- Suleyman, M., with Bhaskar, M. (2023). *The Coming Wave: Technology, Power, and the Twenty-First Century's Greatest Dilemma*. Crown.

I focused much of the chapter on the importance of trust and user confidence in the AI systems we will use in our organizations. I based my thoughts on the work of both AI researchers and senior tech leaders working in business.

Researchers are vigorously discussing the concept of trust in AI. Here are just a few examples, quickly selected from a PsycINFO database search.

- Frank, D.-A., Jacobsen, L. F., Søndergaard, H. A., & Otterbring, T. (2023). In companies we trust: Consumer adoption of artificial intelligence services and the role of trust in companies and AI autonomy. *Information Technology & People, 36*(8), 155–173.

- Jang, C. (2023). Coping with vulnerability: The effect of trust in ai and privacy-protective behaviour on the use of ai-based services. *Behaviour & Information Technology.* Advance online publication.

- Bach, T. A., Khan, A., Hallock, H., Beltrão, G., & Sousa, S. (2022). A systematic literature review of user trust in ai-enabled systems: An hci perspective. *International Journal of Human-Computer Interaction.* Advance online publication.

Many voices at a recent conference on the business implications of AI emphasized the importance of trust and confidence. (The conference: Leading with AI Responsibly: Business Conference, held in Boston, October 2023, organized by The Institute for Experiential AI at Northeastern University).

- Ashok Srivastava, Senior Vice President and Chief Data Officer at Intuit. When asked to name the most critical aspect of using AI in customer interactions, Srivastava said "Confidence!"

- Jay Schuren, Chief Customer Officer at Data Robot, said, "I spend most of my time thinking about [customer] confidence."

- Manish Worlikar, Center of Excellence Leader for Artificial Intelligence and Advanced Analytics at Fidelity Institutional, said his biggest fear in using generative AI in their help and recommendation systems was giving wrong answers to customers.

- Peter Norvig—Educational Fellow at the Stanford Institute for Human-Centered Artificial Intelligence (HAI), Engineering Director at Google, and also co-author with Stuart Russell of the most renowned textbook on artificial intelligence— emphasized that it was more important to focus on AI's stakeholders than the internal consistency of AI models.

Along similar lines, at the Effective Altruism Global Conference in Boston, October 2023, there were many sessions on how to ensure AI is safe.

- Abi Olvera—Senior Fellow at the Council on Strategic Risks, Affiliate at the Institute for AI Policy and Strategy (IAPS), and Board Member at Rethink Priorities—highlighted how important AI has become in the government. Every member of the U.S. Congress has a person on staff devoted to AI. All government agencies are ramping up to learn about AI because of the worry about large-scale AI risks.

- Adam Gleave—CEO of Far AI, an AI research organization dedicated to ensuring that AI systems are trustworthy and beneficial to society—and colleague Adrià Garriga-Alonso, Research Scientist, led a talk titled "The Fragility of AI Systems," where they highlighted how AI systems that are "aligned" (tech-talk for being safe or safely within the bounds of their intended use and ethical guidelines) could be exploited by other non-aligned AI systems.

- Stephen Casper, AI Researcher at MIT, talked about how the most ubiquitous way to improve AI models—called RLHF, Reinforcement Learning with Human

Feedback—was not originally seen as a robust solution to AI alignment, but worryingly it is the main tool in use today. His article, written with over 30 other AI researchers, is available here: https://arxiv.org/pdf/2307.15217.pdf.

Many AI experts have pointed out the need for diverse multidisciplinary teams to ensure safe AI implementations. This was highlighted at the Leading with AI Responsibly: Business Conference, in Boston, October 2023.

- Cansu Canca—Director of Responsible AI Practice at the Institute for Experiential AI at Northeastern University, and Founder and Director at the AI Ethics Lab—highlighted the importance of having multidisciplinary teams in working with AI systems, so that diverse perspectives can be considered.

- John Havens—Executive Director of the IEEE Global Initiative on Ethics of Autonomous and Intelligent Systems and author of the book *Heartificial Intelligence*—asked the question, "When we are creating AI systems, who is NOT in the room? What stakeholders are we missing?"

- Philip Brey—Professor of Philosophy and Ethics of Technology at the University of Twente, and winner of the Weizenbaum Award in Ethics and Information Technology—emphasized the importance of a multi-stakeholder approach to AI.

I argued in the chapter that your learning team is critical to helping your organization upskill for the new reality created by generative AI. To put a finer point on it, here's what a recent Harvard Business Review article said, *"Competitive advantage cannot be achieved without humans in the loop. Rushing to replace talent with AI is a huge mistake."*

- Sanders, N. R. & Wood, J. D. (2023). The skills your employees need to work effectively with AI. Harvard Business Review, November 3, 2023. Available at: https://hbr.org/2023/11/the-skills-your-employees-need-to-work-effectively-with-ai.

If employee skills are critical to successfully using AI, then your learning team is ideally poised to partner with your employees in developing both their AI skills and the skills of collaboration and leadership that are required to work in multidisciplinary and multistakeholder teams.

I also talked about the use of AI to support learning. Unfortunately, there is not yet a ton of research on AI's influence in learning. I could find no research reviews from scientific journals. Still, there are widespread concerns about ethics, and bias, and transparency, given the hidden nature of AI algorithms and the hidden patterns of data influencing machine-learning outcomes. Here is a recent article that expresses some of these concerns.

- Kousa, P., & Niemi, H. (2022). AI ethics and learning: Edtech companies' challenges and solutions. *Interactive Learning Environments.* Advance online publication. https://doi.org/10.1080/10494820.2022.2043908.

Despite the current lack of definitive research, AI is clearly going to impact the practice of learning. Donald Clark, one of the learning industry's most advanced thinkers about learning technology, has written a book on AI in learning. He's not just a passionate advocate but he runs a company that sells AI-based learning interventions. I admire Donald's work and recently awarded him the learning industry's most prestigious award for the use of learning research—the Neon Elephant Award.

- Clark, D. (2020). Artificial Intelligence for Learning: How to use AI to Support Employee Development. Kogan Page.

We should also be wary of the potential dangers of AI. There have been notable problems of bias discussed in machine learning. When AI bases its recommendations on data sets derived from human activity—almost all AI datasets—it tends to repeat the same biases we humans have. AI also has the potential to replace human workers, potentially causing catastrophic labor unrest and economic hardship. Because of AI's ability to create text and images, learning professionals may have difficulty sorting truth from deepfakes. Also, there are worries that AI will be controlled by governments or entities that put special interests above the interests of citizens more generally. Here are just a few recent headline articles (in the New York Times):

- Tugend, A. (2023). *Experts on A.I. Agree That It Needs Regulation. That's the Easy Part.* Available at: https://www.nytimes.com/2023/12/06/business/dealbook/artificial-intelligence-regulation.html.

- Clegg, N, & Alderman, L. (2023). *Are Artificial Intelligence and Democracy Compatible?* (Nick Clegg interviewed by Liz Alderman). Available at: https://www.nytimes.com/2023/10/03/world/athens-democracy-ai.html.

- Roose, K. (2023). *Silicon Valley Confronts a Grim New A.I. Metric.* Available at: https://www.nytimes.com/2023/12/06/business/dealbook/silicon-valley-artificial-intelligence.html.

- Marchese, D. (2022). *An A.I. Pioneer on What We Should Really Fear.* Available at: https://www.nytimes.com/interactive/2022/12/26/magazine/yejin-choi-interview.html.

- Metz, C. (2022). *Lawsuit Takes Aim at How AI is Built.* Available at: https://www.nytimes.com/2022/11/23/technology/copilot-microsoft-ai-lawsuit.html.

- Roose, K. (2022). *We Need to Talk About How Good A.I. Is Getting.* Available at: https://www.nytimes.com/2022/08/24/technology/ai-technology-progress.html.

- Roose, K. (2022). *An A.I.-Generated Picture Won an Art Prize. Artists Aren't Happy.* Available at: https://www.nytimes.com/2022/09/02/technology/ai-artificial-intelligence-artists.html.

And of course, other well-known publications are also highlighting the worries people have about artificial intelligence.

- The Economist (2023). *How to worry wisely about artificial intelligence.* Available at: https://www.economist.com/leaders/2023/04/20/how-to-worry-wisely-about-artificial-intelligence.

- New Scientist (2023). Michael Brooks. *The future of AI: The 5 possible scenarios, from utopia to extinction.* Available at: https://www.newscientist.com/article/mg26034691-600-the-future-of-ai-the-5-possible-scenarios-from-utopia-to-extinction/.

- Scientific American (2023). Tamlyn Hunt. *Here's Why AI May Be Extremely Dangerous—Whether It's Conscious or Not.* Available at: https://www.scientificamerican.com/article/heres-why-ai-may-be-extremely-dangerous-whether-its-conscious-or-not/.

Chapter 22—When Training Pollutes

I've written before about the dangers of air travel in training: https://www.linkedin.com/pulse/when-training-pollutes-will-thalheimer/.

Wikipedia has a very nice review of the environmental impact of aviation: https://en.wikipedia.org/wiki/Environmental_impact_of_aviation.

Even airline CEOs are admitting their industry is a problem. See article from Umair Irfan, writing on Vox: https://www.vox.com/2019/11/21/20974722/climate-change-flying-flight-shame-emirates-air-france-emirates-emissions.

And be aware that there is a global community of folks who want to shame people for flying, and this may rise in prominence enough that it could impact the reputation of your company. See this article from Umair Irfan, writing on Vox: https://www.vox.com/the-highlight/2019/7/25/8881364/greta-thunberg-climate-change-flying-airline.

William Wilkes, writing on Bloomberg, has a nice article describing how airplane pollution is getting worse: https://www.bloomberg.com/news/articles/2019-03-10/airline-pollution-is-soaring-and-nobody-knows-how-to-fix-it.

Deborah Braconnier, on the Phys.org website, has a nice article on the dangers of jet contrails: https://phys.org/news/2011-03-airplane-contrails-worse-co2-emissions.html.

Joseph Schmid has a nice article on how plane manufacturers are being pressured to come up with less polluting options: https://phys.org/news/2019-06-slashing-plane-emissions-lofty-goal.html.

Here is where I got the estimate for the amount of carbon used by a family of four: https://www.carbonfootprint.com/minimisecfp.html.

The ISO folks have an environmental management standard, 14001, which you can read about here: https://www.iso.org/publication/PUB100371.html.

Here is a nice handbook, created by the University of British Columbia, that describes the dangers of air travel and recommends solutions. This kind of document seems worth creating for many organizations, not only helping to reduce air pollution, but in saving a ton of money as well: https://greentravel.sites.olt.ubc.ca/files/2019/11/Climate-Change-and-Air-Travel-UBC-Handbook_.pdf.

Here is a nice travel site that enables your employees and your organization to consider environmentally friendly travel options: https://www.bookdifferent.com/en/sustainable-business-travel/.

Here is a travel website that finds local providers across the world who offer sustainable travel opportunities: https://www.lokaltravel.com/.

Here is a carbon calculator you can use to measure the carbon impact of your activities. As a non-expert, I can't verify that this one is best. There are many calculators available online. https://climatecare.org/calculator/.

A recent 2023 United Nations report on climate change, based on the work of hundreds of scientists, shows clearly that climate change is creating severe harm to people all over the world, that human activity is the cause, and that the problems are getting worse: https://report.ipcc.ch/ar6syr/index.html.

Forbes has reported that the health effects of climate change are worse than was thought. See this article in Forbes in 2023 by Arianna Johnson that details the harms that have been hidden: https://www.forbes.com/sites/ariannajohnson/2023/02/16/air-pollution-more-dangerous-than-previously-understood-here-are-the-biggest-health-risks-and-how-to-reduce-it/.

Niraj Chokshi and Clifford Krauss writing in the New York Times reveal that there are no easy technological solutions to reducing pollution from airplanes. https://www.nytimes.com/2021/05/28/business/energy-environment/airlines-climate-planes-emissions.html. We therefore cannot expect some engineering innovation to bail us out—to quickly circumnavigate the reality that air travel for training is adding to the climate crisis.

Chapter 23—Learning Research: Retrieval Practice

Retrieval practice is one of the most studied phenomena in learning research and is universally touted as one of the most important methods to support people in remembering. There are many recent research reviews on retrieval practice—all of them acknowledging its benefits. In each of these research reviews, dozens and dozens of scientific studies are examined. Here is a list of reviews going back a few decades.

- Agarwal, P. K., Nunes, L. D., & Blunt, J. R. (2021). Retrieval practice consistently benefits student learning: A systematic review of applied research in schools and classrooms. *Educational Psychology Review, 33*(4), 1409–1453.

- Latimier, A., Peyre, H., & Ramus, F. (2021). A meta-analytic review of the benefit of spacing out retrieval practice episodes on retention. *Educational Psychology Review, 33*(3), 959–987.

- Roediger, H. L. III, & Karpicke, J. D. (2018). Reflections on the resurgence of interest in the testing effect. *Perspectives on Psychological Science, 13*(2), 236–241.

- Roediger, H. L. III, & Butler, A. C. (2011). The critical role of retrieval practice in long-term retention. *Trends in Cognitive Sciences, 15*(1), 20–27.

- Roediger, H. L. III, & Karpicke, J. D. (2006). The power of testing memory: Basic research and implications for educational practice. *Perspectives on Psychological Science, 1*(3), 181–210.

- Bjork, R. A. (1988). Retrieval practice and the maintenance of knowledge. In M. M. Gruneberg, P. E. Morris, R. N. Sykes (Eds.), Practical Aspects of Memory: Current Research and Issues, Vol. 1., Memory in Everyday Life (pp. 396-401). NY: Wiley.

To fully appreciate the power of retrieval practice, we need to examine the typical experimental conditions used in retrieval-practice research. I know for most of you this level of detail may feel like overkill, but I'm adding it for those who want to dig deep into the science of learning and remembering.

Let's use a study from Pooja Agarwal, Jeffrey Karpicke, Sean Kang, Henry Roediger, and Kathleen McDermott—all members of Henry Roediger's team at the Washington University in St. Louis. Before I describe the experiment, here is the citation.

- Agarwal, P. K., Karpicke, J. D., Kang, S. H. K., Roediger, H. L. III, & McDermott, K. B. (2008). Examining the testing effect with open- and closed-book tests. *Applied Cognitive Psychology, 22*(7), 861–876.

In their study's first experiment, they had learners read prose passages once and then gave some of them various forms of retrieval practice. Note that I'm describing only some of the experimental conditions they used so I can communicate their findings clearly.

After reading the passages, some learners got a closed-book test, and some got an open-book test. The test consisted of questions requiring short answers. Testing creates retrieval practice. It nudges learners to retrieve what they've learned from their long-term memory. That is the essence of retrieval practice.

The results showed the following. People who did not read a passage scored about 18% correct, presumably responding based on what they knew on their own. People who read the passage without being tested—that is, without being provided with retrieval practice—later scored 46% on the test. Those who got a test later scored about 64% correct.

So, let's look at the learning improvements. Being able to study the passage—that is, spending time in learning—improved test results from 18% to 46%, a substantial improvement. Indeed, the 46% score is a 156% improvement over the 18% no learning score. For those of us thinking about whether training can make a difference, we should be delighted that getting people to process—in this case, read—the learning material improved their knowledge significantly!

So far, we haven't looked at the extra benefits of retrieval practice. What the study showed was that retrieval practice improved results from 46% correct to 64% correct—a percentage improvement of 39%. Now please remember that this is just one study and results will vary. Still, the thing we should understand is that this 39% improvement was created by using a better learning design—by using a simple method to provide learners with retrieval practice. To summarize, in this one study, retrieval practice was better than restudying the material by 39%, and it was 156% better than just being exposed to the material—more than doubling learning results.

Other studies have shown that retrieval practice produces varying levels of improvement, and almost always creates benefits. To give you a sense of these benefits, I'm going to tell you about a number of studies, which I selected largely at random—choosing from some recent studies and from some classic ones I studied in the past. I will include the full research citations in a list below.

- Stamate, Sala, Baddeley, Logie (2022), in two separate experiments, found that retrieval practice compared to no retrieval practice improved memory retention after one month by 103% and 109% for older adults and 23% and 46% for younger adults. This finding is even more remarkable in that the retrieval practice was not for the exact concept to be tested later, but, rather, the retrieval practice was drawn from another concept from a prose passage—a story—that learners were instructed to remember.

- Sana and Yang (2022) found retrieval practice improved remembering by 15% when questions were divided into topics (small effect size of 0.30) and 34% when questions were interleaved—when questions were mixed by topic—(medium effect size of 0.7).

- Sumeracki and Castillo (2022), in their first experiment, found retrieval practice compared with restudying improved remembering by 45% and produced a large effect size of 1.24 when learners had to write down their answers, but only 4% when they were allowed to think of their answers. In their second experiment, both written and mentally generated answering improved remembering by 72% and generated large effect sizes of 1.13 for written answers and 1.01 for covert answers.

- Gupta, Pan, and Rickards (2021), who had learners learn word pairs and used many experimental conditions, found retrieval practice compared to restudying the word pairs improved remembering by 70%, 46%, 44%, 34%, 52%, and 40%, for an average improvement of 48%.

- Roediger and Karkpicke (2006) had learners learn short prose passages and, either two days later or one week later, recall everything they could remember. Retrieval practice proved more effective than extra study time by 26%, 33%, 40%, and 53%—an average improvement of 38%—with large effect sizes of 0.95, 0.83, 1.26, and 0.82.

- Butler and Roediger (2007) presented learners with recorded videos of lectures and allowed them to take notes as they might in a real classroom. After watching the lectures, some of the learners studied an outline of the main learning points, took a multiple-choice test, or took a short answer test. One month later, the multiple-choice test produced better learning by 80% compared to watching the lecture alone but was no better than the opportunity for extra study. The short-answer test—another retrieval-practice method—produced improvement of 135% compared to the lecture alone, and a 31% retrieval-practice benefit.

- Jones (1923-1924), over many studies, found that spending five minutes at the end of a 55-minute lecture asking learners questions—giving them retrieval practice without feedback—increased remembering by an average of 52% compared to asking no questions.

- Runquist (1983), in three separate experiments, had learners learn word pairs and explored whether testing them on the word pairs produced benefits. Learners who were tested—compared to those who were not tested—showed improvements in remembering of 813%, 139%, 184%, 167%, 135%, 192%, and 356% depending on the amount of delay after learning.

- Karpicke and Roediger (2008), having learners learn Swahili–English word pairs, found that having multiple retrieval practice opportunities was 132% better than having only one retrieval practice opportunity.

- Butler and Roediger (2008) found that the benefits of retrieval practice were enhanced when learners got feedback—a topic we'll discuss later. Without feedback, test-induced retrieval practice improved learning by 200%. Adding immediate feedback improved learning by 291%, and delayed feedback improved learning by 391%.

Here are the full research citations for the studies just outlined.

- Stamate, A., Della Sala, S., Baddeley, A. D., & Logie, R. H. (2022). The effect of selective retrieval practice on forgetting rates in younger and older adults. *Psychology and Aging, 37*(4), 431–440.

- Sana, F., & Yan, V. X. (2022). Interleaving retrieval practice promotes science learning. *Psychological Science, 33*(5), 782–788.

- Sumeracki, M. A., & Castillo, J. (2022). Covert and overt retrieval practice in the classroom. *Translational Issues in Psychological Science, 8*(2), 282–293.

- Gupta, M. W., Pan, S. C., & Rickard, T. C. (2022). Prior episodic learning and the efficacy of retrieval practice. *Memory & Cognition, 50*(4), 722–735.

- Roediger, H. L. III, & Karpicke, J. D. (2006). Test-enhanced learning: Taking memory tests improves long-term retention. *Psychological Science, 17*(3), 249–255.

- Butler, A. C., & Roediger, H. L. III. (2007). Testing improves long-term retention in a simulated classroom setting. European Journal of Cognitive Psychology, 19(4-5), 514–527.

- Jones, H. E. (1923-1924). Experimental studies of college teaching: The effect of examination on permanence of learning. *Archives of Psychology, 10*, 1-70.

- Runquist, W. N. (1983). Some effects of remembering on forgetting. *Memory & Cognition, 11*(6), 641–650.

- Karpicke, J. D., & Roediger, H. L. III. (2008). The critical importance of retrieval for learning. *Science, 319*(5865), 966–968.

- Butler, A. C., & Roediger, H. L. III. (2008). Feedback enhances the positive effects and reduces the negative effects of multiple-choice testing. *Memory & Cognition, 36*(3), 604–616.

The research I reviewed above shows clearly that retrieval practice produces profound improvements in learning and remembering. The average of improvements of all the above findings—and please remember that I just sampled willy-nilly from a variety of retrieval practice studies—is well over 100%, more than doubling the learning results!

Now be careful! This doesn't guarantee that your learning team will double its learning results by using retrieval practice! Remember: I picked studies almost at random, or rather studies that were cited often by researchers or that were just well researched and written.

Also, let me add some perspective here. When I look at the studies that found really large improvements, many of them were using learning materials that were *not* like the learning content we would teach in a typical training course. For example, they might be examining relatively low-level knowledge like word pairs—when we as workplace learning professionals are typically teaching higher-level concepts and more complex skills.

But even if your learning team got only one-fifth of the benefits that were found in these research studies—just one-fifth—they'd still get improvements of more than 25% by adding retrieval practice. If they did better and got one-half of the benefits reported above, they would achieve more than 65% improvements in learning by adding retrieval practice. These are very large improvements!

The bottom line is that retrieval practice produces learning improvements, and your learning team can easily provide more retrieval practice in their learning designs.

Chapter 24—Learning Research: Spacing Learning Over Time

Harry Bahrick and Linda Hall, researchers who focused on the spacing effect, said this about the spacing effect: *"The spacing effect is one of the oldest and best documented phenomena in the history of learning and memory research."*

- Bahrick, H. P., & Hall, L. K. (2005). The importance of retrieval failures to long-term retention: A metacognitive explanation of the spacing effect. *Journal of Memory and Language, 52*(4), 566–577.

Note that Bahrick and Hall said that back in 2005, citing research by Bruce and Bahrick who, in 1992, counted the number of scientific articles on the spacing effect and found 321 studies. Every year since, more scientific studies are published—around 10 per year. Why do researchers find the spacing phenomenon so intriguing? Why do learners who get the same learning events—some repeated after long intervals, some with shorter intervals—remember better? There are many theories about the causal factors involved, which is why scientists keep studying the phenomenon.

There have been many meta-analyses and research reviews spanning decades that have confirmed the power of spaced repetitions

- Kim, S. K., & Webb, S. (2022). The effects of spaced practice on second language learning: A meta-analysis. *Language Learning*. Advance online publication.

- Maddox, G. B. (2016). Understanding the underlying mechanism of the spacing effect in verbal learning: A case for encoding variability and study-phase retrieval. *Journal of Cognitive Psychology, 28*(6), 684–706.

- Küpper-Tetzel, C. E. (2014). Understanding the distributed practice effect: Strong effects on weak theoretical grounds. *Zeitschrift für Psychologie, 222*(2), 71–81.

- Cepeda, N. J., Pashler, H., Vul, E., Wixted, J. T., & Rohrer, D. (2006). Distributed practice in verbal recall tasks: A review and quantitative synthesis. *Psychological Bulletin, 132*(3), 354–380.

- Dempster, F. N., & Farris, R. (1990). The spacing effect: Research and practice. *Journal of Research & Development in Education, 23*(2), 97–101.

- Underwood, B. J. (1961). Ten years of massed practice on distributed practice. *Psychological Review, 68*(4), 229–247.

Harry Bahrick did some of the most amazing research on spacing and the "maintenance of knowledge." In one classic study—Bahrick, Bahrick, Bahrick, and Bahrick (1993)—he enlisted the help of his family members over a nine-year period. They tested remembering after one year, two years, three years, and five years. They studied 300 word-pairs in English and in either French or German, depending on the family member. Three wanted to study French; one wanted to study German. They got spaced repetitions after 14 days, or 28 days, or 56 days. The results were remarkable. For example, after five years, those who got the 14-day repetitions remembered 50% of the words; those with 28-day repetitions remembered 59%; those with 56-day repetitions remembered 67%. The 28-day repetitions produced 19% better remembering than the 14-day repetitions, whereas the 56-day repetitions produced 34% more remembering. These results show a typical finding: longer practice intervals tend to produce more remembering.

- Bahrick, H. P., Bahrick, L. E., Bahrick, A. S., & Bahrick, P. E. (1993). Maintenance of foreign language vocabulary and the spacing effect. *Psychological Science, 4*(5), 316–321.

The spacing effect is such a fundamental part of human cognition that it has also been studied in fields outside of learning—for example, marketing and advertising.

- Janiszewski, C., Noel, H., & Sawyer, A. G. (2003). A meta-analysis of the spacing effect in verbal learning: Implications for research on advertising repetition and consumer memory. *Journal of Consumer Research, 30*(1), 138–149.

- Noel, H., & Vallen, B. (2009). The spacing effect in marketing: A review of extant findings and directions for future research. *Psychology & Marketing, 26*(11), 951–969.

The spacing effect has been shown to have an impact in children, too, not just adults.

- Vlach, H. A. (2014). The spacing effect in children's generalization of knowledge: Allowing children time to forget promotes their ability to learn. *Child Development Perspectives, 8*(3), 163–168.

The spacing effect has been studied by neuroscientists.

- Ojea Ramos, S., Andina, M., Romano, A., & Feld, M. (2021). Two spaced training trials induce associative ERK-dependent long term memory in Neohelice granulata. *Behavioural Brain Research, 403*, Article 113132.

- Kim, A. S. N., Wiseheart, M., Wong-Kee-You, A. M. B., Le, B. T., Moreno, S., & Rosenbaum, R. S. (2020). Specifying the neural basis of the spacing effect with multivariate ERP. *Neuropsychologia, 146*, Article 107550.

- Naqib, F., Sossin, W. S., & Farah, C. A. (2012). Molecular determinants of the spacing effect. *Neural Plasticity, 2012*, Article 581291.

The spacing effect was also found in Ebbinghaus's classic memory studies.

- Ebbinghaus, H. (1885/1913). *Memory: A contribution to experimental psychology*, (Translated by H. A. Ruger and C. E. Bussenius). New York: Teachers College, Columbia University. (Also available 1964 and 1987, New York: Dover Publications. Original published in 1885).

Note that there is some debate in the research community about whether there is a difference between spacing repetitions over time by providing downtime between repetitions (no intentional learning events between repetitions) or providing other content to learn between repetitions. This is a relatively recent issue and is still being debated, so I'm not drawing this distinction here. For those interested, you can check out this recent exchange:

- Chen, O., Paas, F., & Sweller, J. (2021). Spacing and interleaving effects require distinct theoretical bases: A systematic review testing the cognitive load and discriminative-contrast hypotheses. *Educational Psychology Review, 33*(4), 1499–1522.

- Sana, F., Yan, V. X., & Carvalho, P. F. (2022). On rest-from-deliberate-learning as a mechanism for the spacing effect: Commentary on Chen et al. (2021). *Educational Psychology Review*. Advance online publication.

- Chen, O., Paas, F., & Sweller, J. (2022). Reply to Sana et al.'s (2022) commentary on rest-from-deliberate-learning as a mechanism for the spacing effect. *Educational Psychology Review*. Advance online publication.

- Rohrer, D., & Hartwig, M. K. (2020). Unanswered questions about spaced interleaved mathematics practice. *Journal of Applied Research in Memory and Cognition, 9*(4), 433–438.

Here are more specific research results from studies on spacing, that I compiled from recent research and from my 2006 research review on spaced learning.

Yamagata, Nakata, and Rogers (2022) had learners who were learning a second language attempt to learn collocated word phrases—for example, "make mention" and "draw a line." It has been shown these collocated words are critical to second-language learning. Over three weeks, they repeated practice either within the same day or over three weeks. They found that spacing the repetition over three weeks improves remembering two weeks later by 156%, a very large improvement.

Katz, Ando, and Wiseheart (2021) had people learn a song—one specifically created for the experiment so that previous learning could be ruled out. After they had been given ample opportunity to learn the song, they then got extra review and practice. Some got this 10-minute review and practice 10 minutes after the original learning session, some got it two days later, and the rest got it one week later. Results showed a clear advantage for the two spaced conditions. The proportion of those who remembered at least half the lyrics improved from the unspaced condition by 55% and 84% for the two-day spacing and 88% and 84% for the one-week spacing. The proportion of those who remembered at least half of the notes improved from the unspaced condition by 37% and 112% for the two-day spacing and 67% and 62% for the one-week spacing.

Krug, Davis, and Glover (1990) asked learners to study a written essay and then gave them an additional five minutes to study the passage either immediately (unspaced) or in one week (spaced). Across three experiments, those in the spaced conditions remembered 40%, 38%, and 30% more of the essay than those in the unspaced conditions.

Singh, Mishra, Bendapudi, and Linville (1994) found that television commercials that were repeated after four intervening commercials (spaced) produced better memory the following day than commercials that were repeated with only one intervening commercial (less-spaced) by 18% for younger adults and 160% for older adults.

Bloom and Shuell (1981) presented learners with three distinct 10-minute exercises to help them learn the same 20 French vocabulary words. The 10-minute exercises were presented back-to-back or spaced over three days. The spaced learning produced only 5% improvement on an immediate test, but 35% improvement on a surprise test given seven days later.

Roediger and Challis (1992) presented learners with lists of words with items repeated after zero intervening items (massed repetitions) or after 9, 10, 21, or 31 intervening items, depending on the experiment. In measuring free recall in three different experiments (Experiments 2, 3, and 4), the spaced repetitions—when they were exact repetitions—produced improvements of 16%, 29%, and 32% over massed repetitions.

Rothkopf and Coke (1963) had learners learn information from short sentences. When the sentences were repeated immediately, those repetitions produced better recall by about 15% than non-repeated sentences (those presented only once). But if the repetition for these sentences was repeated after other unrelated sentences had been presented, improvements in recall more than doubled to 33%.

In a series of experiments simulating the effects of print advertisements, Appleton-Knapp, Bjork, and Wickens (2005) presented people with a series of ads and varied the number of times these ads were presented. Five to eight minutes later they asked people whether they could remember the name of the brand associated with a particular advertising slogan. What they found over three separate experiments was that ads repeated verbatim showed definite spacing effects, with immediate repetitions producing an average of 20% recall, repetitions after 20 seconds producing 33% recall, repetitions after 40 seconds producing 41% recall, and 10-minute repetitions producing 44% recall.

Here are the research citations for the research discussed above:

- Yamagata, S., Nakata, T., & Rogers, J. (2022). Effects of distributed practice on the acquisition of verb-noun collocations. *Studies in Second Language Acquisition.* Advance online publication. https://doi.org/10.1017/S0272263122000225

- Katz, J. J., Ando, M., & Wiseheart, M. (2021). Optimizing song retention through the spacing effect. *Cognitive Research: Principles and Implications, 6,* Article 79. https://doi.org/10.1186/s41235-021-00345-7

- Krug, D., Davis, T. B., & Glover, J. A. (1990). Massed versus distributed repeated reading: A case of forgetting helping recall? *Journal of Educational Psychology, 82*(2), 366–371.

- Singh, S., Mishra, S., Bendapudi, N., & Linville, D. (1994). Enhancing memory of television commercials through message spacing. *Journal of Marketing Research, 31*(3), 384–392.

- Bloom, K. C., & Shuell, T. J. (1981). Effects of massed and distributed practice on the learning and retention of second-language vocabulary. *The Journal of Educational Research, 74*(4), 245–248.

- Roediger, H. L., & Challis, B. H. (1992). Effects of exact repetition and conceptual repetition on free recall and primed word-fragment completion. *Journal of Experimental Psychology: Learning, Memory, and Cognition, 18*(1), 3–14.

- Rothkopf, E. Z., & Coke, E. U. (1963). Repetition interval and rehearsal method in learning equivalences from written sentences. *Journal of Verbal Learning & Verbal Behavior, 2*(5-6), 406–416.

- Appleton-Knapp, S. L., Bjork, R. A., & Wickens, T. D. (2005). Examining the Spacing Effect in Advertising: Encoding Variability, Retrieval Processes, and Their Interaction. *Journal of Consumer Research, 32*(2), 266–276.

Here is the citation for my research review on the spacing effect—the one I mentioned above:

- Thalheimer, W. (2006, February). *Spacing Learning Events Over Time: What the Research Says.* Available at: https://worklearning.com/catalog/.

Chapter 25—Learning Research: Simulating the Work Context

Context alignment—known by different names in the learning research—is a fundamental aspect of human cognition. There is no doubt that contextual stimuli trigger thoughts, actions, and emotions. Researchers are still teasing apart some of the subtleties, but, in general, learning that is designed to link contextual cues with desired thoughts and actions is likely to produce performance benefits.

Steven Smith did a wide range of research using the label "context-dependent memory."

- Smith, S. M., & Vela, E. (2001). Environmental context-dependent memory: A review and meta-analysis. *Psychonomic Bulletin & Review, 8*, 203-220.

- Smith, S. M., Glenberg, A., and Bjork, R. A. (1978). Environmental context and human memory. *Memory and Cognition, 6*, 342-353.

- Smith, S. M. (1979). Remembering in and out of context. *Journal of Experimental Psychology: Human Learning and Memory, 5*, 460-471.

- Smith, S. M. (1982). Enhancement of recall using multiple environmental contexts during learning. *Memory & Cognition, 10*, 405-412.

- Smith, S. M. (1984). A comparison of two techniques for reducing context-dependent forgetting. *Memory & Cognition, 12*, 477-482.

- Smith, S. M. (1985). Background music and context-dependent memory. *American Journal of Psychology, 98*, 591-603.

- Smith, S. M. (1988). Environmental context-dependent memory. In G. M. Davies & D. M. Thomson (eds.) *Memory in Context: Context in Memory* (pp. 13-34), Chichester, UK: Wiley.

Though Smith's work was instrumental in putting a focus on context, it was not the first realization that context matters. For example, in 1926, Shuh Pan from the University of Chicago studied context and learning.

- Pan, S. (1926). The influence of context upon learning and recall. *Journal of Experimental Psychology, 9*(6), 468–491.

Context has been central to other major research paradigms related to learning and cognition, including in Tulving's encoding-specificity principle and Bransford's "transfer-appropriate processing" notion.

- Tulving, E., & Thompson, D. M. (1973). Encoding specificity and retrieval processes in episodic memory. *Psychological Review, 80*, 352-373.

- Bransford, J. D., Franks, J. J., Morris, C. D., & Stein, B. S. (1979). Some general constraints on learning and memory research. In L. S. Cermak & F. I. M. Craik (Eds.), *Levels of processing in human memory* (pp. 331-354). Hillsdale, NJ: Erlbaum.

Context alignment was one of the earliest learning factors I wrote about. In my 2002 research-to-practice report—updated in 2009—I highlighted the power of aligning the learning-and-performance contexts, while also reviewing research that showed when the effect was more likely and less likely.

- Thalheimer, W. (2002, 2009). *Aligning the learning and performance context*: Creating spontaneous remembering. Available at: https://www.worklearning.com/catalog/.

Researchers are continuing to examine the circumstances in which context has its most potent impact. To share a recent example, Ensor and colleagues examined two accounts of context effects in recognition memory and found evidence that supported one theory and contradicted another.

- Ensor, T. M., Surprenant, A. M., Neath, I., & Hockley, W. E. (2022). Using preexperimental familiarity to compare the ICE and cue-overload accounts of context-dependent memory in item recognition. *Journal of Experimental Psychology: Learning, Memory, and Cognition.* Advance online publication.

Another recent study showed that virtual reality can create context effects. Shin and colleagues found a 23% improvement in recall when learners learned and retrieved information from the same context, using virtual reality contexts as background. They also showed that useful information was more likely to produce this effect.

- Shin, Y. S., Masís-Obando, R., Keshavarzian, N., Dáve, R., & Norman, K. A. (2021). Context-dependent memory effects in two immersive virtual reality environments: On Mars and underwater. Psychonomic Bulletin & Review, 28(2), 574–582.

Virtual reality—which can simulate work contexts—seems an ideal tool to use in aligning the learning context to the performance context and is well worth pursuing. But note that virtual reality doesn't always produce benefits. As Shin and colleagues warned: *"...the use of VR does not guarantee a context-dependent memory effect."* The design of the virtual reality interface, content, and activity is critical.

Using simulation to support learning is perhaps the most iconic use of context alignment. Of course, we can also align learning-and-performance contexts with hands-on practice and scenario decision-making. Still, there is something about simulations that energizes our imaginations. In our video games we have flight simulators and war simulators, among other simulations. There are popular movies—especially technology-focused action movies that feature simulation-based learning. *Top Gun* was a box-office smash, but it was based on a real-world simulation—the US Navy's Top Gun school, which significantly improved pilots' ability to be successful in dogfights. Where Navy pilots who learned in the Top-Gun simulation improved their kill-rate success by about six times—a 500% improvement—Air Force pilots who had not gotten simulation training showed no improvement.

- Chatham, R. E. (2009). *20th-Century Revolution in Military Training.* In K. Anders Ericsson (Ed.) Development of Professional Expertise.

The most studied use of simulations is in medical training, where there are numerous meta-analyses that support the benefits of simulation. Simulation training has been shown to improve learning, lower anxiety, and increase self-confidence, among other advantages. Here are a few randomly selected meta-analyses in medical education:

- Oliveira Silva, G., Oliveira, F. S. e, Coelho, A. S. G., Cavalcante, A. M. R. Z., Vieira, F. V. M., Fonseca, L. M. M., Campbell, S. H., & Aredes, N. D. A. (2022). Effect of simulation on stress, anxiety, and self-confidence in nursing students: Systematic review with meta-analysis and meta-regression. *International Journal of Nursing Studies, 133,* 1–15.

- Brydges, R., Manzone, J., Shanks, D., Hatala, R., Hamstra, S. J., Zendejas, B., & Cook, D. A. (2015). Self-regulated learning in simulation-based training: A systematic review and meta-analysis. *Medical Education, 49*(4), 368–378.

- Hatala, R., Cook, D. A., Zendejas, B., Hamstra, S. J., & Brydges, R. (2014). Feedback for simulation-based procedural skills training: A meta-analysis and critical narrative synthesis. *Advances in Health Sciences Education, 19*(2), 251–272.

Interestingly, mental simulations have recently been shown to influence attitudes. Normally our focus in learning is on information or on how knowledge is improved. But here, we see that simulations can influence attitudes as well. People can be nudged to develop—we might say "learn"—to change their attitudes. Paulus, Dabas, Felber, and Benoit prompted people to mentally simulate scenes by pairing people they liked with locations they did not like, and vice versa. By mentally simulating these scenes that contained people and locations, people's attitudes toward the locations improved if paired with people they liked—and worsened if paired with people they didn't like. These kinds of results show that aligning the learning-and-performance context is facilitative generally, not just for knowledge.

- Paulus, P. C., Dabas, A., Felber, A., & Benoit, R. G. (2022). Simulation-based learning influences real-life attitudes. *Cognition, 227,* 1–6.

Now let's turn our attention to the likely percent improvements your learning team might be expected to garner by aligning the learning context to the performance context.

Weiss and Margolis did a remarkable study where they had people learn to associate two-part nonsense syllables (for example, "mot-fud") with four-letter words (like "ring"). This experiment was done a long time ago, before computers were available, so they put the words on cards of different colors. The nonsense syllables were put on the left side of the card and the four-letter words were put on the right side of the card. The right side of the card was covered so learners could guess the four-letter word while seeing the nonsense syllables on the left side of the card. The learners practiced all the pairings until they got them all correct.

A day later, they had to recall the four-letter words while looking at the nonsense syllables. Here's where it got interesting. Sometimes people were presented with the nonsense syllables and the four-letter words on cards that were the same color as those they had learned from the day before. Sometimes the card color was colored gray. That is, sometimes mot-fud and ring were on the same yellow card they had seen the day before. Sometimes they were presented on a gray card.

The results were stunning. Those who saw the pairs on the same-colored cards recalled an average of 7.37 of the 9 possible words. Those who saw the pairs on a gray card recalled only 3.25 words on average. The color context had improved memory by 127%!

Interestingly, presenting the colored cards without any of the nonsense syllables resulted in learners able to recall an incredible 5.37 words. These folks saw completely blank cards! The background context alone was sufficient to trigger remembering.

In one of the most iconic research studies on context-dependent memory, Smith, Glenberg, and Bjork (1978) found that, when people were in the room where they had learned the words, they recalled 28% and 41% more words than when they were in a different room. Effect size improvements were huge, at 2.25 and 1.41.

The following year, Smith found improvements of 30% and 50% when asking learners to remember in the same place they had learned compared to in a different place. Effect size improvements were large, at 0.95 and 1.11.

Godden and Baddeley found that scuba divers who were asked to learn on land or 30 feet underwater were better able to remember what they'd learned in the same context—on land or underwater—with a 47% improvement when asked to remember in the different context. Effect size was large at 1.04.

Grant, Bredahl, Clay, Ferrie, Groves, McDorman, and Dark found context-supported improvements on short-answer tests of 29% and multiple-choice tests of 13% when the contexts were noisy or silent environments. Effect sizes were large, at 0.94 and 1.02.

Marian and Neisser found that having bilingual learners remember in the same language in which they had been taught improved memory by 105% and 53% compared to remembering in the different language. Effect sizes were very large, at 1.65 and 1.30.

Interestingly, it has also been shown that using multiple contexts can improve learning. In a separate experiment to the one already reported, Smith, Glenberg, and Bjork showed that presenting learners with a list of words to memorize in two different rooms improved memory performance by 53% over learning the words in the same-room context twice (a whopping effect-size improvement of 3.80). Smith (1982) found a similar effect in Experiment 1, showing 32% better performance when people learned a list of words in four rooms rather than in just one. In Experiment 3, Smith (1982) found that people who learned in three rooms outperformed people who learned in just one room by 24%, though the difference did not reach statistical significance.

Here are the research citations for the research cited above:

- Weiss, W., & Margolis, G. (1954). The effect of context stimuli on learning and retention. *Journal of Experimental Psychology, 48*, 318-322.

- Smith, S. M., Glenberg, A., and Bjork, R. A. (1978). Environmental context and human memory. *Memory and Cognition, 6*, 342-353.

- Smith, S. M. (1979). Remembering in and out of context. *Journal of Experimental Psychology: Human Learning and Memory, 5*, 460-471.

- Godden, D. R., and Baddeley, A. D. (1975). Context dependency in two natural environments: on land and underwater. *British Journal of Psychology, 91*, 99-104.

- Grant, H. M., Bredahl, L. C., Clay, J., Ferrie, J., Groves, J. E., McDorman, T. A., & Dark, V. J. (1998). Context-dependent memory for meaningful material: Information for students. *Applied Cognitive Psychology, 12*, 617-623.

- Marian, V., & Neisser, E. (2000). Language-dependent recall of autobiographical memories. *Journal of Experimental Psychology: General, 129*, 361-368.

- Smith, S. M. (1982). Enhancement of recall using multiple environmental contexts during learning. *Memory & Cognition, 10*, 405-412.

The results above represent a small subset of the research on context alignment in learning. As the researchers themselves have demonstrated, some contexts are more powerful than others in creating effects. Some learning tasks are more amenable. In my 2002-2009 review I took these inconsistencies into account and estimated that, on average, context alignment was likely to improve learning results by 5-40%. There has been much research done since then, so I can't responsibly advocate for those numbers today, but certainly well-designed practice that targets salient real-world contexts is likely to produce significant improvements in workplace remembering.

What's truly remarkable about the findings above is that the contexts studied were often peripheral to the tasks to be accomplished. How is it that noise, music, smells, and locations had an impact? The contexts were almost incidental, yet they created profound effects. The rooms in the Smith, Glenberg, and Bjork study were just background; they had no relationship to the task of learning. Indeed, in most of these experiments, what fascinated the researchers was that incidental background context had any impact at all.

As learning professionals, we can certainly use incidental background to improve learning—but what's even more powerful is using relevant context. To use one example, in learning algebra, the algebra-equation context is more potent than the classroom context in which the algebra is taught.

To maximize improvements, learning architects should first study which cues are most important in people's work contexts. Realistic practice should focus on the contextual elements that are most central to the task. If we do this well, we are likely to see significant improvements in learning simply due to context alignment—well over the 40% range I reported back in 2002.

Chapter 26—Learning Research: Feedback for Learning

In this chapter, I highlighted another major learning factor: providing feedback to learners. Here in the chapter notes, I will outline some of that research. I once spent hundreds of hours over many months compiling the research on feedback. It was probably the most daunting research translation work I have done. I ended up splitting my research review into two parts—the amount of research on feedback is immense. Here are my two contributions.

- Thalheimer, W. (2008, May). Providing Learners with Feedback—Part 1: Research-based recommendations for training, education, and e-learning. Available at: https://worklearning.com/catalog/.

- Thalheimer, W. (2008, May). Providing Learners with Feedback—Part 2: Peer-reviewed research compiled for training, education, and e-learning. Available at: https://worklearning.com/catalog/.

There are a ton of research reviews and meta-analyses on feedback in the scientific literature. Here are a few recent examples.

The most influential recent review was conducted by Wisniewski, Zierer, & Hattie and published in 2020. They concluded that feedback was a powerful learning factor, with an overall effective size of 0.48. They also noted that feedback was also a very complex phenomenon. *"Feedback cannot be understood as a single consistent form of treatment."* Their meta-analysis also revealed that *"feedback has higher impact on cognitive and motor skills outcomes than on motivational and behavioral outcomes."*

- Wisniewski, B., Zierer, K., & Hattie, J. (2020). The power of feedback revisited: A meta-analysis of educational feedback research. *Frontiers in Psychology, 10,* Article 3087.

Elaborative feedback, in general, has been found to be more effective than just telling learners the correct answer or allowing them to answer until they get the correct answer.

- Mertens, U., Finn, B., & Lindner, M. A. (2022). Effects of computer-based feedback on lower- and higher-order learning outcomes: A network meta-analysis. *Journal of Educational Psychology, 114*(8), 1743–1772.

Researchers have begun to speculate that feedback will have more benefits if it better aligns with learners' cognitive and emotional needs.

- Ryan, T., Henderson, M., Ryan, K., & Kennedy, G. (2021). Designing learner-centred text-based feedback: A rapid review and qualitative synthesis. *Assessment & Evaluation in Higher Education, 46*(6), 894–912.

Feedback is a very active research area, as represented in the following scientific articles, so we should expect further recommendations in the coming decade.

- Panadero, E. (2023). Toward a paradigm shift in feedback research: Five further steps influenced by self-regulated learning theory. *Educational Psychologist, 58*(3), 193–204.

- Van der Kleij, F. M., & Lipnevich, A. A. (2021). Student perceptions of assessment feedback: A critical scoping review and call for research. *Educational Assessment, Evaluation and Accountability, 33*(2), 345–373.

- Huang, C., Tu, Y., Han, Z., Jiang, F., Wu, F., & Jiang, Y. (2023). Examining the relationship between peer feedback classified by deep learning and online learning burnout. *Computers & Education, 207*, 1–18.

There is also work being done on workplace feedback—outside of formal learning—that has implications for employee performance and potentially for workflow learning. For example, here is a recent meta-analysis and an experimental study.

- Katz, I. M., Moughan, C. M., & Rudolph, C. W. (2023). Feedback orientation: A meta-analysis. *Human Resource Management Review, 33*(4), 1–17.

- Xing, L., Sun, J.-M., Jepsen, D., & Zhang, Y. (2023). Supervisor negative feedback and employee motivation to learn: An attribution perspective. *Human Relations, 76*(2), 310–340.

Chapter 27—The Performance Sciences

To highlight the potential and ubiquity of the performance sciences, I will share citations for 25 mainstream nonfiction books from recent years—books I have read (almost all more than once) and found extremely valuable. You can purchase these books at many places or find them in your local library. To make it easy for you to learn more about each book, I've included a link to the books on the United States version of Amazon. Authors are listed in alphabetic order by first name.

- Adam Grant. *Think Again: The Power of Knowing What You Don't Know.* Learn more at: https://amzn.to/3NVzO9b.

- Annie Murphy Paul. *The Extended Mind: The Power of Thinking Outside the Brain.* Learn more at: https://amzn.to/3Pwaw2A.

- Atul Gawande. *The Checklist Manifesto: How to Get Things Right.* Learn more at: https://amzn.to/3JxBkLY.

- BJ Fogg. *Tiny Habits: The Small Changes That Change Everything.* Learn more at: https://amzn.to/46jIDk8.

- Damon Centola. *Change: How to Make Big Things Happen.* Learn more at: https://amzn.to/42XLrAk.

- Daniel Kahneman, Olivier Sibony, Cass Sunstein. *Noise: A Flaw in Human Judgment*. Learn more at: https://amzn.to/3Jqw0K3.

- Daniel Kahneman. *Thinking, Fast and Slow*. Learn more at: https://amzn.to/44iNwbc.

- Daniel Pink. *Drive: The Surprising Truth About What Motivates Us*. Learn more at: https://amzn.to/3NLDl9D.

- David McRaney. *How Minds Change: The Surprising Science of Belief, Opinion, and Persuasion*. Learn more at: https://amzn.to/3qZvRHn.

- Eric Johnson. *The Elements of Choice: Why the Way We Decide Matters*. Learn more at: https://amzn.to/42W4nj8.

- Ethan Kross. *Chatter: The Voice in Our Head, Why It Matters, and How to Harness It*. Learn more at: https://amzn.to/3NM4MjG.

- John Bargh. *Before You Know It: The Unconscious Reasons We Do What We Do*. Learn more at: https://amzn.to/3NMUfoH.

- Jonah Berger. *The Catalyst: How to Change Anyone's Mind*. Learn more at: https://amzn.to/3qZQW4u.

- Judson Brewer. *Unwinding Anxiety: New Science Shows How to Break the Cycles of Worry and Fear to Heal Your Mind*. Learn more at: https://amzn.to/448RpzK.

- Katy Milkman. *How to Change: The Science of Getting from Where You Are to Where You Want to Be*. Learn more at: https://amzn.to/3JzojkX.

- Leidy Klotz. *Subtract: The Untapped Science of Less*. Learn more at: https://amzn.to/3PqlJl9.

- Loran Nordgren, David Schonthal. *The Human Element: Overcoming the Resistance That Awaits New Ideas*. Learn more at: https://amzn.to/3r1ImCj.

- Malcolm Gladwell. Talking to Strangers: What We Should Know About the People We Don't Know. Learn more at: https://amzn.to/3JxAEpY.

- Nir Eyal. *Indistractable: How to Control Your Attention and Choose Your Life*. Learn more at: https://amzn.to/44fUzl1.

- Olivier Sibony, You're About to Make a Terrible Mistake!: How Biases Distort Decision-Making and What You Can Do to Fight Them. Learn more at: https://amzn.to/46ouySD.

- Richard Thaler, Cass Sunstein. *Nudge: The Final Edition*. Learn more at: https://amzn.to/42WBiE8.

- Robert Cialdini, *Influence, New and Expanded: The Psychology of Persuasion*. Learn more at: https://amzn.to/3CRga7z.

- Steven Pinker. Rationality: *What It Is, Why It Seems Scarce, Why It Matters*. Learn more at: https://amzn.to/3qVNsQp.

- Wendy Wood. *Good Habits, Bad Habits: The Science of Making Positive Changes That Stick*. Learn more at: https://amzn.to/44bIDkV.

- Will Storr. *The Status Game: On Human Life and How to Play It*. Learn more at: https://amzn.to/44gG6VX.

Chapter 28—Performance Activation from Within the Work Context

In this chapter, I specified six categories of performance activators. In developing these, I relied on years and years of reading and studying articles from scientific refereed journals and from research-inspired nonfiction books. To recount all the research would take years of investment and the list would still be incomplete given the many sources that influenced my thinking over the six-plus decades of my lifetime.

Still, let me give credit to Jerry Hamburg, my colleague when I was an employee briefly at TiER1 Performance. As I worked on a model to guide learning professionals to think beyond training and consider the work-performance context—what I called the "Performance-Activation Model" or "PA Model"—Jerry jumped with me into a crucible of joyous critical dialogue and helped me refine the ideas.

Thanks also to LDA (the Learning Development Accelerator) and ISPI (the International Society of Performance Improvement) for inviting me to speak about this work at their annual conferences—enabling me to hear more feedback and think with more wisdom about the idea of performance activation.

In the chapter, I used a nautical metaphor—that we humans are like sailboats on the ocean, conscious of the impact of the wind on our behavior and unaware of the influence of the tides.

If you don't like my nautical metaphor, I hope you'll grant me some grace. I wrote this chapter while sitting in a cottage on the coast of Maine. The rest of this chapter note reflects how I was thinking at the time.

<u>Written in the summer of 2022:</u> I have an eerie bodily sensation of floating up and down in the waves. Yesterday, I took my solo canoe out to a nearby island and got caught in a very bad situation: big waves coming at me from two angles. Suddenly, a wave appeared from my left side. My canoe got swamped and I was thrown overboard. As I went underwater, I thought, "This is how people drown." As I plunged beneath the cold North Atlantic water, this thought about drowning seemed to stretch slowly through time toward an infinite horizon.

As I came up out into the air, I saw my stuff scattered about, floating away, and my canoe 10 feet toward shore. The context must have reminded me of my decades-old summer-camp boat-safety training. "Stay with your boat." I swam to my canoe; it was upside-down and filled with water. Waves washed over me and over the canoe as I clung to it. I looked around and noticed my kayak paddle—the one I knew I would need to paddle safely away from the island—was 20 feet behind me in a vortex of angry white waves.

Nobody could see me; there were none of the normally ubiquitous lobster boats within view. The island had one house on it, but it was on the leeward side away from the open ocean, and I was hidden from its view. My tackle box was sinking out of reach; my water bottle and one of my water shoes were too far away to grab.

Then I saw where my canoe and I were headed; the same direction as the waves that were crashing violently against the night-black rock face of the shore, just 50 feet away.

I remembered then that a woman had been killed by a great white shark nearby on the other side of Bailey Island just last year. I tipped my upside-down canoe slightly to add air beneath it so it wouldn't sink. I noticed a small break in the rocks 200 feet down the shore, a place where maybe I could avoid being crushed against the dark foreboding rocks. My canoe and I weren't headed there, but I thought maybe I could swim the boat in that direction fast enough to avoid having the ocean grind me into the barnacles on the face of the rocks.

After a few minutes of dragging the boat, I had enough evidence to gauge my geometric trajectory. My inner Pythagoras calculated that it was too close to call. Maybe the canoe and I would find rocks and waves and barnacles and blood; or, more hopefully, maybe we'd reach rocks and the soft bed of seaweed and shallow water where I could stand up and lift the canoe out of the water into the sky.

At first, I had the canoe in one hand and was swimming beside it—pulling it along. Then I got on top of it, thinking maybe this would move us more quickly, also thinking that maybe, by riding higher in the water, I might be more protected if a great white shark happened to swim nearby. It was as if I was astride a stallion, pushing the great green horse forward with the most powerful frog kicks I could muster. A canoe filled with water moves very, very slowly.

I felt well prepared, reminiscing about the many years my young teenage daughter and I had participated in the "Wacky Canoe Races" at the Rockywold-Deephaven Camps on Squam Lake in New Hampshire. She and I had always done well. Every year we raced the same races. The first race always had us paddling forward. The next race we went backward. Each race was different—we then switched places, then jumped out and got back in, then used no paddles, one person using their hands at the front of the canoe, the other jumping up and down on the seat at the back of the canoe to propel it forward. Then there was the final race—the race that prepared me for my current predicament—the race that really tested our strength and endurance. It was the swamped canoe race, pushing a thousand pounds of canoe through the golden lake-water to the finish line.

I wondered whether my daughter, now grown, would make the connection to our Wacky-Canoe training if my body and canoe were found mangled on the shore. I'll never forget what she said to me as she became an older teenager. Knowing teenagers, one year I suggested she could do the Wacky-Canoe Race without me—with her cousins or aunt or someone else. "No, Dad; the Wacky-Canoe Race is our thing."

It's funny what pops into our heads as we face danger. I didn't feel scared, but I knew my life might end here. On the other hand, my mind seemed to be cranking along in productive ways. I kept the boat moving. I thought of my wife and daughter, my mom and dad, my siblings—but not to the detriment of the mission, to getting myself and the canoe to the relatively quieter waters down the shore.

I did think about my age. Being 64, I considered that my strength and endurance had been slowly degrading for years. I did feel good that I'd rejoined my gym post-COVID a few months before, and that my occasional trail running, tennis, bicycling, and canoeing had kept me reasonably fit. I also thought of the swimming I was doing right then and there, glad that I had finally gotten in the water.

Swimming in the cold Maine water is one of my favorite things—almost spiritual in its importance, given the many years I'd been coming to Maine, swimming with my grandfather and my sister and family, swimming to Pole Island and back when I was 16, having remembered what my father said to me when I was six years old: "When you can swim to Pole Island like your grandfather, then you don't have to wear a life preserver."

I made it. My canoe and I limped toward the relatively quiet part of the shore beyond the sharp perpendicular rocks. I basked in the glorious golden bed of seaweed and the bright rays of the sun. I put on my one remaining water-shoe—the one I was able to grab soon after resurfacing—to help me find a solid purchase so I could stand. It took several attempts to lift the canoe and get the water out. The waves were still fomenting chaos, knocking me off balance at random cycles. The rocks were uneven and the seaweed was slippery. Also, as I began to realize,

I was in a slightly weakened state. The good news was that my backup paddle had stayed in the canoe, under the canoe as I rode it without a saddle. Finally, I was able to lift the canoe into the sky and let the ocean drain out before righting the ship and heading home.

So, even if my nautical metaphor seemed like a stretch, please embrace it! It comes from a special place—one where I am still feeling my body afloat on the waves. Also, note the freedom there is for folks like me who publish their own books. There's no robotically ruthless editor redacting the truth or the soul or the fun from our writings.

Chapter 29—Prompting and Performance-Support Tools

In the classic book *The Checklist Manifesto*, Atul Gawande provides example after example of how simple checklists help humans perform better. As Gawande points out, most human workplace failures can be separated into failures of ignorance (not knowing) and failures of ineptitude (screwing up even because our minds are unfocused or tuned to the wrong thoughts or stimuli). This book revolutionized work in medicine, pilot training, and other high-importance skills. Indeed, as a testament to its continuing influence, even though it was published in 2009, still today it is the #1 book on Amazon in hospital administration and in general surgery.

There are also many examples of research articles supporting the benefits of prompting tools.

- Choi, E., & Johnson, D. A. (2022). Common antecedent strategies within organizational behavior management: The use of goal setting, task clarification, and job aids. *Journal of Organizational Behavior Management, 42*(1), 75–95.

- Hadady, L., Klivényi, P., Perucca, E., Rampp, S., Fabó, D., Bereczki, C., Rubboli, G., Asadi-Pooya, A. A., Sperling, M. R., & Beniczky, S. (2022). Web-based decision support system for patient-tailored selection of antiseizure medication in adolescents and adults: An external validation study. *European Journal of Neurology, 29*(2), 382–389.

- Fletcher, K. A., Bedwell, W. L., Frick, S. E., & Telford, B. N. (2018). Enhancing training with well-designed checklists. *International Journal of Training and Development, 22*(4), 289–300.

- Alpendre, F. T., Cruz, E. D. d. A., Dyniewicz, A. M., Mantovani, M. d. F., Silva, A. E. B. d. C. e, & Santos, G. d. S. d. (2017). Safe surgery: Validation of pre and postoperative checklists. *Revista Latino-Americana de Enfermagem, 25,* Article e2907.

Of course, as with all interventions, prompting tools must be designed to maximize their effectiveness. For example, not just any checklist will do.

- Hales, B., Terblanche, M., Fowler, R., & Sibbald, W. (2008). Development of medical checklists for improved quality of patient care. *International Journal for Quality in Health Care, 20*(1), 22–30.

Even for checklists that are developed by experts and used in sophisticated decision-making, some checklists are superior to others.

- Cwik, J. C., Papen, F., Lemke, J.-E., & Margraf, J. (2016). An investigation of diagnostic accuracy and confidence associated with diagnostic checklists as well as gender biases in relation to mental disorders. *Frontiers in Psychology, 7,* Article 1813.

Checklists, of course, must be utilized to create benefits, so it's not enough to create a checklist—they must be implemented in a way to encourage their use. Research has demonstrated that the use of checklists is not always optimum.

- Nilsen, E. R., Söderhamn, U., & Dale, B. (2019). Facilitating holistic continuity of care for older patients: Home care nurses' experiences using checklists. *Journal of Clinical Nursing, 28*(19-20), 3478–3491.

- Appleby, B. E. (2019). Implementing guideline-checklists: Evaluating health care providers intentional behaviour using an extended model of the theory of planned behaviour. *Journal of Evaluation in Clinical Practice, 25*(4), 664–675.

Decision-support systems—even when they offer evidence-based recommendations—can be ignored by users. In this study, 99% of the time, clinicians ignored or overrode the suggestion of the system.

- Singhal, S., Krishnamurthy, A., Wang, B., Weng, Y., Sharp, C., Shah, N., Ahuja, N., Hosamani, P., Periyakoil, V. S., & Hom, J. (2022). Effect of electronic clinical decision support on inappropriate prescriptions in older adults. *Journal of the American Geriatrics Society, 70*(3), 905–908.

Augmented reality—for example, the ability to overlay prompts or helpful visuals using specialized eyewear—has been shown to be useful in supporting learning, as represented in the following two meta-analyses.

- Baashar, Y., Alkawsi, G., Ahmad, W. N. W., Alhussian, H., Alwadain, A., Capretz, L. F., Babiker, A., & Alghail, A. (2022). Effectiveness of using augmented reality for training in the medical professions: Meta-analysis. *JMIR Serious Games, 10*(3), 1–13.

- Cai, Y., Pan, Z., & Liu, M. (2022). Augmented reality technology in language learning: A meta-analysis. *Journal of Computer Assisted Learning, 38*(4), 929–945.

There are some concerns about cognitive load, as evidenced in the research reviews below, but augmented reality seems to have potential to be useful in both learning and in performance support.

- Suzuki, Y., Wild, F., & Scanlon, E. (2023). Measuring cognitive load in augmented reality with physiological methods: A systematic review. *Journal of Computer Assisted Learning.* Advance online publication.

- Buchner, J., Buntins, K., & Kerres, M. (2022). The impact of augmented reality on cognitive load and performance: A systematic review. *Journal of Computer Assisted Learning, 38*(1), 285–303.

Chapter 30—Research and Practice in Learning

In this chapter, I made the claim that *"I have spent close to 20,000 hours studying, compiling, and reporting on the learning research."* I should probably back that up with evidence. How do I know how many hours I've spent absorbed in the research? Here are my calculations. Admittedly, estimations.

- Eight years in my Columbia University, Teachers College doctoral program. Assuming I read and studied research 15 hours a week for 40 weeks of the year. Total is thus 4,800 hours.

- 25 years at Work-Learning Research and TiER1 Performance reading, studying, compiling research—averaging 200 hours a year. Note: I remember—after doing my work at Work-Learning Research for a handful of years—I estimated I was spending 400 hours a year reading and compiling the research. I am using the lower figure of 200 to be conservative and because I later did less research in some years. Total, using the 200-hour figure, is thus 5,000 hours.

- 25 years at Work-Learning Research and TiER1 Performance creating presentations, workshops, and writing posts and articles about the research. I'm estimating that I did this for 10 hours a week for 40 weeks of each year. This was, and still is, a large part of my work. Total is thus 10,000 hours.

- These figures do not include any time from my 5.5 years as an undergraduate student at West Chester State, Michigan, and Penn State, nor my two years at Drexel getting an MBA and taking courses on instructional design. Certainly, I read some research during these years, but, to be conservative, I won't include it.

- Total estimated hours using the conservative estimates above is 19,800 hours in reading, studying, compiling, using, and presenting on the learning and performance research. That's practically 20,000 hours! Take that, Malcolm Gladwell!

- FYI, Malcolm Gladwell once popularized the 10,000-hour rule, which claimed that world-class performers needed to spend 10,000 hours to reach the highest levels of competence. The theory has been mostly debunked, with findings that the number of hours needed varies across people and by the skill being performed. Hours matter, but also genetics, innate ability, age of early experience, and type of practice/reflection matter too. Some, like me, require extra hours just to reach modest heights of competence. Wink-wink.

- Gladwell, M. (2011). *Outliers: The Story of Success.* Available at: https://amzn.to/44pA4Db.

Why does a research-loving guy like me suggest that L&D teams not read the scientific research themselves? Essentially, because it's too hard!

Like any other complex skill in life, reading journal articles takes training, practice, and experience. There is scientific terminology to learn, statistics to master, research methodology to grasp, and a background in human cognition to comprehend. These skills on their own take years to master! Just as importantly, a person can't read one or two research articles and fully comprehend the meaning of what they're reading. The human sciences are complex because human behavior is infinitely complex.

Of course, you may have a few people on your learning team with the skills to read the research. Let them go ahead if they have the time. Overall, however, there's just no sense in buying your learning team access to scientific journals and having them use valuable time in reading the research.

Chapter 31—Separating Good Research from Bad

Let me provide a few real examples that show how survey research in the learning field causes problems. I won't reveal the perpetrators—the problem is endemic, so it wouldn't be fair to call out these folks specifically.

Here is a question on an industry survey on learning evaluation.

What types of measures do you use to support your evaluation goals?
- *Perception (satisfaction, instructor or format performance, etc.).*
- *Efficiency (completions, enrollment, score, etc.).*
- *Effectiveness (behavior change, on-the-job actions, etc.).*
- *Business Impact (business outcome measures).*
- *We do not have evaluation goals.*
- *I don't know.*

The problem here is that the question doesn't ask about learning factors that might be measured. This is a blackhole-sized oversight that gets respondents thinking too narrowly about learning evaluation and produces data for which the most important constructs have been sucked into oblivion. Because learning professionals must gather data on learning to get feedback they can leverage to maintain and improve effectiveness, this question simply gets respondents and report readers thinking all wrong about learning evaluation!

I was asked recently by a doctoral student to provide feedback on a draft survey—one that will be sent to several thousands of learning professionals. It's not finalized yet, but the guy's dissertation advisor is insisting he only use questions from previously utilized surveys. Unfortunately, the previous surveys were poorly designed. Here's a question that is being contemplated:

Select all levels of evaluation that are used to any extent in your organization.
- *Level 1 (Reaction)—The learner's reaction to the training.*
- *Level 2 (Learning)—The change in the learner's attitude, knowledge, or skills.*
- *Level 3 (Behavior/OJTP)—The learner's ability to apply knowledge, skills, and attitudes to their on-the-job performance.*
- *Level 4 (Results)—The impact on organizational goals or metrics.*

- *Level 5 (ROI)—Financial impact of the training.*
- *None of the above.*

Egads! This is terrible! It reinforces the 1960s-era thinking around learning evaluation. It also, by using the model labels, pushes respondents to think at a surface level, focusing on the labels and likely ignoring the more specific words and meaning behind those labels—thus creating biased and corrupted data. In addition, by smashing all learning metrics into one category (that is, "Level 2 Learning"), the question leaves out important nuances. For example, it does not distinguish between measures of recognition, knowledge, decision-making competence, or skills.

One more. This survey question asks learning professionals to select the practices they have used most frequently. I've modified the question slightly to simplify it and protect the identity of the group who created it.

What processes does your team employ in the design and/or development of your [learning] assets?

- *ADDIE.*
- *Agile.*
- *Design Thinking.*
- *Gagne's Nice Events.*
- *Lean Startup.*
- *Systems View Diagramming.*
- *Understanding by Design.*
- *(And there were several more options as well).*

The answer choices limit what learning professionals might consider selecting, and several of the most proven processes are not even included. For example, where is Cathy Moore's Action Mapping? Where are David Merrill's Five Principles of Instruction? Where are the HPT and HPI models?

In this chapter, I mentioned a few examples of how research on human performance can improve organizational functioning, including brainstorming and onboarding.

Brainstorming has been thoroughly researched, and the findings show that brainstorming individually is more effective than brainstorming in groups.

- Mullen, B., Johnson, C., & Salas, E. (1991). Productivity loss in brainstorming groups: A meta-analytic integration. *Basic and Applied Social Psychology, 12*, 3–23.

- Diehl, M., & Stroebe, W. (1987). Productivity loss in brainstorming groups: Toward the solution of a riddle. *Journal of Personality and Social Psychology, 53*, 497–509.

Brainstorming electronically—rather than in person—has been shown to improve creativity in many situations.

- DeRosa, D. M., Smith, C. L., & Hantula, D. A. (2007). The medium matters: Mining the long-promised merit of group interaction in creative idea generation tasks in a meta-analysis of the electronic group brainstorming literature. *Computers in Human Behavior, 23*(3), 1549–1581.

Interestingly, it matters who is brainstorming. Adding star performers to groups significantly improves groups' creative ideas.

- Kenworthy, J. B., Marusich, L. R., Paulus, P. B., Abellanoza, A., & Bakdash, J. Z. (2020). The impact of top performers in creative groups. *Psychology of Aesthetics, Creativity, and the Arts.* Advance online publication. https://doi.org/10.1037/aca0000365

The following article by long-time creativity researcher Paul Paulus and colleagues provides an excellent overview of how creative ideas can be generated within organizational contexts—and is available to anyone using the link below.

- Paulus, P. B., Baruah, J., & Kenworthy, J. B. (2018). Enhancing collaborative ideation in organizations. *Frontiers in Psychology, 9,* Article 2024. https://doi.org/10.3389/fpsyg.2018.02024.

Onboarding new employees—sometimes called "induction" in parts of the world—is critical for the longevity, satisfaction, and productivity of new hires. Research shows that just providing new hires with information is not enough; that social and emotional considerations are important for success.

- Bauer, T. N., & Erdogan, B. (2011). Organizational socialization: The effective onboarding of new employees. In S. Zedeck (Ed.), *APA handbook of industrial and organizational psychology, Vol. 3. Maintaining, expanding, and contracting the organization* (pp. 51–64). American Psychological Association.

- Klein, H. J., Polin, B., & Sutton, K. L. (2015). Specific onboarding practices for the socialization of new employees. *International Journal of Selection and Assessment, 23*(3), 263–283.

Of course, this doesn't mean socialization is the only critical goal of onboarding; learning new ways of thinking and acting may also be important.

- Becker, K., & Bish, A. (2021). A framework for understanding the role of unlearning in onboarding. *Human Resource Management Review, 31*(1), Article 100730.

Chapter 32—Using A-B Testing in Learning

A-B testing uses the scientific method, especially as practiced by social scientists—scientists who deal with we humans and our vagaries. The ideal is to control for extraneous noise and variability by comparing two things that have only one difference between them. When we compare two things that have multiple differences, we won't know which of the factors is making a difference or whether it's some combination of factors that is making the difference. Of course, because complexity is commonplace, sometimes we must first compare more complex things.

The scientific method is essentially a way to gain accurate knowledge. We begin by observing something in the world, and we make conjectures about what is causing what. These conjectures scientists call "hypotheses."

Note the tone of the word "hypotheses." Scientists know that we humans are imperfect observers. We may think we know what causes what, but the world is so complex that we might be wrong in our conjectures. To gain some sense of certainty, we must test our conjectures under rigorous conditions—for example, by comparing two things that differ in only one way. If you want to learn more, Wikipedia has a nice description, and it relies on our donations, so please consider making a contribution.

- https://en.wikipedia.org/wiki/Scientific_method

Be careful about the common connotation of the scientific method as some techno-mechanistic creation of bookwormy gearheads. In truth, we humans are built with a brain that operates on the scientific method. Even babies in the crib are working to figure out how the world works—what causes what.

- Gopnik, A., Meltzoff, A. N., & Kuhl, P. K. (1999). *The scientist in the crib: Minds, brains, and how children learn.* William Morrow & Co.

- Gweon, H. (2021). Inferential social learning: Cognitive foundations of human social learning and teaching. *Trends in Cognitive Sciences, 25*(10), 896–910.

Of course, this doesn't mean we humans don't need help in perfecting our ability to think scientifically.

- Winne, P. H. (2022). Modeling self-regulated learning as learners doing learning science: How trace data and learning analytics help develop skills for self-regulated learning. *Metacognition and Learning.* Advance online publication. https://doi.org/10.1007/s11409-022-09305-y

Those who know more and know better—they tend to do better. This has always been true. In our world today, we see this play out in experimentation, iterations, and agile project management. We now try to fail faster. We do this by testing our hypotheses.

Here's a question we might ask: Why should learning teams do A-B testing when scientists are doing A-B testing all the time, and they're better at it? Great question! Here's my answer: In practice, not everybody has access to the science. Not everybody agrees with the science or makes accurate interpretations of the science. Even when members of your learning team know the science, they may not be able to convince your organizational permission-granters or resource-providers based on the science—but, if a learning team shows that A is better than B with your learners, the icy indifference begins to melt.

And one more thing: Scientists cannot study every little variation in a learning program. Their incentives tend to cleave toward general theories rather than specifics. In the parlance of science, they do basic research much more than they do applied research.

Ideally, your learning team would be able to rely on your learning vendors to do the applied research, but they're not doing it! Their incentives are to get your organization the learning programs or learning tools you ask for—and, as of now, your organization isn't smart enough to ask for programs and tools that are rigorously tested.

Chapter 33—Data Should Help People Make Decisions

In this chapter, I argued that the following key learning outcomes are critical for learning success:

- Whether learners COMPREHEND key concepts and skills.

- Whether learners REMEMBER key concepts and skills.

- Whether learners are MOTIVATED TO APPLY the learning.

- Whether learners can MAKE WORK-REALISTIC DECISIONS.

- Whether learners can PERFORM WORK-REALISTIC TASKS.

- Whether learners ATTEMPT TO PERFORM the newly learned skills IN THEIR WORK.

- Whether, and to what extent, learners are SUCCESSFUL in using their newly learned skills IN THEIR WORK.

In a very real sense, this list represents a causal chain from learning to results. Learners must first engage in learning and pay attention to the learning material in a manner that leads to learning. My dissertation advisor, the legendary Ernie Rothkopf, coined the term "mathemagenic," meaning to give rise to learning. Mathemagenic attention begins the process of learning and enables all the rest.

As learners attend to the learning messages, they must COMPREHEND key concepts and skills clearly and correctly. If they do this, then they must BE PREPARED TO REMEMBER what they've learned and BE MOTIVATED TO APPLY what they've learned. Then, when they encounter key workplace situations, they must REMEMBER and ATTEMPT TO APPLY what they've learned in making appropriate and beneficial DECISIONS and performing WORK TASKS successfully—possibly even overcoming or circumventing any obstacles that might get in the way.

This causal chain of learning outcomes is where your learning team can leverage its efforts in supporting your employees to help them achieve organizational results. It's also where they need to measure their success to maximize learning outcomes.

Let's look at some examples. If a learner pays attention but incorrectly comprehends key concepts, the causal chain breaks before it begins. If, while in training, your employees comprehend incorrectly, they are likely to remember and use that incorrect information as they make decisions. Their decisions and performance will thus be poor, as will their work actions and work outcomes.

Suppose that learning goes further up the causal chain but still breaks down. Learners pay attention and comprehend correctly but later they forget. Or learners pay attention, comprehend correctly, remember, but are not motivated to apply. Or learners pay attention, comprehend correctly, remember, are motivated to apply, make good decisions, and take productive actions but still don't get good results. Each of these breakdowns requires different fixes. But if we don't measure along the causal chain, we won't know which fixes to apply.

The LTEM framework can help in examining learning outcomes because it specifically targets many of these key outcomes. It specifically targets knowledge (LTEM Tier-4), decision-making competence (LTEM Tier-5), task competence (LTEM Tier-6), and work performance (LTEM Tier-7)—and reminds learning teams to focus not just on comprehension but also remembering.

Chapter 34—Learning Evaluation As Decision Support

In this chapter I detailed the LEADS process—Learning Evaluation As Decision Support. Moreover, I specifically detailed over a dozen decision categories to evaluate and, for each one, I described "input data" and "output data." I also detailed the problem of focusing only on output data. While doing that I quoted Jacob

Bernoulli, famous Swiss mathematician: *"One must not decide about the value of human actions from their outcomes."* I also quoted from Olivier Sibony's brilliant book on cognitive biases in business decision-making: *"In many circumstances, there's a lot to be said for the simplicity of focusing on results, and the accountability it creates. But the price we pay for this simplicity is steep."* Both quotes come from Sibony's book.

- Sibony, O. (2019). *You're About to Make a Terrible Mistake!: How Biases Distort Decision-Making and What You Can Do to Fight Them*. Little, Brown Spark of the Hachette Book Group.

For each of the 14 decision categories listed in the chapter, I provide an in-depth discussion, including suggestions for exploring both the input and output data and evidence. While my 14 categories detail decision categories that are critical to the performance of any learning team, the list certainly could be expanded, and I encourage your learning team to add decision categories for which evidence demonstrates their importance.

One warning: The text below is really detailed!

- **Outcome Targeting**

  Focus: Here we determine whether our learning-and-performance initiatives are clearly targeting important outcomes, including business/organizational goals and impacts on key constituencies.

  Input Data: What evidence can we examine to determine how well our initiatives are targeting important goals? At one level we can simply check to see that each program was designed specifically to target important goals. Taking a cue from LTEM Tier-8 recommendations, we can explore whether our programs are specifically designed to provide benefits to (1) learners, (2) coworkers/family/friends, (3) the organization, (4) the community, (5) society, and (6) the environs. Not all constituencies need to be targeted, but we can seek evidence that all were considered and some specific important outcomes were outlined. At a deeper level, we can examine whether the goals we are targeting are truly important to our organization and our various constituencies. We can do this by gathering input through unbiased interviews, surveys, or focus groups of representative knowledgeable stakeholders. We can also utilize rigorous research methodologies, scientific reviews, data analytics, or artificial intelligence to help us evaluate our goal selections.

  Output Data: After our programs have been implemented, how do we evaluate that we've targeted appropriate outcomes? This is difficult. Indeed, because our ultimate outcomes are really our benchmark, it's hard to know how to measure our success in selecting good outcome targets. One method is to gather feedback from our key stakeholders several months after a program has ended and ask whether the original targeted goals were the right ones.

- **Outcome Evaluation**

  Focus: Here we determine whether our programs were effective and whether our evaluation practices are well crafted.

Input Data: To determine whether we are using good learning evaluation practices, we can look to LTEM (described in the next chapter) to guide us. Specifically, we need to measure more than attendance, completion rates, and learner activity. We need to use performance-focused learner surveys instead of surveys focused on learner satisfaction and course reputation. We should also be evaluating beyond learner surveys—periodically measuring critical knowledge, decision competence, task competence, and work performance. We also ought to be using this LEADS approach, focusing first on the decisions to be made and designing our evaluation approach to help us make those decisions.

Output Data: To evaluate our learning programs, we must look at our targeted outcomes and evaluate how we did on these metrics. For work performance and outcome metrics (LTEM Tier-7 and Tier-8), it's critical we isolate the impact of our programs—ensuring that our programs are making a difference outside of effects from the economy, new management practices, operations changes, and all other external factors. Evaluating learning is complex and must be undertaken with rigor and good practices.

- **Behavior Targeting**

  Focus: Here we determine which behaviors are most critical for a particular job—behaviors that can be leveraged for improvement.

  Input Data: What evidence can we use in making behavior targeting decisions? First, we need to focus on a particular job rather than a constellation of jobs. Second, we need specifics, not broad categories of competences. Learning architects can use sophisticated diagnostic methods, such as cognitive task analysis, that break down a job into its constituent parts. Or they can use simpler, less intensive methods to uncover key behaviors—for example, focusing on the best practices of experts and common mistakes on both novices and more experienced workers. The goal is to select key points to target in training, coaching, or experience design. Some useful questions to gauge important job behaviors include the following: *What makes people who are successful in this role effective? What do they do that less-successful people don't do? What common mistakes do new people make? What common mistakes do experienced—but less successful—people make? What skills will people learn on the job even if we don't teach them? What are the top skills people need to be taught so they can avoid the most common mistakes?*

  Output Data: Later, to validate our behavior-targeting decisions, we can pilot our learning or performance-improvement programs and determine whether the behaviors targeted were useful. In evaluating behaviors, we first need to determine whether the behaviors were utilized as envisioned. If they were, we can then evaluate whether they were effective—most pointedly, whether they were more effective than other behavior options.

- **Motivational Targeting**

  Focus: Here we determine the motivational influences that energize people to take deliberate and beneficial actions.

  Input Data: Because motivation is influenced by many factors, we need to look broadly at the individual and situational characteristics that may move people to learn and perform. We can examine things like: (1) people's sense of identity as it relates to the job, (2) their moral/ethical view of the behaviors targeted, (3) their belief in the benefits of the work for the organization, for their team, for society, etc., (4) their sense of self-efficacy in relation to learning and performing the work, (5) the situational cues that exert an influence, (6) the career or job benefits that may accrue, and (7) any financial incentives that may have an influence. Note that asking learners general questions about what motivates them should probably be avoided or should be done with great care because we humans often don't clearly understand what propels us to action.

  Output Data: Motivation can be inferred—albeit imperfectly—from people's observed tenacity, perseverance, and effort. People can also be asked directly about their level of motivation to engage in some work or achieve some goal. To determine which motivational techniques create the best learning and performance, we can do a series of A-B tests—for example, seeing whether reminding people that they care about safety (using their sense of identity to motivate them), is more effective than reminding them that their job success depends on how well they promote safety (using job security as a motivator). By comparing the success of different motivators, we can learn which motivators to utilize with our different audiences and contexts.

- **Solution Selection**

  Focus: Here we are selecting the methods that can be leveraged in supporting people in learning or in their work performance.

  Input Data: Essentially, we are asking about which learning and performance tactics are likely to be effective and workable given the behavior improvement targets we've already outlined. Traditionally—in the past—instead of looking at a broad set of solutions, we would just default to providing training. However, because we have other options besides training, our first step is to list all the learning and performance methods available to us (I've hinted at these options throughout the book and have provided a list in Chapter 44 on learning strategy). We then develop hypotheses on which combination of methods might work—ideally using historical data from previous efforts to make those predictions.

  Output Data: How do we decide whether the learning-and-performance solutions we've chosen were effective? In practice, this is difficult because it's hard to separate the choice of solution from the quality of its implementation. There are several strategies available. We can compare solutions to each other (determining which is best). We can simply assume our solution implementation was of sufficient quality, and then make our conclusions based on targeted outcomes. We can also evaluate the constituent parts of our solution, determining how well each solution tactic added or subtracted from the outcomes.

- **Management Enlistment**

  <u>Focus</u>: Here we are aiming to get managers on board and prepared to provide encouragement, guidance, monitoring, and feedback.

  <u>Input Data</u>: To determine how to enlist managers in support of learning, we first need a checklist of all the things managers can do to support learning—and then determine which of these supports we will need to leverage for our learning initiative. Here's a short list of how managers can help: (1) management permission or acceptance for the learner to apply the learning, (2) management encouragement to apply the learning, (3) management coaching and feedback, (4) management goal setting and monitoring for accountability, (5) management resourcing for critical equipment and supplies, and (6) management requisition for coworker support and encouragement.

  <u>Output Data</u>: To evaluate whether employee managers are providing the targeted supports, the easiest and most straightforward thing we can do is ask their direct reports—our learners/performers—to share their perceptions of those supports using surveys, interviews, focus groups, etc. We can also ask for the manager's assessment of their learning-support actions. Where objective data is available—for example, if there is a goal-setting system that records goals and actions—we might be able to use this data as part of our evaluation efforts.

- **Support Enlistment**

  <u>Focus</u>: Here we are looking to ensure that additional supports and resources are provided and easily accessible.

  <u>Input Data</u>: To determine what additional supports and resources are needed to augment the solutions that have been selected—besides management support, because that is important enough to be in a separate category—we need to first understand the supports available to us. Here's a short list: (1) Resources to apply what was learned, (2) time to apply the learning, (3) organizational prioritization to apply the learning, (4) tangible incentives, (5) needed tools and equipment, (6) changes in rules, principles, and accepted practices, and sometimes even (7) changes in values and work culture. Yes, there are many overlapping elements here involving management support, but that's okay—it's helpful to separate the two because, while they can and should work toward the same ends, they can be marshaled separately.

  <u>Output Data</u>: How do we evaluate these supports, whether they were present and effective, if needed? The simplest way is to survey the learners/performers, but we can also survey their coworkers and managers. We can utilize other methods for gathering perceptions as well, including focus groups, structured interviews, and observations from trained observers. We can also use A-B testing.

- **Content Vetting**

  <u>Focus</u>: Here we are focused on ensuring we are teaching good content and that the

tools we are teaching are useful.

<u>Input Data</u>: How do we get evidence to determine whether the content we aim to teach or incorporate in our performance tools is accurate, backed by science or evidence, and credible to the targeted learners? It's a tough question—sometimes more important to answer than at other times. Sometimes our content is obvious and indisputable. For example, in teaching people how to submit their timesheets, there is likely one good method we can teach, and even if another method might be slightly better, it's just not that important to distinguish between the two. On the other hand, there are many topics that need vetting. If we're teaching people how to safely pick up a heavy package, or how to secure a gas pipe, or how to defuse a bomb, we better damn well validate that our methods are sound. Similarly, interpersonal practices like leadership or coaching often err in following unproven—even if popular—practices, and we would do well to seek research validation by experts before we invest heavily in faulty bromides. Finally, we may need to pilot some of our recommendations with a representative subset of our target learners to determine whether and how our content can be made to seem credible to those audiences.

<u>Output Data</u>: How do we evaluate whether our content was useful? It's difficult because content and learning design and support go hand in hand in creating outcomes. Sometimes it's easy to tell. When we hear people say the new method—even when we see it has been correctly applied—just doesn't work, we know the content was problematic. But often it's more difficult to differentiate content from other factors. When our leadership training fails to achieve all that was hoped, was it the leadership content that failed or the learning design or the after-learning support—or some combination? To separate out the effects of content, we need to design our evaluations to capture data specifically related to content. Alternatively, and probably a better practice, is to test our content recommendations in the pre-decision phase to ensure our content is solid. Then, when we evaluate, we assume the content is solid, but we use a small part of our evaluation efforts to double check—for example, adding an after-learning survey item that assesses whether learners experienced the techniques they learned as effective.

- **Engagement Design**

  <u>Focus</u>: Here we focus on whether our solutions are doing a good job of focusing attention.

  <u>Input Data</u>: How do we decide which learning or performance designs are likely to be effective in getting the attention of our learners—during learning or while working? Oh my! There are hundreds if not thousands of ways to grab and keep learner attention, so gathering input data here may be counterproductive if we try to get too specific. Instead, we ought to ask ourselves some broad questions like: (1) Are the engagement activities meaningful in supporting learning as opposed to being just attention getting?, (2) Will an overwhelmingly large majority of our learners see the activities as useful and relevant to them?, and (3) Do our engagement activities follow

science-based factors that support learning, remembering, action, and perseverance? Output Data: Here we can use learner surveys that ask questions about how well the learning kept people's attention, but we can also go beyond these subjective responses. Trained observers can watch learners in face-to-face learning sessions. When using elearning, we can track learner behaviors to see how long they watch or read learning content, how long they engage in exercises or answer questions, etc.

- **Comprehension Design**

  Focus: Here we are focused on whether learners can correctly and fully comprehend what we teach.

  Input Data: How do we prepare to make decisions about our learning designs that will support our learners in understanding the knowledge and skills targeted for performance? The input data we can look toward are many, including (1) the clarity of the words and descriptions, (2) clear ties to actual work tasks, (3) whether both positive and negative examples are provided (i.e., what to do and what to be careful to avoid), (4) whether worked examples are provided for novices, (5) whether sufficient confirmatory practice is provided (i.e., practice that enables learners to confirm their comprehension), and (6) whether boundary conditions and contingencies are clarified (i.e., are learners clear about when and where principles should be applied).

  Output Data: How do we evaluate learner comprehension? In the LTEM learning-evaluation framework, three levels of comprehension are tracked: knowledge, decision-making, and full task competence (LTEM Tiers 4, 5, and 6). We can test learners on their knowledge using a variety of testing methods. We can provide learners with realistic decision-making exercises or questions. We can ask learners to demonstrate their ability to carry out actual work-relevant tasks.

- **Remembering Design**

  Focus: Here we are focused on whether our learning designs are doing a good job supporting learners in remembering what they've learned.

  Input Data: To support remembering, what should we examine in our learning designs? We should ensure that we keep learners focused on real work situations and realistic tasks and skills. We should provide realistic practice and lots of it. We should spread repetitions of instruction and practice over time. We should focus on providing practice in the most likely performance situations, but also provide some variety within that range of possibilities.

  Output Data: How do we know if our learners have been prepared to remember what they've learned? We must test their actual remembering, preferably waiting a week (or longer) after the main learning ends. Again, LTEM guides us to measure knowledge, decision-making, and task competence—but after a significant time delay (at least three days) to ensure that learners have actually remembered. Care must be taken to measure remembering and not restudying. If learners cram for your delayed tests, you're not measuring remembering—you're measuring the momentary effects of cramming.

- **Action Design**

  Focus: Here we are focused on whether learners are supported in applying what they've learned.

  Input Data: How do we ascertain whether our learning designs include supports for action? We can look at whether (1) our learners will be nudged to formalize their own set of goals for applying the learning to their work, (2) learners will be prompted to set work-context triggers and associate these with specific action plans, (3) learners will be inoculated against obstacles (i.e., practicing how to handle the several likely obstacles they will face), (4) learners will be nudged or required to enlist other people in supporting them or in working together, and (5) prompting tools will be thoroughly practiced to increase the likelihood that they will be used in work situations.

  Output Data: How do we evaluate whether our action designs are working? This is tricky because work performance is the goal of action design as well as the goal of the overall learning-to-performance program! To separate out the benefits of our action designs, we ideally would compare initiatives that utilized our action designs to initiatives that didn't utilize them. We could also do some A-B analyses by comparing one action design to another or several to one, or by tracking compliance on each action-design element. If, for example, we discovered that none of our learners were inoculated against obstacles, but 97% set goals and 93% set context triggers, we would know that inoculation had no impact—and would focus our analysis on the impact of goal setting and trigger setting.

- **Prompting Tool Design**

  Focus: Here we are focused on how well prompting tools like job aids, checklists, and performance support are working.

  Input Data: What input data should we look at for prompting tool design? First, we can do an inventory of all the types of prompting tools and consider which are appropriate for our learning design. Our inventory should include such prompting tools as job aids, checklists, signage, performance-support systems, embedded help systems, information search, visual reminders, time-based reminders, context-based reminders, action planners, and event reviewers. Not all will be relevant, but we likely will want to utilize at least one prompting tool. Also, we should see whether a plan is in place for having learners engage in substantial practice using the chosen prompting tools. And, of course, we ought to determine whether the prompting tool prompts useful thoughts and behaviors. We can do this by getting reviews from experts and/or piloting with real users.

  Output Data: Prompting tool evaluation can have the same issue as action design—when the goal of the whole program is similar to the goal of the prompting tool, it's hard to ascribe the cause to the prompting tool alone. Where the prompting tool supports a subset of actions, this is not an issue. To assess the effects of a prompting tool, we can compare the use of the prompting tool to its non-use or do an A-B test comparing one prompting tool to one or more other tools.

- **Work-Context Performance Activators**

  Focus: Here we focus on the objects in the work context that influence people's thoughts and actions—or could if added or activated.

  Input Data: How can we determine which objects in people's work environments are nudging them to think and act? This is an extremely difficult task given there are thousands of salient stimuli in every setting—some that are already nudging behavior and some that could be if activated. The task becomes even more difficult when we begin brainstorming stimuli we might add to the work situation to support people's thinking and performance. Nevertheless, because contextual stimuli are so influential in human thinking and action, analyzing potential performance activators is critical. We can gain insights on potential sources of activation by looking specifically at: (1) goals and expectations, (2) common phrases, especially if suggestive of desired action, (3) terminology, especially terms that guide or constrain thinking, (4) signs and signage, (5) intuitive cues and affordances of tools and equipment, (6) workspace design, especially aspects that guide or constrain action, (7) work practices, especially those that guide or constrain action, (8) rules and procedures, (9) leader words and behaviors, and (10) organizational mission and stated values. By brainstorming possible activators, we can explore the sources of activation that are likely to have an influence and which sources are likely to be underutilized.

  Output Data: How can we tell which sources of performance activation have made a difference? This is tricky because many activators exert influence at the same time. When we add an activator—say we add a sign to encourage safety—we can compare output measures before and after the activator was added. Same thing when we activate an activator. Activation is the process by which we connect a contextual cue to an action or make such a cue-action connection more accessible in memory. We can also test activators by comparing the outcomes when we activate one and ignore another.

All right! Wow! There are certainly a ton of complexities in what I conveyed above. Don't expect your learning team to quickly utilize or be able to focus on all these decision areas at once. Still, by exploring these decision-making targets, they will see opportunities to get better insights and improve their practices!

Chapter 35—LTEM—The Learning-Transfer Evaluation Model

The LTEM webpage includes the LTEM framework, plus the article I wrote explaining the need for LTEM and recommendations for how to use it, plus a call for LTEM case studies to gather lessons learned. The link is in these first two citations.

- Thalheimer, W. (2018, version 12). *The Learning-Transfer Evaluation Model*. Available at: https://www.worklearning.com/ltem/.

- Thalheimer, W. (2018). The Learning-Transfer Evaluation Model: Sending Messages to Enable Learning Effectiveness. Available at: https://www.worklearning.com/ltem/.

Here is a recent article I wrote about LTEM, reflecting on LTEM's first five years and outlining both its strengths and limitations.

- Thalheimer, W. (2023). *LTEM After Five Years*. Available at: https://www.linkedin.com/pulse/ltem-after-five-years-will-thalheimer/.

Here is a citation for the first doctoral dissertation completed featuring LTEM, researched by Elham Arabi, who is now my dear friend.

- Arabi, E. (2021). *Training design enhancement through training evaluation: Effects on training transfer*. Dissertation Abstracts International: Section B: The Sciences and Engineering, 82(6-B).

Here is a recent scientific article published on LTEM, based on Elham Arabi's dissertation:

- Arabi, E., & Garza, T. (2022). Training design enhancement through training evaluation: Effects on training transfer. *International Journal of Training and Development*. Advance online publication. https://doi.org/10.1111/ijtd.12295

Chapter 36—Performance-Focused Learner Surveys

The second edition of my book, winner of the International Society for Performance Improvement's Outstanding Human Performance Communication in 2022:

- Thalheimer, W. (2022). Performance-Focused Learner Surveys: Using Distinctive Questioning to Get Actionable Data and Guide Learning Effectiveness—Second Edition. Work-Learning Press. Available at Amazon worldwide and in the United States here: https://amzn.to/3x62Zxt.

The original edition of the book, winner of the International Society for Performance Improvement's Outstanding Human Performance Communication in 2016:

- Thalheimer, W. (2016). Performance-Focused Learner Surveys: A Radical Rethinking of a Dangerous Art Form. Work-Learning Press.

Chapter 37—Customer Education

Customer education creates many benefits for organizations that provide it. Sun, Eisingerich, Foscht, Cui, and Schloffer reviewed the research on customer education and found that well-designed customer education can create the following benefits for organizations: *"trust, purchase growth, customer loyalty, customer engagement, positive brand word of mouth, customer engagement and value co-creation for firms."*

They also found important distinctions between learners who are more motivated and those who aren't, and between those who are more experienced and knowledgeable about the product being learned and those who are novices. With experienced users, those motivated to increase their competence might learn better when the learning design "arouses curiosity and enhances enjoyment." For learners who are motivated to share knowledge, the learning design might focus on social interaction and job aids or guidance on how best to help others learn.

- Sun, X., Eisingerich, A. B., Foscht, T., Cui, X., & Schloffer, J. (2022). Why do customers want to learn? Antecedents and outcomes of customer learning. *European Journal of Marketing, 56*(3), 677–703.

Bell, Auh, and Eisingerich found that customer education creates a strong positive impact on customer loyalty when it is "directed toward firm-specific elements" of an organization's product or services. But they also found that customer education focused on general market-related knowledge could backfire—enabling customers to seek out competitive products or services. They caveated this finding, so we should be somewhat circumspect before shrinking our customer-education investments. Indeed, they warned that, as customers increasingly self-educate from social-media sources, it may be best to proactively shape the information available to the market. They also noted that providing balanced and foundational information may build trust with customers.

- Bell, S. J., Auh, S., & Eisingerich, A. B. (2017). Unraveling the customer education paradox: When, and how, should firms educate their customers? *Journal of Service Research, 20*(3), 306–321.

In the chapter, I made the case that customer education should be considered part of an organization's overall customer success management strategy. Although a new field, there is clear evidence that customer success management (CSM) is on the rise. Harvard Business Review is writing about it.

- Zoltners, A. A., Sinha, P., Lorimer, S.E. (2019). What Is a Customer Success Manager? Harvard Business Review, November 2019. Available at: https://hbr.org/2019/11/what-is-a-customer-success-manager.

A quick search on the LinkedIn job board searching for "customer success manager" found over 80,000 listings in the United States alone.

Researchers Hilton, Hajihashemi, Henderson, and Palmatier reviewed the nascent literature on customer success management and concluded that it "*represents a departure from traditional customer management practices by proactively prioritizing customers' experience and engagement towards maximum value-in-uses.*"

- Hilton, B., Hajihashemi, B., Henderson, C. M., & Palmatier, R. W. (2020). Customer success management: The next evolution in customer management practice? *Industrial Marketing Management, 90,* 360–369.

CSM researchers Prohl-Schwenke and Kleinaltenkamp did an extensive analysis of what customers want, and they found such factors as fast problem solving, low cost, process improvement, avoiding downtime, reduced risk, innovativeness, and competitive advantage. And, as mentioned in the chapter, customers also value personal factors like task simplicity, perceived control, pressure reduction, uncertainty reduction, social comfort, and personal reputation.

- Prohl-Schwenke, K., & Kleinaltenkamp, M. (2021). How business customers judge customer success management. *Industrial Marketing Management, 96,* 197–212.

CSM ideas are also reflected in customer research that doesn't use the term but does align with CSM's key factors. For example, it's not good enough to have satisfied customers; rather, we'd like "customer advocates."

- Sweeney, J., Payne, A., Frow, P., & Liu, D. (2020). Customer advocacy: A distinctive form of word of mouth. *Journal of Service Research, 23*(2), 139–155.

Product and service failures happen occasionally, even in the best organizations. When they happen, companies need to recover or they'll lose that customer and perhaps others. Researchers have found that, when a company is known for generally engaging in socially responsible behaviors and when it also has deep relationships with its customers, recovery from product/service failures is greatly improved.

- Alhouti, S., Wright, S. A., & Baker, T. L. (2021). Customers need to relate: The conditional warm glow effect of CSR on negative customer experiences. *Journal of Business Research, 124,* 240–253.

Good customer education then should model (not preach about) the organization's socially-desirable values while also developing strong bonds between its educators and customer learners.

Let me make this real. Imagine new employees who are sent off to a customer education program by their managers. They not only learn how to use an important product—Product XYZ from Company ABC—but they grow comfortable and bond with their program facilitators. Over the next few years, they get additional training and coaching and they develop close ties to these Company ABC facilitators. Their sense of identity and work competence becomes associated with the product and the brand. After a few years, they move into supervisory roles and make decisions to maintain the relationship with Company ABC and Product XYZ. Some move on to other companies and make decisions or influence decisions to purchase XYZ and bring in Company ABC—already a trusted advisor.

The bottom line is that customer education can provide a competitive advantage for organizations that utilize it effectively.

Chapter 38—Adding Learning to Leadership Development

In this chapter I started with a critique of traditional leadership training. Let me be clear that I'm not dismissing all leadership training as ineffective. Indeed, in Chapter 5 I shared a meta-analysis showing that our leadership programs are generally providing benefits. I'll reshare that citation here:

- Lacerenza, C. N., Reyes, D. L., Marlow, S. L., Joseph, D. L., & Salas, E. (2017). Leadership training design, delivery, and implementation: A meta-analysis. *Journal of Applied Psychology, 102*(12), 1686–1718.

However, as these researchers warn in their summary of the article: *"the strength of these effects differs based on various design, delivery, and implementation characteristics."* This has two implications. First, we must use good leadership-development practices to create benefits. Second, our leadership training can be improved. Here is one example of how researchers are calling for improvements in leadership development programs:

- Allen, S. J., Rosch, D. M., & Riggio, R. E. (2022). Advancing leadership education and development: Integrating adult learning theory. *Journal of Management Education, 46*(2), 252–283.

One of the critiques of leadership development content is that it is based on popular books that too often promote ideas that don't work. Perhaps the best example is Pfeffer and Sutton's book that details many bestselling business books that get things wrong.

- Pfeffer, J. & Sutton, R.I. (2006). Hard Facts, Dangerous Half-Truths And Total Nonsense: Profiting From Evidence-Based Management Available at: https://amzn.to/3NIuXa0

Also in this chapter, I suggested that leadership recommendations were often too fuzzy to be practical. In this recent research article, the authors suggest that leadership can be more fruitfully focused on situations rather than on more global conceptions:

- Green, J. P., Dalal, R. S., Fyffe, S., Zaccaro, S. J., Putka, D. J., & Wallace, D. M. (2023). An empirical taxonomy of leadership situations: Development, validation, and implications for the science and practice of leadership. *Journal of Applied Psychology*. Advance online publication.

Along similar lines, here is a recent study that focuses leadership training on practical situation-based behaviors:

- Grill, M., Pousette, A., & Björnsdotter, A. (2023). Managerial behavioral training for functional leadership: A randomized controlled trial. *Journal of Organizational Behavior Management*. Advance online publication.

And here is a recent article positing that, because the practice of leadership is so complex, leadership development can benefit from exposing evolving leaders to experiences where they get to try out the leadership practices they are learning about.

- Kjærgaard, A., & Meier, F. (2022). Trying out loud: Leadership development as experimentalism. *Leadership, 18*(3), 383–399.

Chapter 39—Integrating Values and Ideas Across Your Learning Efforts

In this chapter, I advocated for learning teams to stop thinking in silos—in courses—and think about how to use repetition to support key messages across many learning assets. The power of repetition is undeniable. Earlier in this book we talked about spacing repetitions over time to support long-term remembering. There are hundreds if not thousands of research studies that spaced repetitions work. See my extensive chapter notes for Chapter 23 on the spacing effect.

If your learning team can integrate your organization's values and key ideas across courses and other learning events, your employees are much more likely to be energized and activated to use them in their work. But advantages may also flow beyond work performance to the way your company's brand is transmitted beyond your organization.

Your company's brand image impacts sales and customer loyalty, but it also impacts recruiting—helping you recruit high performers. In this recent research review on employee recruitment, the authors refer to "brand," "brands," or "branding" more than 25 times, an indication of branding's importance in recruiting talent.

- Dineen, B. R., Yu, K. Y. T., & Stevenson-Street, J. (2023). Recruitment in personnel psychology and beyond: Where we've been working, and where we might work next. Personnel Psychology, 76(2), 617–650.

Spaced repetitions not only improve remembering; they also increase belief in concepts, values, and ideals—the very kind of constructs that are the lifeblood of organizational success. Sometimes we scoff at the ham-handed ways organizations talk about values, mission statements, and the like, but our employees' beliefs about our organization certainly impact their performance, loyalty, tenure, and happiness.

In these studies, increases in repetitions increased beliefs.

- Fazio, L. K., Pillai, R. M., & Patel, D. (2022). The effects of repetition on belief in naturalistic settings. *Journal of Experimental Psychology: General, 151*(10), 2604–2613.

- Unkelbach, C., & Speckmann, F. (2021). Mere repetition increases belief in factually true COVID-19-related information. *Journal of Applied Research in Memory and Cognition, 10*(2), 241–247.

- Hawkins, S. A., Hoch, S. J., & Meyers-Levy, J. (2001). Low-involvement learning: Repetition and coherence in familiarity and belief. *Journal of Consumer Psychology, 11*(1), 1–11.

Interestingly, these studies overall may suggest that earlier repetitions have more impact than additional repetitions, that people may habituate to rote repetitions and thus be more attentive to repetitions that are varied in content or delivery, and that false information can be made more believable through repetitions as well.

The bottom line is that spaced repetitions have value in terms of learning, remembering, and believing—but they must be properly implemented to create desirable effects.

The good news is that not many learning teams are integrating values and ideas across their learning activities. It's good news because this is an excellent way for your organization to gain a competitive advantage. Yes, your learning team will have to experiment and vary their approaches to maximize effectiveness, but this is a huge opportunity!

Chapter 40—Training to Help Your Employees

In their decade-long effort focusing on organizational excellence, the American Psychological Association advocated that organizations take seriously the importance of providing employees with professional development. *"The opportunity to gain new skills and experiences can increase employee motivation and job satisfaction and help workers more effectively manage job stress. This can translate into positive gains for the organization by enhancing organizational effectiveness and improving work quality, as well as by helping the organization attract and retain top-quality employees."*

This quote is available for viewing through the WayBack Machine at webarchive.org.

- Original website: https://www.apaexcellence.org/resources/creatingahealthyworkplace/employeegrowth/

Employees are more likely to be engaged in work if they feel their organization supports them. In David Pincus's excellent research review of employee engagement, he cites Saks's work that shows *"that perceived organizational support is far and away the top predictor of engagement with the organization."*

- Pincus, J. D. (2022). Employee engagement as human motivation: Implications for theory, methods, and practice. *Integrative Psychological & Behavioral Science.* Advance online publication. https://doi.org/10.1007/s12124-022-09737-w

- Saks, A. M. (2006). Antecedents and consequences of employee engagement. *Journal of Managerial Psychology, 21*(7), 600–619.

Investments in training, as perceived by employees, tend to lower turnover. It appears that employees—even when their skills become more marketable outside their current companies—prefer to stay with a company where they get useful training.

- Martini, M., Gerosa, T., & Cavenago, D. (2022). How does employee development affect turnover intention? Exploring alternative relationships. *International Journal of Training and Development.* Advance online publication. https://doi.org/10.1111/ijtd.12282

There is also evidence that employees who engage more fully in learning may have better mental health outcomes. The advocacy group Mental Health America views employee professional development as so important they highlight it on their website.

- Kleine, A.-K., Rudolph, C. W., Schmitt, A., & Zacher, H. (2022). Thriving at work: An investigation of the independent and joint effects of vitality and learning on employee health. *European Journal of Work and Organizational Psychology.* Advance online publication. https://doi.org/10.1080/1359432X.2022.2102485

- Mental Health America webpage: https://mhanational.org/what-professional-development-opportunities-can-we-offer

Employees are more motivated when they have a sense of autonomy. As Pincus tells us, at least seven theories of motivation include autonomy as a central element. Autonomy seems to be a critical part of what it means to be human. In David Graeber and David Wengrow's well-received book on the history of humankind, they provide evidence that human groups have quite often formed their practices to be the opposite of practices of neighboring groups—as if they aspired to demonstrate autonomy.

- Graeber, D. & Wengrow, D. (2021). *The Dawn of Everything: A New History of Humanity.* Farrar, Straus and Giroux.

The U.S. Surgeon General's report on Workplace Mental Health & Well-Being—which I cited in the chapter to highlight the importance of learning—is available online.

- U.S. Surgeon General (2022). *The U.S. Surgeon General's Framework for Workplace Mental Health & Well-Being.* Available at: https://www.hhs.gov/sites/default/files/workplace-mental-health-well-being.pdf

Chapter 41—Compliance Training: Effectiveness and the Law

There are many areas of compliance training. Let's look at one area that has been studied extensively: health and safety training. In general, reviews of the scientific literature, done by researchers with expertise in this type of training, show that content-focused training is not as effective as practice-focused training. Here are a few review articles—those that look at many scientific studies—published over the past two decades.

Casey, Turner, Hu, and Bancroft reviewed research studies and recommended that learning teams delivering safety training should consider what happens before, during, and after training—considering factors like employee characteristics and using effective learning designs that align the training to the work and that support application by aligning the training effort to the systems and routines already existing in the work situation.

- Casey, T., Turner, N., Hu, X., & Bancroft, K. (2021). Making safety training stickier: A richer model of safety training engagement and transfer. *Journal of Safety Research, 78,* 303–313.

Burke, Salvador, Smith-Crowe and three other researchers conducted a meta-analysis of how exposure to workplace hazards and safety training interact to motivate workers to fully engage in safety training. They found that safety training was most effective if it was both highly engaging and if a recent safety issue had occurred.

- Burke, M. J., Salvador, R. O., Smith-Crowe, K., Chan-Serafin, S., Smith, A., & Sonesh, S. (2011). The dread factor: How hazards and safety training influence learning and performance. *Journal of Applied Psychology, 96*(1), 46–70.

Burke, Sarpy, Smith-Crow and three other researchers conducted a meta-analysis of worker safety and health training methods and found that the more learners were actively engaged in the learning—being involved in behavior modeling, substantial practice, and two-way dialogue—the better the training outcomes.

- Burke, M. J., Sarpy, S. A., Smith-Crowe, K., Chan-Serafin, S., Salvador, R. O., & Islam, G. (2006). Relative Effectiveness of Worker Safety and Health Training Methods. *American Journal of Public Health, 96*(2), 315–324.

Chapter 42—Learning in the Workflow

In this chapter, I introduced the concept of workflow learning and made the case that learning teams could be tasked with doing more to support individuals and teams in learning on the job.

There is complexity behind the seemingly simple concept of learning in the workflow. Indeed, informal learning has been a topic of interest going back over a century, even being traced back to 1900s figures in education like John Dewey, Mary Parker Follett, Eduard Linnemann, and Malcolm Knowles. For more background, see the following sources:

- Wikipedia on Informal Learning: https://en.wikipedia.org/wiki/Informal_learning

- Linnemann, E. C. (1926). *The Meaning of Adult Education*, New York: New Republic, Inc.

- Messmann, G., Segers, M. S. R., Dochy, F. (2018). Informal Learning at Work (New Perspectives on Learning and Instruction). Routledge.

In the 1990s, led by Victoria Marsick and Karen Watkins, informal and incidental learning became a renewed topic of interest.

- Marsick, V. J. & Watkins, K. (1990). *Informal and Incidental Learning in the Workplace*, London and New York: Routledge.

Watkins and Marsick have continued their work over the past three decades, recently leading to a new book.

- Watkins, K. E. & Marsick, V. J. (2023). Rethinking Workplace Learning and Development (Rethinking Business and Management series). Edward Elgar Publishing.

In 2006, Jay Cross introduced the idea of informal learning to L&D professionals in his book on informal learning.

- Cross, J. (2006). Informal Learning: Rediscovering the Natural Pathways That Inspire Innovation and Performance. Pfeiffer.

In 2018, the L&D field's most widely recognized industry analyst, Josh Bersin, used the phrase "learning in the workflow" to describe how learning technologies could be used to augment learning and performance as people are working.

- Bersin, J. (2018). *Learning in the Flow of Work: Arriving Now*. Video available at: https://joshbersin.com/2018/11/learning-in-the-flow-of-work-arriving-now/

There are many thought leaders in the L&D field who have championed workflow learning, informal learning, and the like over the past 10 years, including folks like Jos Arets, Charles Jennings, Paul Matthews, Saul Carliner, and Robin Hoyle. Jos Arets has been indispensable to me over the years as we've discussed workflow learning.

There is a very active scholarship on informal learning. For example, here are a few recent scientific articles I've selected largely at random:

- Tannenbaum, S. I., & Wolfson, M. A. (2022). Informal (field-based) learning. *Annual Review of Organizational Psychology and Organizational Behavior, 9,* 391–414.

- Gerards, R., de Grip, A., & Weustink, A. (2021). Do new ways of working increase informal learning at work? *Personnel Review, 50*(4), 1200–1215.

- Pejoska, J., Bauters, M., Purma, J., & Leinonen, T. (2016). Social augmented reality: Enhancing context-dependent communication and informal learning at work. *British Journal of Educational Technology, 47*(3), 474–483.

- Markouzis, D., Baziakou, A., Fesakis, G., & Dimitracopoulou, A. (2022). A systematic review on augmented reality applications in informal learning environments. *International Journal of Mobile and Blended Learning, 14*(4), 1–16.

Despite all this work, we are just beginning to figure out how to leverage workflow learning. Too often we are still focused on short formal learning events like microlearning, undirected social discussion groups, and fuzzy exhortations to enable reflection. These aren't useless, but they are just getting us started.

I expect we'll make real progress when we focus on how managers and organizations can create a culture of learning, when we parlay scientific knowledge of human cognition into workflow-learning hacks, and when we develop technologies that seamlessly support people in the work they do. The bottom line? Workflow learning provides a rich opportunity for organizations to grab a competitive advantage. While competitors dither in providing traditional training, enlightened organizations will be led by learning teams experimenting with a variety of workflow-learning methods.

There are many other types of workflow-learning interventions beyond the seven I mentioned in the chapter. No definitive list has been published, but here's a sampling of other workflow learning interventions I've encountered or can imagine:

- Using data to make decisions.

- Seeking help from others.

- Being open to new ideas.

- Following one's curiosity to learn more.

- Being sensitive to environmental stimuli related to identified knowledge gaps.

- Brainstorming and ideation.

- Performance reviews.

- After-action reviews.

- Audits.

- Seeking feedback or criticism.

- Trial and error.

- Reflection, whether guided or not, whether intentional or not.

- Being bold in taking action.

- Taking notes.

- Journaling.

- Conversations.

- Engaging consultants or experts to provide insights.

- Managerial accounting, thinking about our finances and operations by organizing the numbers into meaningful nuggets.

- Creating a plan.

- Being open to feedback.

- Using a visual interface or tool to clarify or discover relationships between objects, ideas, or events.

- Using a performance-support tool to guide action and learn.

- Job shadowing.

- Interviewing.

- Focus groups.

- Surveys.

- Augmented reality.

Chapter 43—Your Learning Leader

Leaders who have more knowledge of the work are more able to lead their teams to be creative. This finding has huge implications for organizational effectiveness. Where creativity is a key to success, managers must not only have expertise in the domain of the work they are managing, but they also must know how to utilize that expertise.

The following research has found that managers who know more about the area in which they are managing are more likely to have teams that produce creative outcomes.

- Mumford, M. D., Scott, G. M., Gaddis, B., & Strange, J. M. (2002). Leading creative people: Orchestrating expertise and relationships. *The Leadership Quarterly, 13*(6), 705-750.

- Stenmark, C. K., Shipman, A. S., & Mumford, M. D. (2011). Managing the innovative process: The dynamic role of leaders. *Psychology of Aesthetics, Creativity, and the Arts, 5*(1), 67-80.

- Hemlin, S., & Olsson, L. (2011). Creativity-stimulating leadership: A critical incident study of leaders' influence on creativity in research groups. *Creativity and Innovation Management, 20*(1), 49-58.

- Leone, S. A., & Reiter-Palmon, R. (2022). Leading creative teams: A process-perspective with implications for organizational leaders. *Translational Issues in Psychological Science, 8*(1), 90–103.

Chapter 44—How to Tell If Your Learning Leader Is Doing a Good Job

In the chapter I alluded to Bill Gates's work in education. Here is an article that describes how Bill and Melinda Gates learned that educational reform is not easy.

- Strauss, V. (2020). Bill and Melinda Gates have spent billions to shape education policy. Now, they say, they're 'skeptical' of 'billionaires' trying to do just that. https://www.washingtonpost.com/education/2020/02/10/bill-melinda-gates-have-

spent-billions-dollars-shape-education-policy-now-they-say-theyre-skeptical-
billionaires-trying-do-just-that/

Chapter 45—Your Learning Team Should Have a Strategy

In this chapter, I provided a list of 28 focus areas for learning teams. The science behind this approach is simple. We humans are easily distracted. We forget what we want to focus on. Also, most of us simply don't know what to focus on. In the learning-and-performance field, my colleagues and I have been educated to focus on only a relatively narrow range of performance targets. To provide a few examples, we've been told to get the content of our courses right, but we haven't been fully educated about the importance of the work context in triggering thoughts and action. We've been focused on how to deliver content in ways that are engaging, but not on how people can best learn on their own or in groups. We are well practiced in developing courses but have virtually no experience in teaching managers how to support their teams in learning.

By providing learning teams with a list of 28 focus areas, we help overcome the limitations of our human cognitive architecture. First, we help learning teams know where to focus. Second, we help them avoid distractions from current fads and fancies, and channel popular new ideas into an actionable framework. Third, we help them remember their leverage points, so they don't limit themselves to traditional training practices.

Chapter 46—A Full-Factor Learning Request Process

In this chapter, I laid out a comprehensive learning-request process. For creating an immediate impact, it's one of the most important chapters in the book. If learning teams would use a process like this, they would regularly remind themselves—and other important organizational players—about critical considerations in learning and performance design.

Some people are concerned about the first question in the process: *"If you have a preference, what type of learning or performance-improvement intervention are you requesting? Because learning-and-performance interventions can blend methods, feel free to select more than one:"* It then lists 10 potential solutions before giving the respondents a chance to choose, *"I'm not sure—but want to partner with you on the learning team to determine what might be effective."*

The objection is based on the presumption that we should first ask about the business need and work from there to design the learning intervention. Here's the subtlety. It is good practice to start with our ultimate goals and work backwards from there, but the Full-Factor Learning Request Process is *not* our design process; it is a process for beginning a conversation with a key stakeholder.

By first asking them if they have a solution in mind, we are meeting them where they are, not shocking them with our idiosyncratic process. Because they are human, they likely have some idea of what they want. We should honor them by listening to them. Later, we'll focus on their ultimate goals—after we have acknowledged that they are looking for us to help them with a specific solution.

The first question also nudges them to see that training may not be the only solution—even though most likely that's what they're thinking.

To summarize, the Full-Factor Learning Request Process is designed to gather valuable information while also educating our stakeholders to the full range of options available to help them solve their problem or seize an opportunity. The process is designed to get a conversation started—a conversation that is directed toward productive decision-making.

Chapter 47—Outsourcing Your Learning Team?

As the authors of this recent review of outsourcing describe, *"Outsourcing can produce positive, negative, mixed, moderated or no significant impact on the firm."*

- Lahiri, S. (2016). Does outsourcing really improve firm performance? Empirical evidence and research agenda. *International Journal of Management Reviews, 18*(4), 464–497.

Chapter 48—What If Your Learning Team Wins Awards?

Awards are hard! It is extremely difficult to run an awards program, especially if you want to use a fair and rigorous process. We shouldn't beat up on awards sponsors too much. Indeed, even though I'm raising the issue, I myself am not above criticism. My Neon Elephant Award process is far from perfect! It is fair game to criticize it, just as it is fair game to criticize other award sponsors in the hopes of improving awards programs.

Awards can produce positive benefits. I've detailed this previously in an article on my blog—worth repeating:

- Those who apply for awards have the potential to reflect on their own practices and thus learn and improve based on this reflection and any feedback they might get from those who judge their applications.

- Those who apply (and even those who just review an awards application) maybe be nudged toward better practices based on the questions or requirements outlined.

- Selected winners and the description of their work can set aspirational benchmarks for other organizations.

- Selected winners can be acknowledged and rewarded for their hard work, innovation, and results.

- Individuals selected for awards can be deservedly promoted or recruited to new opportunities.

- Learning departments can earn reputation credits within their organizations that can be cashed in for resources and permission to act autonomously and avoid micromanagement.

- Vendors that win can publicize and support their credibility and brand.

- Organizations that need products or services can be directed to vendors that have been vetted as excellent.

- Judges who participate can learn about best practices, innovations, and trends they can use in their work.

Given these benefits, it would be helpful to the learning industry if award sponsors improved their awards programs. I've previously used an awards-funnel diagram to detail suggestions for improvement, which you can find in the article cited below. Here are the 11 principles I recommended:

- *Award Eligibility*—Open to all, low cost, opportunity widely known?

- *Criteria*—Valid, relevant, critical to learning effectiveness?

- *Application*—Does it promote clear, relevant applicant responses that judges can evaluate?

- *Applicant Responses*—Honest, substantial enough to judge?

- *Information Verification*—Can data/information be verified as accurate/true?

- *Judge Quality*—Sufficiently knowledgeable and experienced?

- *Judge Impartiality*—Impartial, unbiased, blind to applicant identities, no conflicts of interest?

- *Judge Time and Attention*—Adequate time devoted in reviewing applications?

- *Judging Rubric*—Are judges provided with a rubric that has clear options?

- *Judge Reliability*—Do at least three judges review each applicant?

- *Sponsor Non-Interference*—Does award sponsor accept results?

Here is the article I wrote, which goes into greater detail about how to design improved awards programs:

- Thalheimer (2019). *Futility and Error in Learning Industry Awards.* Available at: https://www.worklearning.com/2019/12/20/futility-and-error-in-learning-industry-awards/.

As CEO, I hope this discussion gives you some idea about how to judge the awards and honors your team may be winning or your vendors may be touting. The bottom line is that currently most awards in the learning-and-development field are not good enough.

Chapter 49—Learning Vendor Awards Are Just as Problematic

There's not much more to add here. Most of the details that apply to learning vendor awards were detailed in the chapter notes above. Still, it may be worth telling the story of Bill Ellet's Training Media Review.

Bill Ellet is a hero of mine. Two or three decades ago, as learning technology began to become mainstream in the learning-and-development field, Bill realized that companies like yours could use help separating the wheat from the chaff—separating effective learning programs and technology from those that were not effective or were less effective. He started a company, Training Media Review, to fill this need. He hired highly knowledgeable and skilled judges to review training programs.

For many years, Bill and his colleagues published important reviews of training media. Unfortunately, Training Media Review's business model just didn't work. Revenues came from subscribers only, and not enough learning-and-development folks needed the information. Vendors were not invited to fund operations, so no revenues came from them. Contrast this honest independent approach to some of today's shenanigans, where vendors pay to be included on top-20 lists, to get special reviews, to influence what is published, and to win awards.

Now let me be clear. There are fine organizations that promote vendors fairly and transparently. Not all awards are biased and corrupt.

Chapter 50—Investing in Learning for a Competitive Advantage

In this chapter, I summarize the main recommendations in the book by suggesting what organizations should budget more for and less for—in terms of learning and performance.

In thinking about what to budget less for, I highlight the work of Leidy Klotz, whose research has found that we humans tend to add new practices, resources, and concepts to our work while simultaneously ignoring the incredible benefits that can come when we subtract things that aren't working that well.

- Leidy Klotz. *Subtract: The Untapped Science of Less*. Learn more at: https://amzn.to/3PqlJl9.

Index
Of Critical Concepts and Names

Some names are alphabetized by first name.

70-20-10, 38, 184

A-B Testing, 80, 81, 84, 87, 88, 125, 134, 159, 221, 222, 227

Adam Neaman, VII

Agarwal, 183, 198, 199

Alderman, 196

Alhouti, 234

Allen, 234

Alliger, 167

Alpendre, 216

Al-Shawaf, 190

Alter, 188

Anders Ericsson, 82, 208

Anderson, 183

Andris, 111

Annie Murphy Paul, 212

Appleby, 217

Appleton-Knapp, 205, 206

Arnicane, 182

Attention, 94, 95, 97, 106, 108, 110, 114, 139, 150, 175, 181, 182, 223

Atul Gawande, 212, 216

Awards, 128, 153, 155, 243, 244

Baashar, 217

Bach, 194

Baddeley, 199, 201, 209, 210

Bahrick, 202, 203

Bailey, 173, 174

Baldwin, 170

Bauer, 221

Becker, 221

Bedi, 186, 187

Behavioral Guidance, 76

Bell, 233

Benjamin, 173

Bersin, 239

Bertilsson, 181

Big Five, 190

Bill Ellet, 244

Bish, 221

BJ Fogg, 212

Bjork, 173, 174, 179, 185, 199, 205, 206, 209, 210

Bloom, 206

Bloom's Taxonomy, 37, 38, 183

Blume, 170

Bob Mager Allusion, 27

Braconnier, 197

Bransford, 207

Brey, 195

Brooks, 197

Brown, 123, 167, 176, 189, 190, 224

Bruce, 202

Brydges, 208

Buchin, 181

Buchner, 218

Buczel, 188

Bui, 173, 174

Bureau of Labor Statistics, 165, 166

Burke, 238

Butler, 172, 198, 200, 201

Cai, 217

Calderón Carvajal, 180

Calvo-Ferrer, 184

Campbell, 188, 208

Canca, 195

Cao, 186

Carl Hulshof, 41

Carpenter, 185, 192

Carvalho, 192, 204

Casey, 170, 238

Casper, 167, 194

Castillo, 178, 200, 201

Cathy Moore, 220

CEO Research, 170

Cepeda, 202

Chang, 174, 175, 177

Change Championing, 141

ChatGPT, 40, 50, 86

Chatham, 208

Chen, 187, 193, 204

Chief Learning Officer, viii, 2, 6, 17, 21, 78, 80, 83, 93, 127, 129, 131, 132, 133, 170, 241

Choi, 216

Chokshi, 198

Christina Reagle, VII

Chung, 165

Clardy, 184

Clark Quinn, v, VII, 38, 41, 82, 162

Classroom Training, 34, 49, 53, 182, 192

Clegg, 196

Coaching, 4, 8, 26, 43, 56, 66, 76, 120, 137, 143, 145, 225, 227

Coaching for Learning, 114

Coke, 205, 206

Cokely, 188

Communities of Practice, 28, 108, 110, 112, 123, 145

Competitive Advantage, V, 4, 6, 10, 12, 16, 30, 44, 57, 61, 71, 73, 74, 79, 80, 83, 85, 87, 92, 96, 103, 111, 116, 118, 127, 128, 130, 131, 137, 139, 143, 160, 233, 234, 236, 240

Compliance Training, 108, 121, 238

Conference Board, V

Content Vetting, 94, 143, 227

Context, 32, 56, 62, 67, 68, 75, 207, 209

Context Alignment, 63, 64, 182, 206, 207, 208, 210

Context Enablers, 142

Context Obstacles, 142

Context Triggering, 14, 68, 71, 72, 73, 74, 75, 76, 77, 103, 142, 230, 242

Cook, 180

Corbière, 187

Course Repositories, 40, 49, 55, 56, 123, 136, 157, 193

Crap Data, 19, 21, 30, 167

Creativity and Innovation, 18, 30, 43, 44, 45, 46, 72, 73, 74, 79, 83, 88, 114, 115, 116, 117, 118, 124, 130, 131, 141, 143, 159, 220, 221, 241

Cross, 239

Curse of Knowledge, 31, 32, 176

Customer Education, 6, 107, 109, 110, 111, 112, 160, 232

Customer Success Management, 111, 233, 234

Cwik, 217

Damon Centola, 212

Daniel Kahneman, 103, 213

Daniel Pink, 213

D'Arcy, 174, 175, 177

Datu, 188

David McRaney, 74, 213

David Merrill, 38, 220

David Schonthal, 74, 213

Debbie Smith, VII

Decisive Dozen, 37, 162

Degado, 190

Dekker, 180

Dempster, 202

DeRosa, 220

Diehl, 220

Dignity and Respect, 119, 143

DiMenichi, 175

Dineen, 236

Donald Clark, v, VII, 38, 82, 196

Donald Kirkpatrick, 24, 162, 168

Donovan, 184

Double, 179

Dunlosky, 173, 174, 176

Dunning-Kruger Effect, 29

Ebbinghaus, 166, 204

ECRA, 44, 185

Education, 11, 12, 33, 35, 133, 135, 145, 191, 241

Effective Altruism, 194

Ekuni, 192

eLearning, v, vi, VI, 34, 49, 50, 53, 54, 106, 140, 162, 182, 191, 192

Elham Arabi, v, VII, 102, 232

Employee Empowerment, 143

Enablers and Obstacles, 76, 142

Ensor, 207

Erdogan, 221

Esterman, 181, 182

Ethan Kross, 213

Ethics, 6, 43, 57, 130, 136, 194, 226

Experimentation, 125

Farris, 202

Fay, 174, 175, 177, 178

Fazio, 236

Feedback, VII, 12, 24, 32, 33, 35, 40, 43, 44, 54, 62, 63, 64, 65, 68, 69, 70, 76, 82, 94, 116, 120, 135, 148, 149, 159, 170, 175, 176, 178, 179, 182, 184, 200, 201, 211, 212, 214, 219, 224, 227, 240, 243

Finn, 173, 211

First Do No Harm, 1, 7, 41, 163

Fisher, 177

Flanagin, 177

Fletcher, 216

Ford, 170

Forgetting Curve, 7, 13, 14, 102, 166

Fortenbaugh, 181, 182

Frank, 193

Furst, 183

Gale Stafford, VII

Garavan, 9, 10, 163, 164

Generations, 39

Generative AI, 50, 52, 57, 58, 86, 132, 193

Gerards, 239

Giessner, 185, 186

Gleave, 194

Gneezy, 188

Godden, 209, 210

Gollwitzer, 189

Gopnik, 222

Graeber, 237

Grant, 190, 209, 210, 212

Green, 235

Grill, 235

Grossmeier, 188

Guided Cognition, 126

Gupta, 200, 201

Guy Wallace, v, VII, 82

Gweon, 222

Habits, 14, 40, 46, 71, 72, 73, 74, 83, 103, 113, 123, 142

Hadady, 216

Hales, 216

Hall, 202

Hatala, 208

Hattie, 211

Havens, 195

Hawkins, 236

Hemlin, 241

Henly, 174, 177

Herppich, 179

HEXACO, 190

Hilton, 233

Hinds, 176, 178

Hoch, 189, 236

Hofseth, 173

Huang, 170, 212

Hughes, 164, 167, 180

Huisman, 179

Human Resources, 17, 129, 130

Hunt, 197

Ilona Boomsma, VII

Incentives, 46

Ingeborg Kroese, 106

Irfan, 197

Jack Phillips, VII, 168, 171

Jackson, 169

Jane Bozarth, VII, 82

Jang, 193

Janiszewski, 203

Jeroen van Merriënboer, 38

Jerry Hamburg, vi, VII, 38, 214

Jerry Muller, 103

John Bargh, 213

Johnson, 184, 198, 213, 216, 220

Jonah Berger, 74, 213

Jones, 200, 201

Jos Arets, vi, VII, 239

Josh Cavalier, VII

Judson Brewer, 213

Julie Dirksen, VII, 38, 82, 162

Kähkönen, 187

Kang, 199

Karkpicke, 200

Karl Kapp, vi, VII, 82

Karpicke, 172, 198, 199, 200, 201

Katy Milkman, 213

Katz, 204, 205, 212

Kehoe, 189

Keiser, 165

Kellie Chamberlain, VII

Kendeou, 172

Kenworthy, 221

Keysar, 174, 175, 176, 177

Kim, 180, 181, 186, 187, 202, 203

Kirkpatrick-Katzell Model, 19, 24, 47, 90, 98, 102, 154, 156, 161, 162, 168

Kjærgaard, 235

Klein, 82, 221

Kleinaltenkamp, 111, 233

Kleine, 237

Kleinlogel, 174, 175, 177

Klitmøller, 180

Knowledge Access, 140

Koriat, 173, 174

Kousa, 195

Kozma, 191

Kraiger, 164, 168, 183

Krathwohl, 183

Krauss, 198

Krug, 205

Küpper-Tetzel, 202

Lacerenza, 164, 167, 234

Lahiri, 243

Lai, 184

Lake, 190

Lance Crow, VII
Latimier, 198
Lau, 174, 175, 176
Leadership Development, 107, 113, 116, 141, 158, 164, 190, 234
LEADS, 89, 90, 93, 95, 96, 97, 103, 161, 223, 225
Learner Surveys, 21, 105
Learners Don't Always Know, 20, 170, 172
Learning Acceleration, 141
Learning Development Accelerator, 162
Learning Effectiveness, 16, 29, 92, 105, 134, 168, 191, 232, 244
Learning Evaluation, 19, 23, 89, 90, 93, 97, 161, 162, 168, 223
Learning Myths, v, vii, 8, 11, 12, 15, 16, 20, 33, 34, 41, 110, 157, 159, 162
Learning Pyramid, 35
Learning Sciences, 61, 182
Learning Styles, 33, 179, 181
Learning Support, 19, 27, 28, 35, 137
Lee, 165
Leidy Klotz, 159, 213, 245
Levari, 179
Linnemann, 238
Loran Nordgren, 74, 213
LTEM, 24, 37, 48, 90, 92, 96, 97, 98, 99, 100, 101, 102, 103, 161, 162, 168, 223, 224, 225, 229, 231, 232
Maddox, 202
Malcolm Gladwell, 213, 218
Managers, 3, 4, 6, 8, 14, 17, 18, 19, 20, 25, 26, 27, 28, 29, 30, 32, 33, 38, 40, 43, 44, 45, 46, 47, 48, 54, 55, 59, 66, 68, 69, 74, 78, 83, 84, 93, 94, 101, 106, 107, 111, 112, 113, 114, 115, 116, 117, 118, 120, 122, 123, 124,

128, 130, 133, 134, 141, 142, 143, 145, 148, 149, 150, 152, 155, 169, 178, 185, 187, 189, 227, 234, 240, 241, 242
Managers' Performance Checklist, 45
Marchese, 196
Margolis, 209, 210
Marian, 209, 210
Mark Nilles, VII
Markouzis, 239
Markus Bernhardt, VII
Marsick, 239
Martini, 237
Mason, 181
Matt Richter, vi, VII, 162
Mayer, 82, 183, 191, 193
Mazzetti, 186
McDaniel, 82, 176, 179
McDermott, 199
Megan Torrance, vi, VII
Meier, 235
Memory Accessibility, 76, 142
Mental Health America, 237
Merriënboer, 38, 82, 176
Mertens, 211
Mesmer-Magnus, 165
Messmann, 238
Metz, 196
Michael Allen, vii, VII, 162
Michelle Ockers, vii, VII
Micklos, 178
Microlearning, 34, 51, 181
Mirjam Neelen, 82
Moehring, 188
Mullen, 220
Mulligan, 181
Mumford, 241

Myers-Briggs Type Indicator, 47, 189, 190

Nancekivell, 180

Naqib, 203

Navy SEALs, 12

Needs Analysis, 78, 159

Nelson, 173, 174

Network Science, 72

Neuroscience, 36, 51

Nick Howe, VII

Nickerson, 176

Niemi, 195

Nikki Vassallo, vii, VII

Nilsen, 217

Nir Eyal, 213

Noel, 203

Norvig, 194

Noticing, 113, 114, 115

Nückles, 178, 179

Nudging, 71, 72, 73, 75, 76, 78, 88, 102, 103, 118, 142, 166, 199, 231, 242

O'Driscoll, 170, 171

Ojea Ramos, 203

Oliveira Silva, 208

Olsen, 180

Olvera, 194

Oppenheimer, 177

Order Taker, 169

Organizational Literacy, 140

Organizational Success, 9

Outsourcing, 128, 151, 152, 243

Pan, 207

Panadero, 212

Pashler, 179, 202

Patti Phillips, VII, 156, 170, 171

Patti Shank, VII, 38, 82

Paul Kirschner, 38, 41, 82, 176

Paul Matthews, VII, 239

Paulus, 208, 209, 221

Pedro De Bruyckere, 82

Pejoska, 239

Performance Activation, 38, 71, 75, 214

Performance Sciences, 8, 71, 72, 73, 74, 75, 130, 132, 139, 159, 212

Performance Support, 72, 77, 216

Personal States, 76

Persuasion, 72, 73, 74, 107, 115

Pfeffer, 178, 235

Pieschl, 177

Pincus, 237

Pintrich, 183

Pittenger, 189

Pollution, 59

Posner, 182

Pre-Mortems, 125

Preparatory Cognition, 125

Presentation Science Bootcamp, 53

PricewaterhouseCoopers, V

Prinz, 172

Prior Knowledge, 172, 181, 185

Proactive Behaviors, 76

Prohl-Schwenke, 111, 233

Prompting, 46, 72, 77, 95, 142, 145, 216, 230

Prompting Tools, 8, 77, 103, 142, 145

Pyc, 173, 174

Rapp, 184

Realistic Practice, 32, 35, 56, 61, 62, 63, 103, 106, 110, 122, 157, 159, 229

Remembering, 172

Remembering Support, 141

Reminding, 141

Renkl, 172, 173, 178, 179

Repetition, 29, 32, 34, 40, 64, 65, 66, 68, 107, 108, 117, 118, 172, 203, 204, 205, 206, 229, 235, 236

Research and Practice, 79, 81, 218
Retrieval Practice, 61, 63, 64, 68, 70, 82, 114, 172, 181, 182, 183, 192, 198, 199, 200, 201, 202
Rhodes, 176
Richard E. Clark, vii, VII, 38, 82, 169, 190, 191, 193
Riley, 182
Robert Brinkerhoff, viii, VII, 156
Robert Cialdini, 74, 189, 214
Robey, 175, 176
Robinson, 180, 181, 191
Rodriguez, 187
Roediger, 82, 172, 176, 185, 198, 199, 200, 201, 205, 206
Roelle, 173, 174
Rohrer, 179, 202, 204
ROI, viii, 5, 24, 47, 158, 170, 171
Roose, 196
Ross Edwards, VII
Rothkopf, 205, 206, 223
Roy Pollock, VII
Roy V.H. Pollock, viii
Runquist, 200, 201
Ruth Clark, viii, VII, 82
Ryan, 211
Saks, 237
Salas, 9, 96, 164, 167, 168, 183, 220, 234
Salovich, 184
Sana, 200, 201, 204
Sanders, 165, 195
Schaerer, 178
Schaufeli, 186
Schuren, 194
Scientific Research, 1, 2, 6, 8, 22, 27, 29, 49, 62, 63, 79, 80, 81, 82, 83, 84, 85, 86, 88, 103, 136, 176, 189, 190, 191, 192, 219

Seddon, 183
Self-Direction, 142
Sharon Castillo, VII
Shaughnessy, 172
Shin, 207, 208
Sibony, 96, 213, 224
Simulation, 67, 68, 82, 161, 205, 206, 208
Singh, 205, 206
Singhal, 217
Sitzmann, 167, 168
Smile Sheets, 7, 21, 22, 51, 85, 90, 105, 106, 157, 159, 172
Smith, 164, 168, 178, 183, 206, 207, 209, 210, 220, 238
Social Learning, 115, 140
Spaced Learning, 15, 35, 61, 62, 64, 65, 66, 68, 182, 198, 202, 203, 204, 205, 206, 235
Spaced Repetitions, 47, 62, 66, 82, 106, 122, 159, 202, 203
Srivastava, 194
Stamate, 199, 201
Stella Lee, viii, VII
Stenmark, 241
Steve Foreman, VII
Steven Pinker, 214
Strauss, 241
Subconscious, 126
Sugrue, 170, 171
Suleyman, 193
Sumeracki, 200, 201
Sun, 233
Sung, 191
Sunstein, 73, 189, 213
Sutton, 221, 235
Suzuki, 217
Talent Strategy, 142
Tang, 182

Tannenbaum, 96, 164, 167, 168, 183, 239

Technology and Learning, 28, 49, 51, 52, 58, 60, 151, 190, 192, 193

Thaler, 73, 189, 213

The Economist, 197

Thibault, 188

Thomas Harrell, VII

Thompson, 207

Travel, 59

Tricomi, 175

Triggered Cognition, 126

Trinh, 178

Tugend, 196

Tullis, 176

Tulving, 207

U.S. Surgeon General, 120, 237

Ulrich Boser, 82

Underwood, 203

Unkelbach, 236

Uslu, 164

Uttl, 167

Vallen, 203

Vallesi, 182

van den Broek, 172, 179

Van der Kleij, 212

Vince Han, VII

Vlach, 203

von Hoyer, 175, 177

Vona, 170, 171

Wakslak, 178

Wang, 175, 187, 217

Watkins, 239

Webb, 202

Weiss, 209, 210

Well-Being, 120, 143, 237

Wendy Wood, 73, 214

Wengrow, 237

Wieber, 189

Wilkes, 197

Will Storr, 214

Will Thalheimer, v, vi, vii, viii, v, vi, 4, 15, 157, 161, 162, 168, 169, 183, 191, 192, 206, 207, 211, 231, 232, 244

Willingham, 179, 180

Winne, 222

Wisniewski, 211

Witherby, 185, 192

Wittrock, 183

Wittwer, 172, 178, 179

Wood, 195

Work Context, 4, 62, 67, 68, 71, 72, 73, 75, 76, 82, 93, 95, 108, 110, 111, 115, 123, 125, 141, 142, 159, 164, 206, 208, 209, 210, 214, 230, 231, 242

Work Contexts, 75, 95, 137, 142, 207, 208

Work Culture, 142

Work Performance, 72, 75, 76, 78, 94, 101, 129, 134, 142, 167, 223, 225, 230

Workflow Learning, 30, 83, 93, 108, 116, 123, 126, 134, 152, 212, 238, 239, 240

Work-Learning Research, 81, 160, 161, 162

Worlikar, 194

Wu, 187

Xing, 212

Xu, 192

Yamagata, 204, 205

Yan, 180

Yang, 187, 200

Yu, 179

Zechmeister, 172

Zhang, 176, 192, 212

Zhao, 192

Zhou, 187

Zoltners, 111, 233